Domestic and international trials, 1700–2000

MANCHESTER
UNIVERSITY PRESS

Domestic and international trials, 1700–2000

The trial in history, volume II

edited by R. A. Melikan

Manchester University Press
Manchester and New York

distributed exclusively in the USA by Palgrave

Published by Manchester University Press
Oxford Road, Manchester M13 9NR, UK
and Room 400, 175 Fifth Avenue, New York, NY 10010, USA
www.manchesteruniversitypress.co.uk

Distributed exclusively in the USA by
Palgrave, 175 Fifth Avenue, New York,
NY 10010, USA

Distributed exclusively in Canada by
UBC Press, University of British Columbia, 2029 West Mall,
Vancouver, BC, Canada V6T 1Z2

British Library Cataloguing-in-Publication Data
A catalogue record for this book is available from the British Library

Library of Congress Cataloging-in-Publication Data applied for

ISBN 0 7190 6486 4 *hardback*

First published 2003

10 09 08 07 06 05 04 03 10 9 8 7 6 5 4 3 2 1

Typeset in Photina
by Graphicraft Limited, Hong Kong
Printed in Great Britain
by Bookcraft (Bath) Ltd, Midsomer Norton

Contents

List of figures and tables — *page* vi
List of contributors — vii
Acknowledgements — ix
List of legal abbreviations — x

Introduction *R. A. Melikan* — 1

1 Evidence law and the evidentiary objection: a view from the *British Trials* collection *T. P. Gallanis* — 12

2 *Sense and sensibility*: fateful splitting in the Victorian insanity trial *Joel Peter Eigen* — 21

3 Trials of character: the use of character evidence in Victorian sodomy trials *H. G. Cocks* — 36

4 Pains and penalties procedure: how the House of Lords 'tried' Queen Caroline *R. A. Melikan* — 54

5 The invention of trials *in camera* in security cases *A. W. Brian Simpson* — 76

6 War crimes trials before international tribunals: legality and legitimacy *Dominic McGoldrick* — 107

7 An embarrassing necessity: the Tokyo trial of Japanese leaders, 1946–48 *Peter Lowe* — 137

8 The trial of Maurice Papon for crimes against humanity and the concept of bureaucratic crime *Robert Boyce* — 157

9 The trial of Slobodan Milosevic: a twenty-first century trial? *Dominic McGoldrick* — 179

Index — 195

List of figures and tables

Figures

1.1 Objections to oral evidence in civil cases, 1745–1820 *page* 13

1.2 Length of pamphlet accounts of civil cases, 1745–1820 14

3.1 Indictments for sodomy, indecent assault, and other homosexual offences presented at the Old Bailey, 1750–1830 38

Tables

1.1 Lawyers raising objections to oral evidence in civil cases, 1765–1820 16

4.1 Non-attendance on the first day of the Queen's trial 59

4.2 Attendance in the House of Lords, 1815–25 60

List of contributors

Robert Boyce is a Senior Lecturer in International History at the London School of Economics and Political Science. He has written or edited four books including *French Foreign and Defence Policy, 1918–1940: the Decline and Fall of a Great Power* (Routledge, 1998).

H. G. Cocks is a Lecturer in History at Birkbeck College.

Joel Peter Eigen is the Charles A. Dana Professor of Sociology at Franklin and Marshall College in Lancaster, Pennsylvania. He is the author of *Witnessing Insanity: Madness and Mad-Doctors in the English Court* (Yale University Press, 1995) and is currently completing a manuscript, *Missing Persons: Consciousness and Criminality in the Victorian Courtroom*, under contract to The Johns Hopkins University Press.

T. P. Gallanis is an Associate Professor of Law and History at Ohio State University and, during 2000–1, was Mellon Fellow in Historical Studies at the Institute for Advanced Study, Princeton. His essay 'The rise of modern evidence law', *Iowa Law Review*, 84: 3 (1999), 499–560, was awarded the Selden Society's David Yale Prize.

Peter Lowe is a Reader in History at the University of Manchester. He is the author of *Containing the Cold War in East Asia* (Manchester University Press, 1997) and *The Korean War* (Macmillan, 2000), and he is currently preparing a study of British policy in South-East Asia after 1945.

Dominic McGoldrick is Professor of Public International Law and Director of the International and European Law Unit, Liverpool Law School, University of Liverpool. He has written books on the Human Rights Committee and International Relations Law of the European Union. Among his recent works are articles on the Permanent International Criminal Court, racist and hate speech, human rights in the European Union, accommodating national identity in the Former Yugoslavia, the United Kingdom's Human Rights Act 1998, and state responsibility.

R. A. Melikan is a Fellow of St Catharine's College, Cambridge. She is the author of *John Scott, Lord Eldon (1751–1838): the Duty of Loyalty* (Cambridge University Press, 1999), and has also published articles dealing with the intersection of law and politics in late Georgian England.

A. W. Brian Simpson is the Charles F. and Edith J. Clyne Professor of Law at the University of Michigan. His recent publications include *Human Rights and the End of Empire. Britain and the Genesis of the European Convention* (Oxford University Press, 2001).

Acknowledgements

Most of the essays in this volume were presented at a conference on 'The Trial in History' held in Manchester on 17–19 September 1999. This conference was organised by the Department of History in the University of Manchester in association with the Faculty (now the School) of Law, and with the advice and help of members of the Wellcome Unit for the History of Medicine and of the Departments of Philosophy and Social Anthropology. Further financial contributions in support of the conference were made by the British Academy Humanities Research Board, the University of Manchester, Messrs Eversheds, Solicitors of Manchester, and the J. K. Hyde Centre for Late Medieval and Renaissance Studies. A companion volume, *Judicial tribunals in England and Europe, 1200–1700*, edited by Maureen Mulholland and Brian Pullan of the University of Manchester, is also being published by Manchester University Press. The editors of both volumes are deeply grateful to Dr Bill Smith, the conference administrator, for his efficiency and good humour.

As the editor of the present volume, I would like to add my thanks to Professor J. H. Baker for the cover print, to Dr Quentin Stafford-Fraser for technical and other assistance, and to Professor Brian Pullan, for his support, friendship, and dedication to this project.

List of legal abbreviations

A.C.	Law Reports, Appeal Cases
All E.R.	All England Law Reports
Cox C.C.	Cox's Criminal Law Cases
E.C.H.R.	European Court of Human Rights
I.C.C.	International Criminal Court
I.C.J. Reports	International Court of Justice
I.L.M.	International Legal Materials
I.L.R.	International Law Reports
L.J.K.B.	Law Journal, King's Bench
L.J.R.	Law Journal Reports
L.T.R.	Law Times Reports
S.I.	Statutory Instrument
S.T.	State Trials
T.L.R.	Times Law Reports
W.L.R.	Weekly Law Reports

Introduction

R. A. Melikan

I have been asked, in the context of this volume, to explain how one ought to write a history of the trial. Like a lawyer, rather than answering this question, I pose a counter-question and attempt to answer it instead – do you mean a history of *a trial* or a history of *trials*? The distinction is not, I hope, a pedantic one, as the former seems to focus upon a particular event and the latter upon a process. If we examine *a trial*, we are interested in the experiences, in so far as they can be understood, of the various participants – the parties, judge, jury, witnesses, and counsel. We want to know the facts – not only the basis for the dispute, but also the reason why it is being litigated, which may not be the same thing. We want to know the principles of law that led to the decision. Were they misapplied? Did a new principle emerge? Did the judge and/or jury simply ignore the law and do as they pleased? And we want to know the consequences of this trial, for the individual parties, certainly, but also for the subsequent development of the law, and for its political and social impact. However, if we examine *trials*, while we are still concerned with participants, facts, law, and outcomes, we want to know how all of these components functioned over time or, perhaps because that task is so large, we may concentrate on the developments of one or two components. To take a few examples from criminal litigation, which for many people is synonymous with trials, what effect did public prosecutors, the availability of capital punishment, or the law of contempt of court have upon the conduct of English criminal trials in the nineteenth century?

Is either method of analysis – that of a trial or of trials – preferable? No, although the state of the historical record and individual scholarly temperament may militate in favour of one or the other. One need only mention Brian Simpson's *Leading Cases in the Common Law* and John Langbein's work on English criminal trials to appreciate the value of either perspective.[1] What these and other successful examples of trial/trials scholarship have in common is their wide range of sources, and this brings me to a second matter for consideration – whether historical scholarship on individual or groups of trials ought to be written from within or without. This has sometimes divided lawyers and 'lawyerly' legal historians from their non-lawyer colleagues in legal, social, and political history. Lawyers, it might be said, can examine a trial from so deeply *within* that they lose all sense that it is an actual dispute involving real people, with influences and effects beyond the exposition of legal principles.[2] A completely external view of a trial or series of trials, however, creates its own problems. Litigation does involve substantive rules that will be applied, at some level, to the facts of the dispute, as well as procedural rules that will be imposed, at some level, upon the various participants and even upon outsiders. It is important to understand these rules, if only to appreciate what the lawyers and judges *thought* they were doing, even if one might argue that they were mistaken, or duplicitous, or unwittingly influenced by other, non-legal, factors.

To avoid an excessive bias towards either internal or external factors, one needs to take full advantage of the trial literature of the period under consideration. To take the example of eighteenth- and nineteenth-century England, here one has a wealth of official and unofficial sources. Accounts of civil and criminal litigation were published in this period for two general reasons: to provide technical information to the legal profession; and to provide moral edification and/or entertainment to the public. The genres of trial literature that fulfilled these purposes were discrete, but the trial scholar will want to make use of both.

Lawyers had been producing reports of trials and appellate proceedings in order to understand the law and practices of the Westminster courts since the Middle Ages, and printed reports had appeared in the late fifteenth century. Reporting was inconsistent, both in the quantity and the quality of reports produced, until the late eighteenth century, when professional reporters undertook to provide a periodical series for each of the four superior courts. These and other series continued until 1865, when they were joined by the *Law Reports*, produced under the aegis of the Council of Law Reporting. The *Law Reports*, along with several parallel and specialist series, still constitute the 'official' sources of case law, which are cited in court, discussed in law faculties, and dissected in legal journals.[3] They are essential to understand the substantive law being applied, but they do not provide much information either about an individual trial or collection of trials. Facts which might have explained what was actually going on in court but which shed no light on the legal principles at issue tend to be excluded, and with them goes much of the sense that litigation is anything more than the tidy legal discourse between lawyers and judge, resulting in the jury's verdict or the judge's reasoned judgement.

This somewhat clinical approach to litigation can be corrected by reference to other materials. First, and perhaps surprisingly, one can look to the further records produced by and for the courts. The various classes of documents that were generated in support of litigation can provide considerable information about individual litigants as well as patterns of litigation. This generally means navigating the awkward seas of the Public Record Office, though friendly beacons do exist with respect to some courts.[4] Nor are these the only relevant materials. The *Eighteenth-Century Short-Title Catalogue* contains many examples of judges' charges to grand juries.[5] Trial notebooks, kept by judges from the eighteenth century when their erroneous jury directions and mistakes on the admissibility of evidence became grounds for a new trial, constitute another important resource.[6] James Oldham has identified nine areas in which judicial notebooks can enhance the printed case reports, and several of these relate particularly to the actual process of litigation: by revealing further factual details, unreported portions of judges' opinions, suppressed reports of testimony, and jury instructions.[7] Documentation produced after criminal trials, in the form of petitions for mercy and judges' reports to the Home Secretary, rounds off our understanding of how the legal process operated. V. A. C. Gatrell includes considerable information on these sources as part of his larger study of capital punishment in the eighteenth and nineteenth centuries, and Roger Chadwick has written on the capital case files of the Victorian Home Office.[8]

Even more enlightening, however, are the trial accounts that were never prepared for the lawyer's eye. From the late seventeenth century commercial publishers began producing popular accounts of trials in pamphlet form. In the eighteenth century they were often compiled by well-known court and parliamentary shorthand writers, and they included many details of the courtroom proceedings excluded from the professional accounts. The majority of the pamphlets concerned trials of serious criminal offences, but civil trials also featured. Many of these accounts are available to scholars via two important collections. *The Old Bailey Sessions Papers* are pamphlets written on trials at the Old Bailey, the trial court for cases of felony committed in the city of London and Middlesex.[9] The modern compilation, *British Trials 1660–1900*, includes pamphlet accounts of civil and criminal trials from a variety of courts in Scotland, Wales, Ireland, and provincial England, as well as London.[10]

A particular version of the popular trial account emerged in 1712 with the publication of the *Accounts* of the ordinary, or chaplain, of the Newgate prison. These embellished the trial with a synopsis of the sermon preached to the condemned criminal, a narrative of his life and crimes, any statement provided (or allegedly provided) by the condemned, and details of his execution.[11] The inclusion of sermons and defendants' speeches from the scaffold imposed a moral tone on these accounts, however sensational their subject-matter. The object of raising the reader's moral standards by warning of the fatal consequences of bad conduct was made explicit in the genre that succeeded the *Accounts* in the later eighteenth century. Known as *Newgate Calendars*, but also published under such inspiring titles as *The Bloody Register* and *The Malefactor's Register*, these handsome volumes were designed as moral reference books to grace the libraries, and perhaps the nurseries,[12] of the high-minded members of the middle class. The frontispiece of the four-volume *Bloody Register* of 1764 features the inscription 'Learn to be wise from others Harms, And you shall do full well.'[13] Thomas Boyle has said of the *Calendar* genre, 'it functioned for its readers as a reassuring set of parables which illustrated virtue rewarded and immorality punished.'[14] Sir Samuel Romilly, who read the *Newgate* accounts as a child, admitted that they had given him nightmares.[15]

It would be wrong, however, to ascribe generally to the trial literature of the eighteenth and nineteenth centuries the goal of moral edification. More widespread, and of growing significance, was the aim of entertainment. Peter Wagner has argued that a focus on crime in combination with sex, shifting to the sexual aspects of trials and particularly trials concerning the sexual misbehaviour of the aristocracy, was a characteristic of some eighteenth-century trial reporting.[16] This trend is certainly noticeable in the many surviving collections of trials for criminal conversation, the common law action in which a husband sued his wife's lover for damages, and actions for annulment or separation in the ecclesiastical courts. An interest in sexuality was not always openly acknowledged in these texts. In a 'Notice' explaining a seven-volume compilation in 1780, the publisher primly explains that its aim is 'to deter the wavering wanton from the completion of her wishes', and also suggests that the collection 'may be of service to the practicers in the law, as they may have recourse to these trials for information, which will answer the same purpose in this, as the Law and Equity Reports in other courts'. Such a disclaimer may have been felt necessary, given the fact that the title has an arresting quality quite unlike that of the professional reports: *Trials for Adultery: or, The History of Divorces, Being Select Trials at Doctors Commons for ADULTERY, CRUELTY, FORNICATION, IMPOTENCE, &c.*[17] Another compilation, the two-volume *A New Collection of Trials for Adultery: or, General History of Modern Gallantry and Divorce*, published in 1799–1802, advertised that it was 'embellished with an elegant set of plates', another feature absent from the professional reports. That sex, criminality, and high society continued to exert a fascination for the readership of popular trial accounts is suggested by some of the titles chosen for compilations in the nineteenth century: *English Causes Célèbres* (1840), *Celebrated Trials Connected with the Aristocracy and the Upper Classes of Society in Relations of Private Life* (1848–51), *Sensational Trials: or, Causes Célèbres in High Life* (1865).

The public interest in trials was also reflected, and probably enhanced, by newspapers, and these provide a valuable resource to scholars less interested in particular 'celebrated' trials. In the late eighteenth century newspapers such as *The Times* provided limited coverage of important trials, but in the nineteenth century this coverage grew, and particularly after the abolition of stamp and paper taxes in the 1850s the number of newspapers exploded. Many, if not all, seem to have been interested in reporting on trials. *The Times*, Martin Wiener notes, developed a healthy appetite for murder, reporting on approximately 97 per cent of all murder trials listed in the Home Office files after 1840.[18] David Philips found a very extensive coverage of local criminal trials of all kinds in the mid-century newspapers of south Staffordshire,[19] and Patrick Polden has shown that the local newspaper reporter was a familiar figure in the county courts that came into existence in 1847, reporting on local disputes and revealing judicial styles, manners, and idiosyncrasies.[20] Moreover, because it was unclear whether reporting pre-trial investigations would render the author liable to prosecution for contempt of court, many Victorian criminal trials were not merely closely *followed* in the press; reports of the evidence against the accused were often published months before the trial.[21] The apparently insatiable appetite for stories about trials and courtroom conduct, which we associate with the late twentieth century, certainly has a longer pedigree.

The chapters that comprise this volume occupy a rather different niche. Versions of seven were presented at the 'Trial in History' conference, held at the University of Manchester. Written, as they were, without a more specific brief, it would be absurd to argue that they present a coherent picture of litigation between the eighteenth and twentieth centuries. The authors too come from a range of scholarly disciplines on both sides of the Atlantic, being three legal historians, one lawyer, three historians, and a sociologist. A glance at the titles of the chapters reveals that some focus on individual trials and some upon many trials. As a group the chapters are not confined to the courts of a single country, much less the work of a single court. Despite their diversity, however, all these chapters have an important point of contact. Central to each is the notion that trial litigation is permeated by influences that are not specifically legal – not fundamental to the legal adjudicative process. While recognising the importance of the practical and intellectual life of the law, these chapters demonstrate that the armour of legal rules and practices is particularly vulnerable in the courtroom. In that setting social, political, and cultural influences can have dramatic consequences. They violate (or perhaps transform?) legal rules, upset (or perhaps confirm?) expectations of legal certainty, and undermine (or perhaps redefine?) what we mean by *the trial*.

The first three chapters concern trials in the regular English criminal courts in the eighteenth and nineteenth centuries. Generally speaking, criminal trials in this period began with an accusation made before a lay magistrate. The accusation was brought by a member of the public or, increasingly during the nineteenth century, by a member of the newly created police forces. The office of Director of Public Prosecutions was not created until 1879. If the accusation concerned a very minor offence, the magistrate might try the matter himself, or with a colleague, without a jury. Since the sixteenth century, statutes had authorised such summary proceedings, often by a pair of magistrates at what became known as petty sessions. Where that process was not authorised, a misdemeanour or non-capital felony was tried by magistrate and jury, following a grand jury indictment. Trials of this kind occurred at quarter sessions, which were held four times annually in county towns. If the accusation concerned a capital offence the magistrate would almost certainly not undertake to try it, but would instead imprison or bind over the accused until the assizes, when royal justices would visit the designated assize towns, trying those persons indicted by grand juries, with the assistance of trial juries.

Lawyers themselves constitute the first 'external influence' in the present volume. Tom Gallanis considers the contribution of criminal lawyers in developing the modern rules of evidence. It may seem strange to regard lawyers as in any way *joining* the trial process because they are so integral to modern litigation, but ordinary English criminal trials largely functioned without them for hundreds of years. Their involvement gradually became more common during the eighteenth century, but restrictions on their role in court were not fully lifted until 1836, when defence counsel were placed upon an equal footing with prosecution counsel and permitted to address the jury in felony cases.[22] By examining the instances of evidentiary objections in civil cases between 1745 and 1820, Gallanis argues that lawyers' experiences in the new forum of the criminal courtroom equipped them with the skills and the sensibilities to create 'rules' of evidence to control the conduct of litigation in the civil courts.

Joel Eigen and Harry Cocks explore the influence of scientific and pseudo-scientific knowledge in chapters 2 and 3 on Victorian insanity trials and trials for homosexual offences, respectively. Eigen uses the murder trial of one William Newton Allnut as the springboard to a wider discussion of expert medical testimony in pleas of insanity. He shows us the medical expert, scientific conceptions of mental disease, and popular notions of the unconscious invading the courtroom and threatening traditional 'legal' categories of fact and opinion. In contrast, Victorian society's understanding of homosexuality seeped inconsistently into criminal trials for homosexual offences, not through medical testimony but through character evidence. Drawing on a number of trials, Cocks explains that contemporary views of homosexuality as a species of mental deficiency emerged in the character evidence admissible against an accuser. Character evidence of that type was not, however, admissible against a defendant. Neither Eigen nor Cocks argues for a sharp distinction between legal and non-legal influences in their respective trials. Defence lawyers, Eigen notes, played a crucial role in introducing new ideas about the mind, consciousness, and responsibility in the service of their clients. Men charged with homosexual offences, on the other hand, often resisted the admission of scientific evidence on homosexual propensity – they did not wish to admit the offence and plead mental deficiency in mitigation.

The next two chapters consider examples of litigation in more unusual English tribunals, Parliament and courts-martial. The House of Lords, where Queen Caroline's 'trial' took place in 1820, had an established civil and criminal appellate jurisdiction as well as jurisdiction in respect of impeachments by the House of Commons and trials of peers for treason or felony. The accusation of adultery made against the wife of George IV, however, occurred in the context of *legislation* to deprive her of her royal status and affect a divorce. Debate on the bill assumed a judicial character during the second reading stage when counsel presented a 'prosecution' and 'defence' consisting of witness testimony, documentary evidence, and professional legal argument, and the 'verdict' of the House determined the bill's fate. Brian Simpson's chapter on modern trials *in camera* concerns litigation in the regular English criminal courts, but also in courts-martial. During the first part of the twentieth century, British military personnel could be tried by court-martial for offences of a particularly military nature and for ordinary criminal offences, as the latter were deemed to constitute offences under military law.[23] Trial before a civil court barred a subsequent court-martial on the same or similar charge, but the same rule did not operate in reverse.[24] There were several types of court-martial available, depending on the status of the accused, the seriousness of the offence, and the circumstances in which the offence was to be tried. When forces were on active service, for example, a field court-martial could dispense with several of the procedural safeguards that characterised the general court-martial, the tribunal having ordinary authority to try capital offences.[25]

One might argue that, because courts are created by the state, staffed by judges who are often government appointees, and apply rules enacted by national legislatures, politics can never be far from the trial process. In some situations, however, political influence has a particularly disruptive, and arguably corrosive, effect. Simpson examines the practice of excluding the public from the courtroom, particularly in the context of espionage and other cases of national security. He identifies the roles of MI5, the War Office, Home Office, and government lawyers in achieving greater levels of public exclusion, and discusses how legislation, enacted ostensibly to protect the public from foreign and domestic treachery, helped to undermine one of the basic elements of the trial process. Further, the chapter shows how patriotism, deference, and the self-replicating culture of secrecy could result in the trial, conviction, and execution of British citizens in conditions of almost complete anonymity. In 'Pains and penalties procedure', on the other hand, I focus on the political influences in a single, high-profile trial. I attempt to show how the Earl of Liverpool's government was obliged to set in motion a complex legal process, the significant burdens that decision placed upon all who participated in the trial, and the very indifferent results of the experiment.

With the chapters of Dominic McGoldrick, Peter Lowe, and Robert Boyce we leave the specifically English trial setting. McGoldrick and Lowe examine international trials for war crimes – what are sometimes referred to as breaches of international humanitarian law – and human rights violations. The twentieth century witnessed the creation of an apparently impressive range of international tribunals with authority to consider such offences: the International Court of Justice, the European Court of Human Rights, the Inter-American Court of Human Rights, and the African Court of Human Rights. All of these, however, adjudicated state responsibility for violations of international law; they did not have jurisdiction over individuals or the power to determine individual accountability for international crime. A permanent international criminal court was proposed by the League of Nations as early as 1937, but it failed to receive any significant support.[26] After the Second World War the United Nations undertook a long and what looks to be a successful campaign to create a court, but the century ended with the ratification process incomplete. Such international criminal prosecutions as occurred during the twentieth century, therefore, took place in tribunals specifically created to deal with particular examples of extreme and sustained criminality: the atrocities committed during the Second World War, and during the conflicts in Rwanda and the former Yugoslavia.

McGoldrick and Lowe show that the obstacles to achieving a satisfactory process can multiply when trials take place outside a traditional legal system. That war crimes tribunals were strongly influenced by international politics should come as no surprise. Called into being by such organisations or nations that claimed, however imperfectly, to act on behalf of the international community, in the immediate aftermath of horrific conduct, they could hardly be compared to judicial bodies with less-dramatic creations and life spans measured in centuries, rather than years. In his first chapter McGoldrick surveys the trials in Nuremberg, Tokyo, Yugoslavia, and Rwanda, but gives primary attention to the latter two. In the course of examining how the various tribunals were established and functioned, he identifies the particular problems that their international status provoked. These included identifying the 'international community' to which they were accountable and assessing its expectations, maintaining sufficient levels of co-operation with individual states who might otherwise refuse to extradite suspects or support the court financially, and achieving an acceptable relationship with the government and people of the state in which the court had been placed. Lowe focuses on a particular trial, that of the Japanese leaders for planning and carrying out aggression in Asia and the Pacific region between 1928 and 1945. In addition to querying the general parameters of the trial in terms of its fairness, he examines its particular legal and non-legal features. By highlighting the conduct of the lawyers and judges involved, the signals sent from the British and American governments in London and Washington, and the influence exerted by the effective government in Japan, General Douglas MacArthur, Lowe illustrates the range of extra-legal difficulties that plagued the proceedings. These included friction within the Anglo-American prosecution team and questionable competence among the panel of Allied judges. Allied and Japanese public opinion played a significant role, influencing the decision to hold the trial in the first place, as well as the decision to exclude Emperor Hirohito.

Enforcement of international human rights and humanitarian law during the twentieth century was not restricted to international tribunals. The various treaties and other international instruments on these subjects anticipated the involvement of domestic courts by permitting or requiring states to penalise offences under their own laws, if their legal systems did not permit a domestic prosecution directly on the basis of international law.[27] German courts tried suspected war criminals following the First World War, and a number of states, including Germany, conducted prosecutions for war crimes or common crimes after the Second World War. Domestic trials of offences related to that conflict continued sporadically for the rest of the century, and included the trial in Israel of Adolf Eichmann for war crimes, crimes against humanity, and crimes against the Jewish people; and the trials in France of Klaus Barbie, Paul Touvier, and, most recently, Maurice Papon, for war crimes and crimes against humanity.[28] Robert Boyce's chapter focuses on the last of these.

It is perhaps fitting that, having begun with a chapter focusing upon the 'external influence' of lawyers in trials, we turn to a chapter focusing on the comparable role of history. Prior to Papon's trial, commentators perceived it as an opportunity for history. They believed it would expose and dispel the lingering demon of France's wartime experiences, as well as educate a new generation in the dangers of anti-semitism. Historians were recruited to participate in the process as expert witnesses, drawing on their scholarly expertise to inform the *Papon* jury on military and political conditions during the Second World War. However Boyce queries whether the trial actually served its 'historical' function by helping to reveal the character of the Vichy civil service as personified in the defendant. Indeed, perhaps history itself was put 'on trial' along with Papon, as the historian's tools – documentation, memory, and professional objectivity – vied with legal analysis and social imperatives as providing the best means of revealing truth.

A trial's 'historical' function is queried again in Dominic McGoldrick's chapter on the trial of Slobodan Milosevic, which concludes this volume. In the spring of 2002 Milosevic became the first former head of state to be tried by an international tribunal for war crimes. This fact alone renders the trial a historic occasion. As McGoldrick notes, however, far more than Milosevic's own conduct may be on trial at The Hague. These proceedings may constitute the last significant chapter in the history of the ad hoc international criminal tribunal – will it confirm or undermine the validity of such an institution? Moreover, the prosecution has claimed that this trial will form an important part of the long, bloody history of the Balkans – will it help to exorcise the spectre of ethnic hatred or contribute to further conflict? Lawyers and historians must wait to see whether this trial will change history, or whether history will overwhelm this trial.

Notes

1 A. W. B. Simpson, *Leading Cases in the Common Law* (Oxford: Clarendon Press, 1995). See, for example, J. Langbein, 'The criminal trial before the lawyers', *University of Chicago Law Review*, 45 (1978), 236–316; J. Langbein, 'Shaping the eighteenth-century criminal trial, a view from the Ryder sources', *University of Chicago Law Review*, 50 (1983), 1–136; J. Langbein, 'The prosecutorial origins of defence counsel

in the eighteenth century: the appearance of solicitors', *Cambridge Law Journal*, 58: 2 (1999), 314–65.

2 See, for example, Simpson, *Leading Cases*, p. 10.

3 J. H. Baker, *An Introduction to English Legal History*, 3rd edn (London: Butterworths, 1990), pp. 204–11.

4 See, for example, M. Cale, *Law and Society: an Introduction to Sources for Criminal and Legal History from 1800* (Kew: PRO Publications, 1996); H. Horwitz, *Chancery Equity Records and Proceedings 1600–1800. A Guide to the Documents in the Public Record Office*, 2nd edn (London: H.M.S.O., 1995, 1998). For a less comprehensive, but informative, treatment of the equity proceedings in the court of Exchequer, see J. Milhous and R. D. Hume, 'Eighteenth-century equity lawsuits in the court of Exchequer as a source for historical research', *Historical Research*, 70 (1997), 231–46.

5 See, for example, H. L. Snyder, 'Charges to grand juries: the evidence of the eighteenth-century Short Title Catalogue', *Historical Research*, 67 (1994), 286–300.

6 The notebooks held in the Harvard Law School, Lincoln's Inn, Gray's Inn, and the Bodleian Library have been reproduced on microfiche by the English Legal Manuscripts Project. For details of the specific materials, see J. H. Baker, *MSS Sources – English legal Manuscripts*, 2 vols (Zug, Switzerland: Inter Documentation Company AG, 1975, 1978).

7 J. Oldham, 'Eighteenth-century judges' notes: how they explain, correct, and enhance the reports', *The American Journal of Legal History*, 31 (1987), 9–42, 10. Oldham has also written extensively on Lord Mansfield's notebooks, *The Mansfield Manuscripts and the Growth of English Law in the Eighteenth Century*, 2 vols (Chapel Hill: University of North Carolina Press, 1992).

8 V. A. C. Gatrell, *The Hanging Tree: Execution and the English People 1770–1868* (Oxford: Oxford University Press, 1996); R. Chadwick, *Bureaucratic Mercy: the Home Office and the Treatment of Capital Cases in Victorian Britain* (New York: Garland, 1992).

9 Compilations of Old Bailey trials were also produced in book form during the eighteenth century, and four volumes of trials from the early eighteenth century have been published as part of the series, R. Trumbach (ed.), *Marriage, Sex, and the Family in England 1660–1800*, 34 vols (New York: Garland, 1985).

10 *British Trials 1660–1900* microfiche and guides (Cambridge: Chadwyck-Healey, 1990).

11 P. Linebaugh, 'The ordinary of Newgate and his *Account*', in J. S. Cockburn (ed.), *Crime in England 1550–1800* (London: Methuen & Co., 1977), pp. 246–69.

12 The idea that children could be influenced, not merely by the accounts of how criminals had come to grief but by participating in actual 'trials' of their fellows, seems to have been behind *Juvenile Trials for Robbing Orchards, Telling Fibs, and Other Heinous Crimes*. Published in 1786 by R. Johnson, *Juvenile Trials* describes how a tutor and governess organise a tribunal in which their young charges can prosecute, judge, and impose punishments on each other, the 'sessions' being presided over by the aptly named Master Meanwell and Miss Sterling.

13 *The Bloody Register*, ed. N. Groom, facs. edn, 4 vols (London: Routledge, 1999).

14 T. Boyle, *Black Swine in the Sewers of Hampstead: Beneath the Surface of Victorian Sensationalism* (London: Hodder & Stoughton, 1990), p. 44.

15 Sir S. Romilly, *Memoirs of Sir Samuel Romilly*, 3 vols (London: John Murray, 1840), vol. 1, p. 11.
16 P. Wagner, 'Trial reports as a genre of eighteenth-century erotica', *British Journal for Eighteenth-Century Studies*, 5: 1 (1982), 117–21.
17 A facsimile edition is published as part of Trumbach (ed.), *Marriage*.
18 M. J. Wiener, 'Judges v. jurors: courtroom tensions in murder trials and the law of criminal responsibility in nineteenth-century England', *Law and History Review*, 17: 3 (1999), 467–506.
19 D. Philips, *Crime and Authority in Victorian England: the Black Country 1835–1860* (London: Croom Helm, 1977).
20 P. Polden, 'Judicial Selkirks: the county court judges and the press, 1847–80', in C. Brooks and M. Lobban (eds), *Communities and Courts in Britain, 1150–1900* (London: The Hambledon Press, 1997), pp. 245–62.
21 J. Knelman, 'Trial by newspaper in nineteenth-century England', *Media Law and Practice*, 15: 4 (1994), 106–10.
22 6 & 7 Will. IV *c.* 114 (1836). See D. J. A. Cairns, *Advocacy and the Making of the Adversarial Criminal Trial 1800–1865* (Oxford: Clarendon Press, 1998).
23 44 & 45 Vict. *c.* 58 (1881) s. 41.
24 See J. Stuart-Smith, 'Military law: its history, administration and practice', *Law Quarterly* Review, 85 (1969), 478–504, 491.
25 See 44 & 45 Vict. *c.* 58 (1881) as modified by Army Rules of Procedure 1900, S.I. 1900/31, and Army Rules of Procedure 1926, S.I. 1926/989.
26 S. R. Ratner and J. S. Abrams, *Accountability for Human Rights Atrocities in International Law* (Oxford: Clarendon Press, 1997), p. 177.
27 For example, the War Crimes Act (1991), criminalises war crimes and human rights offences linked to war crimes under UK law.
28 *Attorney-General of the Government of Israel* v. *Eichmann*, 36 I.L.R. 5 (1961); *Fédération Nationale des Déportés et Internés Résistants et Patriotes and Others* v. *Barbie*, 78 I.L.R. 125 (1985); *Touvier*, 100 I.L.R. 338 (1992).

1

Evidence law and the evidentiary objection: a view from the *British Trials* collection

T. P. Gallanis

'When a man raises his eyes from the common-law system of evidence', wrote Professor Thayer in 1898, 'he is struck with the fact that our system is radically peculiar'.[1] Thayer explained: 'Here, a great mass of evidential matter, logically important and probative, is shut out . . . by an imperative rule, while the same matter is not thus excluded anywhere else. English-speaking countries have what we call a "Law of Evidence"; but no other country has it; we alone have generated and evolved this large, elaborate, and difficult doctrine'.[2] Today, more than a century later, Thayer's observations retain nearly all of their original force. Despite statutory modifications, Anglo-American law remains devoted to the exclusion of otherwise probative testimony,[3] an attitude wholly unfathomable to lawyers trained, for example, in the civilian systems of Continental Europe.[4]

How, when, and why did this quintessentially Anglo-American approach to testimony develop? There seems to be a working assumption among legal historians that it emerged first in civil trials, where lawyers had been active for centuries, and spread to criminal trials in the late eighteenth century when lawyers began doing regular criminal work.[5] On its face, this assumption is plausible. The only problem is that newly available sources point in exactly the opposite direction. Chadwyck-Healey has recently released on microfiche more than one thousand pamphlet accounts of civil and criminal trials. This collection, entitled *British Trials 1660–1900*, contains the only readily accessible and near-verbatim accounts of civil trials from the 1760s, 1770s, and 1780s, decades crucial to understanding how the rules of evidence developed.[6] An examination of these pamphlets suggests that the routine use of the objection to oral evidence in civil cases developed only *after* lawyers had begun to appear regularly in criminal trials.

I conducted a sample of the civil trial pamphlets in the *British Trials* collection dating from the years 1745 to 1820.[7] The average number of objections per case is displayed in Figure 1.1. The data in this chart tell the story. Between

Figure 1.1 *Objections to oral evidence in civil cases, 1745–1820*

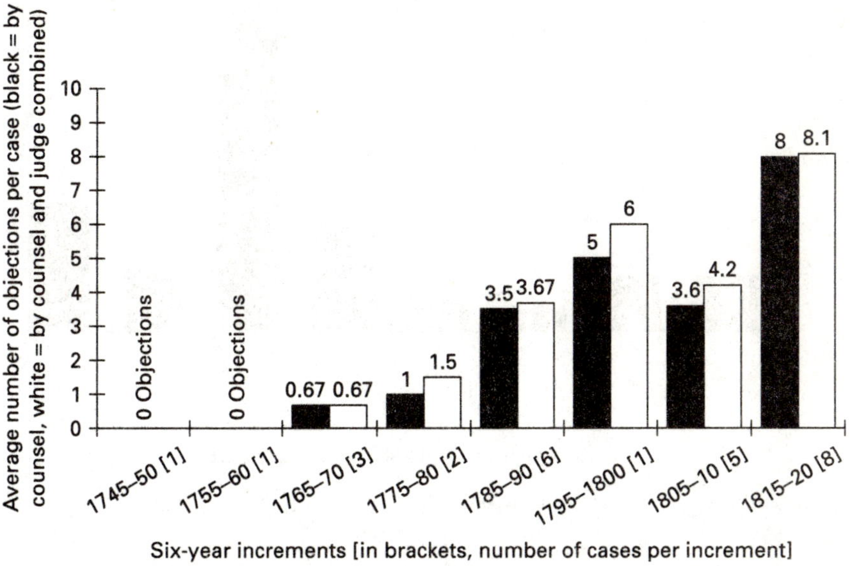

Source: *British Trials 1660–1900* (Cambridge: Chadwyck-Healey, 1990–), Units 1–3.

1745 and 1760, the cases in the sample contained no objections whatsoever to oral evidence. Between 1765 and 1780, the average number of such objections per case increased slightly, first to 0.67 and then to 1.0.[8] This pattern of minimal growth was replaced by a noticeable jump between 1785 and 1790, when the average number of objections per case rose to 3.5. A moderate increase then brought the number to 5.0 between 1795 and 1800, followed by a mild downturn between 1805 and 1810. Finally, in the last set of cases (between 1815 and 1820) another increase raised the number to 8.0.

Lord Jowitt was fond of saying that the secret of a good lawyer's success is to discover the worst thing an opponent can say and then to say it oneself.[9] With this admonition in mind, I should say a few words about two possible weaknesses in the data. First, the number of cases in the sample is very low. Each six-year average is based on somewhere between one and eight cases, and the mean number of cases for each calculation is only 3.4. These numbers are quite small and candour requires me to say that it is theoretically possible that the phenomenon I have described – a significant increase in the use of objections – did not actually exist. My reading of the cases, however, leads me to discount this possibility. There is a marked change in tone between the cases at each end of the sample. Even today, trials at which witnesses can testify unimpeded sound very different from trials interrupted by constant objections. The cases in the middle of the eighteenth century flow much more naturally

Figure 1.2 *Length of pamphlet accounts of civil cases, 1745–1820*

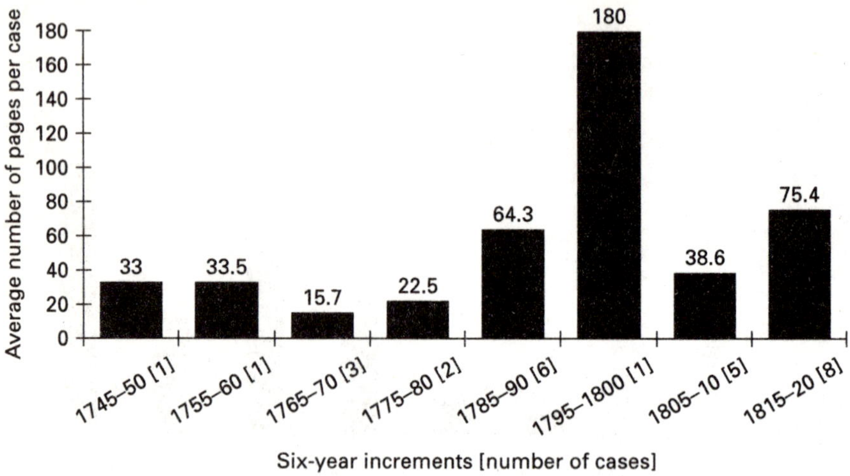

Source: *British Trials 1660–1900* (Cambridge: Chadwyck-Healey, 1990–), Units 1–3.

than those in the late 1810s, a phenomenon that did not go unnoticed by observers at the time.[10] Accordingly, I am inclined to think that the sample, although small in overall numbers, does reflect a real change in trial practice.

The second potential weakness in the data is that the trials are of varying length. The fourteen-fold increase in the number of objections per case would be less significant if the trials at the beginning of the sample were fourteen times shorter. I have therefore graphed in Figure 1.2 the average page length of the trial reports in each six-year sample. As the numbers reveal, there is not much of an upward or downward pattern in the data. The cases at the end of the sample are approximately twice as long as those at the beginning, but between the starting and ending points, the graph moves up and down erratically. It therefore seems sensible to say that the observed increase in the use of objections is not just a reflection of the length of the trial.

Having examined and rejected these two possible weaknesses, let us assume that the numbers in the sample reflect reality. What then? What could have caused the use of testimonial objections in civil cases to develop in the late eighteenth century? The answer, I argue, is the influence from criminal procedure. I base this argument on three grounds: first, chronology; second, the restrictions in criminal cases on counsel's power; and third, the particular lawyers raising most of the objections.

According to the data, a noticeable increase in the number of objections to oral evidence began sometime in the 1780s. I have been unable to find any reason particular to civil cases that would explain this phenomenon. To take just two examples, the procedural reforms introduced by Lord Mansfield were either unrelated or too early,[11] and the *nisi prius* reports – which Professor Wigmore saw as an important factor in the history of evidence[12] – did not begin until 1790.[13] All of this led me to ask: if there was no obvious cause in civil practice, might the chronology fit better with developments in criminal litigation? The answer to this question is yes. Thanks to the work of Professor Langbein and others, we know that the use of lawyers at the Old Bailey rose sharply in the late eighteenth century.[14] Professor Beattie has quantified this increase, which seems to have begun around the year 1780.[15] According to Beattie, the percentage of cases with defence counsel stayed at or below 6 per cent until 1780; in that year, the percentage rose to 7.3, followed by 12.8 per cent in 1782, 17.6 per cent in 1784, and 20.2 per cent in 1786.[16] A similar rise occurred on the prosecution side, where counsel appeared in less than 1 per cent of the cases in 1775, 3.8 per cent in 1780, more than 7 per cent in 1782 and 1784, and 10.9 per cent in 1786.[17] What these numbers show is a dramatic rise in legal representation in criminal trials. In the short time between 1775 and 1786, the use of counsel at the Old Bailey increased approximately ten-fold.[18] It is highly suggestive that the use of testimonial objections in civil cases rose only a few years after an increase in the appearance of lawyers on the criminal side. But to be persuasive, the connection between the two must rest on more than mere chronology.

More than chronology supports this article's thesis. Certain aspects of criminal practice suggest that the objection was more likely to develop there than in the civil trial. In particular, lawyers representing criminal defendants had much less power than their counterparts in civil practice. In the late eighteenth century, even as the use of lawyers in criminal cases was rising rapidly, the prisoner's counsel was allowed to do little more than cross-examine the victim and the other witnesses supporting the charge.[19] Significantly, he was not allowed to address the jury.[20] On this point, an Old Bailey judge in 1790 was emphatic; as he told the prisoner, 'Your counsel cannot speak for you. If you have any account to give of yourself to the jury . . . or if you have any thing to observe on the evidence, you must do it yourself.'[21]

This restriction on defence counsel remained formally in place until 1836[22] and had important implications for evidentiary practice. On the civil side, lawyers were well equipped to deal with potentially dangerous testimony. Not only did they have the right to examine and cross-examine witnesses, but they routinely spoke directly to the jury, which enabled them either to explain away unsafe testimony or to disparage its reliability.[23] Lawyers representing criminal defendants, however, were forced to focus their energies on vigorous cross-examination and the use of evidentiary objections.[24] To use a theatrical metaphor, we can think of lawyers in criminal cases spending comparatively little time on stage; while the curtain was up, they had to make every moment count. And this new level of courtroom warfare did not go unnoticed. One observer remarked in the late 1780s that ordinary citizens did not want to report crimes and go to court for fear of being 'entangled' in cross-examination.[25]

Another observer writing in the 1790s argued that defence counsel had become so powerful that only a system of public prosecution could bring back a level playing field.[26] Although potentially alarming at the time, the vigorousness of lawyers in criminal trials was the logical response to the limited ways in which they were able to act on behalf of their clients.

All of this made sense in the criminal context. But how did the objection migrate into civil litigation? To answer this question, we need to look closely at the particular lawyers who made the most use of evidentiary objections. One advantage of the *British Trials* pamphlets is that they often identify the lawyers involved in each civil action. As I was reading the cases in the sample, I noticed that some lawyers raised objections to oral evidence much more frequently than others. In fact, a small set of lawyers seemed to be doing most of the objecting. The precise data are contained in Table 1.1, which lists the

Table 1.1 *Lawyers raising objections to oral evidence in civil cases, 1765–1820*

	Number of objections						
Name	*1765–70*	*1775–80*	*1785–90*	*1795–1800*	*1805–10*	*1815–20*	*Total*
Messing	2						2
Davy		1					1
Thurlow		1					1
Bearcroft			5				5
Adair			7				7
Grose			2				2
Garrow			2	4	2	4	12
Lawrence			1				1
Baldwin			2				2
Bower			2				2
LeBlanc				1			1
Shepherd					1		1
Gibbs					5		5
Best					8	9	17
Dauncey					1		1
Gurney					1	1	2
Lens						13	13
Copely						2	2
Vaughn						5	5
Topping						3	3
Scarlett						17	17
Hullock						2	2
Raine						1	1
Cross						7	7

Source: *British Trials 1660–1900* (Cambridge: Chadwyck-Healey, 1990–), Units 1–3.
Note: Lawyers raising five or more objections are shown in italics.

lawyers in the order in which they first raised an objection. The total number of objections made by each person is contained in the final column.

Who were the big objectors? In the first half of the table, and therefore reflecting the early development of this new practice, the lawyers raising the most objections were Edward Bearcroft (five objections), James Adair (seven objections), and William Garrow (six objections before 1800 and six objections thereafter). Comparatively little biographical information exists about Bearcroft.[27] Various sources reveal that he practised on the Oxford Circuit,[28] and he was described in a book of legal sketches as an 'eminent advocate'.[29] But no information appears to survive about the range of matters he handled, and to what extent (if at all) he acted in criminal cases. With respect to Adair and Garrow, however, biographical material is far more plentiful. Both men had extensive experience with criminal trials and, in particular, with the proceedings at the Old Bailey. For Adair, this experience came during his tenure as recorder of London, a post he held from 1779 to 1789.[30] One of the recorder's duties was to sit as an Old Bailey judge, and during his ten years on the job, Adair presided over exactly eighty sessions.[31] After stepping down, he worked predominantly on civil cases, concentrating his practice in the Court of Common Pleas.[32] Adair's tenure as recorder straddled the benchmark year 1780, around which time lawyers began appearing more and more in criminal trials. One of these lawyers, and perhaps the most well known, was William Garrow. So much has been written about him that only a few words are needed here.[33] Garrow's early career centred on the Old Bailey, and he quickly distinguished himself as a master at cross-examination.[34] By the early 1790s, less than ten years after being called to the bar, Garrow was widely regarded as the leading criminal barrister in London.[35] He also practised in civil cases, and in 1793, after being named a King's Counsel, began to work exclusively on the civil side.[36]

No two men by themselves could have established the evidentiary objection as a regular feature of civil practice, but I would argue that it is right to think of Adair and Garrow as members of a larger group of lawyers whose experiences in criminal practice had an influence on their conduct in civil litigation. As lawyers began working more and more in criminal trials, it is natural that the skills and techniques needed for success in that arena would, over time, be deployed on the civil battlefield as well.

Mindful of Lord Jowitt's advice, let me be the first to say that the surviving sources do not contain the proverbial smoking gun, but then few sources ever do. Instead, this hypothesis relies on three important pieces of the puzzle: chronology, the limits on counsel's power in criminal cases, and the particular lawyers raising these objections in civil trials. It is highly suggestive that, in civil litigation, the use of the objection to oral evidence rose just after the appearance of lawyers in criminal practice did the same. This chronological connection makes sense, because the restricted role of counsel in criminal cases naturally led them to focus their adversarial energies on vigorous cross-examination and the repeated use of evidentiary objections. The connection can also be demonstrated empirically, because the lawyers raising the most objections in the late eighteenth century – Adair and Garrow – had extensive experience with criminal practice at the Old Bailey.

The conventional wisdom has long held that the distinctively Anglo-American approach to evidence law and evidentiary practice must have developed first in civil cases, where lawyers had been practising since the Middle Ages, and then migrated much later into the criminal context. But the pamphlets examined in this article tell a different story. Indeed, they point in exactly the opposite direction. They suggest that a crucial impetus for the development of the modern rules limiting oral evidence – a more aggressive attitude on the part of lawyers striving to keep problematic testimony from the ears of the jury – manifested itself first in the criminal courts and spread from there into civil litigation.

Notes

This chapter is a revised version of the introduction and Part IV of T. P. Gallanis, 'The rise of modern evidence law', *Iowa Law Review* 84: 3 (1999), 499–560, which received the Selden Society's David Yale Prize for 1999. The present article was prepared while the author was a Mellon Fellow at the Institute for Advanced Study, Princeton, and he thanks the Andrew W. Mellon Foundation and the Institute for Advanced Study for their support of his research.

1 J. B. Thayer, *A Preliminary Treatise on Evidence at the Common Law* (Boston: Little Brown, 1898), pp. 1–2.
2 *Ibid.*
3 E.g., R. Bagshaw (ed.), *Cross and Wilkins: Outline of the Law of Evidence*, 7th edn (London: Butterworths, 1996), p. 2.
4 See J. H. Langbein, 'The English criminal trial jury on the eve of the French Revolution', in A. P. Schioppa (ed.), *The Trial Jury in England, France, Germany: 1700–1900* (Berlin: Duncker & Humblot, 1987), pp. 33–4; J. H. Langbein, 'The German advantage in civil procedure', *University of Chicago Law Review*, 52: 4 (1985), 829.
5 E.g., J. Oldham, *The Mansfield Manuscripts and the Growth of English Law in the Eighteenth Century* (Chapel Hill: University of North Carolina Press, 1992), p. 144. Professor Langbein has questioned this working assumption but has left it to other scholars to test it. J. H. Langbein, 'Historical foundations of the law of evidence: a view from the Ryder sources', *Columbia Law Review*, 96: 5 (1996), 1202.
6 On the importance of these decades, see Gallanis, 'Rise', pp. 536–7.
7 I read all cases that fell within six-year increments between 1745 and 1820 (in other words, 1745–50, 1755–60, and so on).
8 Please note that I am referring here to objections raised by counsel, shown in Figure 1.1 in black. Interventions by judges also occurred, but these were very infrequent. See Figure 1.1, where the white bars represent the combined number of objections raised by counsel and judges.
9 R. F. V. Heuston, *Lives of the Lord Chancellors, 1940–1970* (Oxford: Clarendon Press, 1987), p. 115.

10 As one writer put it in 1819: 'There are few abuses at the Bar more crying . . . than the mode in which the examination of witnesses is sometimes conducted. . . . [A witness] may enter the box with a resolution to tell a plain straight-forward story, and to adhere closely to the facts within his own knowledge; but if he be not a man of more than ordinary firmness and acuteness, his purpose will be defeated by those who have attained such skill in confusing what is clear, and involving what is simple'. [J. P. Collier,] *Criticisms on the Bar* (London: W. Simpkin & R. Marshall, 1819), pp. 109–10.

11 For discussions of these reforms, see C. H. S. Fifoot, *Lord Mansfield* (Oxford: Clarendon Press, 1936), pp. 52–81; Oldham, *Mansfield Manuscripts*, pp. 140–60.

12 J. H. Wigmore, *A Treatise on the Anglo-American System of Evidence in Trials at Common Law*, 3rd edn (Boston: Little Brown, 1940), vol. 1, p. 238.

13 J. H. Baker, *An Introduction to English Legal History*, 4th edn (London: Butterworths, 2002), p. 412.

14 J. H. Langbein, 'Shaping the eighteenth-century criminal trial: a view from the Ryder sources', *University of Chicago Law Review* 50: 1 (1983), 124–6; J. M. Beattie, 'Scales of justice: defense counsel and the English criminal trial in the eighteenth and nineteenth centuries', *Law and History Review*, 9: 2 (1991), 226–30.

15 Beattie, 'Scales', pp. 227–8.

16 *Ibid.*, p. 227.

17 *Ibid.*

18 These numbers concentrate on criminal practice in London. Information about lawyers on assize is considerably sketchier. There are a few hints here and there that lawyers were more prominent on assize, but none of these dates from the late eighteenth century. E.g., C. Cottu, *De l'Administration de la justice criminelle en Angleterre et de l'esprit du gouvernement anglais* (Paris: H. Nicolle, 1820), p. 93; Oldham, *Mansfield Manuscripts*, p. 137. For the moment, the best guide is probably Professor Beattie's study of the Surrey Assizes. The relevant records in Surrey do not survive for the years after 1774; but at least until then, Beattie argues persuasively, the appearance of counsel in Surrey and at the Old Bailey followed the same 'broad pattern'. J. M. Beattie, *Crime and the Courts in England, 1660–1800* (Oxford: Oxford University Press, 1986), p. 360. It therefore seems reasonable to assume that the use of lawyers on assize also increased during the 1780s, even though at this point we have no way to quantify that rise.

19 Langbein, 'Shaping', p. 129; e.g., *R.* v. *Smith*, *Old Bailey Sessions Papers* [hereafter *OBSP*] July 1755 (no. 268), pp. 234–5.

20 E.g., *R.* v. *Davis*, *OBSP*, October 1755 (nos 390–2), p. 354.

21 *R.* v. *Newton*, *OBSP*, January 1790 (no. 128), p. 139.

22 Beattie, 'Scales', pp. 250–8.

23 For two examples out of many in the *British Trials* pamphlets, see *Onslow* v. *Horne* (1770) *British Trials 1660–1900* (Cambridge: Chadwyck-Healey, 1990–) [hereafter *BT*], no. 59, pp. 5–19, 31–9; *Knowles* v. *Gambier* (1757), *BT*, no. 57, pp. 4–11, 33–9, 51–6.

24 For recent commentary, see Beattie, 'Scales', pp. 232–6; S. Landsman, 'The rise of the contentious spirit: adversary procedure in eighteenth-century England', *Cornell Law Review*, 75: 3 (1990), 548–57.

25 J. Hawkins, *The Life of Samuel Johnson LL.D.* (Dublin: Chambers, 1787), p. 462. I owe this reference and the next one to Professor Beattie.

26 P. Colquhoun, *A Treatise on the Police of the Metropolis* (London: H. Fry, 1796), pp. 31–2, 246–7.

27 For example, Bearcroft's obituaries in the *Annual Register* (Chron. 1796, p. 44) and the *Gentleman's Magazine* (1796, p. 44) contain little information about his legal practice.

28 *Masters of the Bench of the Honourable Society of the Inner Temple, 1450–1883, and Masters of the Temple, 1540–1883* (privately printed, 1883), p. 81 (available in the University Library, Cambridge, under shelfmark LE.7.122); J. A. Venn (ed.), *Alumni Cantabrigienses: Part II, 1752–1900*, vol. 1 (Cambridge: Cambridge University Press, 1940), p. 202; T. A. Walker, *Admissions to Peterhouse or S. Peter's College, 1615–1911* (Cambridge: Cambridge University Press, 1912), p. 304.

29 [A. Polson,] *Law and Lawyers*, 2 vols (London: Longman, 1840), vol. 1, p. 182.

30 *Dictionary of National Biography* [hereafter *DNB*], vol. 1 (London: Smith Elder, 1908), pp. 69–70.

31 According to the *OBSP*, Adair's first session was held in October 1779; his last session was held in June 1789.

32 *DNB*, vol. 1, p. 69; e.g., *Brown* v. *Phoenix Assurance Company* (1789), BT no. 896.

33 For sketches of his life, see *DNB*, vol. 7, pp. 907–8; E. Foss, *A Biographical Dictionary of the Judges of England* (London: John Murray, 1870), pp. 289–90; Polson, *Law and Lawyers*, vol. 1, pp. 216–18. For more recent commentary, see Beattie, 'Scales', pp. 236–47.

34 *DNB*, vol. 7, p. 908.

35 Beattie, 'Scales', p. 237.

36 *Ibid.*

2

Sense and sensibility: fateful splitting in the Victorian insanity trial

Joel Peter Eigen

Sometime before Sunday dinner on 22 October 1848, 12-year-old William Newton Allnutt added arsenic to the family sugar bowl. There could have been no mistake about his intended victim: only the boy's grandfather was in the habit of sprinkling sugar on his after-dinner fruit, and this Sunday was no exception. Recovering from this first attempt on his life, the victim attended church accompanied by his murderous grandson, but he would not survive a second poisoning. Allnutt's eventual trial and conviction in London's central criminal court, the Old Bailey, took place five years after the celebrated 1843 insanity acquittal of Daniel McNaughtan.[1] Unlike the famous would-be assassin of Robert Peel, however, the young poisoner did not have nine prominent medical practitioners and authors to explain his mental state to the jury. William Newton Allnutt's three medical witnesses included only a family physician, a relative who happened to be a doctor, and a mad-house superintendent who had never actually met him.

Although Allnutt and his trial have received nowhere near the attention accorded to McNaughtan, the testimony medical witnesses offered on the 12-year-old's behalf affords today's legal historian an invaluable glimpse into courtroom dynamics that shaped the assertion of expert medical opinion in the mid-Victorian insanity trial. Forensic-psychiatric opinion was hardly a novel occurrence to the English courtroom; at the time of the Allnutt trial, mad-doctors had been appearing in English courts for almost one hundred years.[2] The simple fact of participation, however, tells one little of the substance of early forensic-psychiatric testimony, and in the case of the juvenile poisoner, may easily obscure the qualitative shift that such opinion would take. William Newton Allnutt's trial would be no ordinary Victorian insanity case; jurors would not hear testimony about delusion or delirium *leading* the young boy to his murderous deed. Instead, medical men would use the occasion to introduce into the English courtroom a 'species' of derangement that had nothing to do with confusion, incoherence, or insensibility. In their testimony, they would proceed to place Allnutt among an emerging population of mid-Victorian defendants whose mental process was split between the functions of understanding and feeling: between the resources of *sense* and *sensibility*.

I Fact or opinion

The unique province claimed by medical witnesses in this, and other nineteenth-century trials, rested initially on the question of mental derangement's status as a fact – no different from other facts entered into evidence. Traditionally, English law considered facts to be direct sensory products: what neighbours saw, heard, or smelled. Neither judgement nor inference was thought to be required. Facts were conceived to be unproblematic reports of on-scene impressions.[3] This was, after all, the reason that witnesses were called into court to begin with: to inform the jury of the physical circumstances surrounding the offence. By considering such observations, the jury drew its own inferences regarding the sequence of reported events, the probable identity of the perpetrator, and the consequent criminal liability, if any.

Not all observations were free from ambiguity, however, and not all testimony was free from equivocation. As early as 1311 one finds the appearance of specialist witnesses, called to the court to draw their own inferences regarding ambiguous observations. Saddled with the unfortunate name of 'expert witnesses', these persons were thought to possess knowledge beyond the ken of the ordinary lay person.[4] Because their job description ran perilously close to that of the jurors' in that they also drew inferences and rendered opinions, the use of expert witnesses has historically provoked disquiet among members of the legal community who feared that the expert would eventually usurp the lay juror's role. Although usually voiced in contemporary legal texts, this sentiment could also be expressed in open court. In his instructions to a jury at the Old Bailey in 1877, Mr Justice Lash addressed the prosecution counsel's objection to a medical witness giving his opinion regarding the mental state of the accused at the time of the crime. '[T]his was the form of question often put and objected to, and it was in reality not a question of medical science, but was the question which the Jury alone could properly decide.'[5]

Were these fears justified? It is difficult to say how much importance lay people attached, or indeed currently attach, to the opinions of an expert witness. In any criminal trial there are likely to be contradictory or disputed observations reported by on-scene witnesses, and sometimes persons of particular training have been deemed necessary to assist the lay juror in determining the facts of a crime. One has little way of knowing, however, how readily the lay juror relinquished *his* role as fact finder. Certainly there are some situations when lay persons would welcome the testimony of a physician to explain, for example, whether a head wound could have resulted from a fall or from the blow of a blunt instrument. Or why some wounds bled, while others remained dry. Or how a drowned man could have been found with no water in his lungs.

There was one medical condition, however, that even when grounded in physical, and hence 'specialist', knowledge encountered a dubious lay public when proffered as a *scientific* specialty. English juries had been considering the possibility that debilitating mental states were responsible for some defendants' criminal behaviour for at least two hundred and fifty years *before* the first medical witness walked into a trial to comment on the defining characteristics of insanity. Appearing in the House of Lords in 1760, physician superintendent of Bethlem John Monro testified that Earl Ferrers suffered from 'occasional insanity', only to hear the Lords unanimously reject the legal significance of a defence based on a *partial* degree of derangement. Ferrers's conviction for murder underscored eighteenth-century law's dismissal of any state but total madness – a total want of memory or understanding – as the grounds for an insanity acquittal.[6]

The standard of complete and total insanity had necessarily restricted the scope of forensic-psychiatric opinion, since raving madness was hardly an ambiguous skull fracture or a mysterious bloodless-wound. Eighteenth-century madness, in Roy Porter's words, was 'spectacularly on view . . . few doubted nature's legibility'.[7] When medical witnesses appeared late into the 1700s – and infrequently, at that – they did little more than legitimise the testimony of the neighbour, the lover, or the co-worker who was, after all, in a much better position to comment on the verbal pandemonium and behavioural histrionics of the accused. There was certainly no animus between the medical practitioner and the jurist in the early years of forensic psychiatry for the most understandable of reasons. Mad-doctors were only offering *facts* to the court: the appearance of insanity, the incoherence of delirious ranting, the seemingly legible signs conveyed by the expression, '[he behaved] like a mad bullock'. These reports could have been supplied by the defendant's neighbours, and indeed usually were. Most often it was, in fact, the neighbour's vivid depiction that was merely affirmed by the medical men who then advised the jury, 'I have looked upon him as a man insane.'[8]

Fact or opinion? In the eighteenth-century context, insanity was most definitely a 'fact'.

II *Opinion* and dispute

The emergence of medical testimony *as opinion* can be timed to the dissolution of total madness as the grounds for an insanity acquittal. Beginning in 1800, medical witnesses employed terms for certain states of mind – delusion, monomania, circumscribed delirium – that depicted insanity in cognitive, not restrictively behavioural, terms. Delusion appears, in retrospect, to have been the first forensic-psychiatric concept: hidden from public view, resisting exposure to any but the most adroit medical excavator, and, finally, impelling in its power.[9] It was the last element that gave early nineteenth-century insanity its critical courtroom significance, since criminal responsibility had long rested on the individual's capacity to choose evil. Only someone who understood the nature and consequences of his actions had been thought to exercise will. This is precisely why delusion had potential consequences for the law: sensations filtered through a delusory lens left the sufferer in such a confused state of misperception that he could not be said to have *chosen* to do evil.

At the level of misperception and error, delusion was an unexceptionable term. Lay persons were certainly well familiar with the ravages of religious delusions and persecution paranoia. Where medical testimony began to diverge from lay belief was in the clinician's pronouncing the *consequences* of delusion for vanquishing human agency. In the *McNaughtan* trial, for example, the jury heard from medical witnesses of the power exerted by the Scotsman's delusion: 'I mean that black spot on his mind . . . the commission of the act is placed beyond his moral control.' Subsequent medical testimony depicted McNaughtan's delusion as one that 'grinds' on his mind . . . 'impels . . . destroys moral liberty . . . carr[ies] a man quite away'.[10]

Although delusion may have appeared to challenge fundamentally the law's notion of human agency, it was far less provocative to the court than the diagnosis of *moral insanity*, which had been introduced into the court three years before *McNaughtan*. One who suffered from this particular derangement suffered no errors in judgement, no confusion, no delirium. It was rather the 'moral sentiments' that were deranged – how one ought to feel towards others, not what one *believed* about others. Medical witnesses alleged that criminal activity so motivated was no more *chosen* than the acts of the delusional, thereby calling attention to the critical element of voluntariness, again said to be missing. Moral insanity had made its conspicuous courtroom debut in medical testimony during the trial of Edward Oxford, prosecuted in 1840 for an unmotivated, unprovoked, indeed seemingly *indifferent* attack on Queen Victoria. As Oxford informed one of the medical witnesses who visited him prior to the trial, 'Oh, I might as well shoot at her as any body else.'[11]

For present purposes, moral insanity marked the first true migration of insanity from neighbour's fact to medical witness's opinion. Lay people were well familiar with hidden delusion – with an insanity limited to a particular subject – activated only when a 'trip-wire' was pulled. Medical witnesses may have distinguished themselves in their speculation regarding the implications of delusion for choice and self-control, but they were hardly sketching out a departure in cultural notions about derangement. Oxford's insanity was something altogether different, and its existence as a medical phenomenon was restricted to the testimony of the medical expert. A crime motivated by no discernible motive and offering the perpetrator little chance of escape was only possible if one were to accept the possibility of independently deranged moral sensibilities. The judge in the *Oxford* trial clearly took exception to the very term 'moral insanity', and asked the following question to discredit the cloaking of inexplicable criminality with explicable medical imagery: 'Do you consider this is really a medical question at all which has been put to you?'

The medical witness replied, 'I do – I think medical men have more means of forming an opinion on that subject than other persons.'[12]

In answer to the judge's further query, 'Why could not any person form an opinion whether a person was sane or insane from the circumstances which have been referred to,' the medical witness answered, 'Because it seems to require a careful comparison of particular cases, more likely to be looked to by medical men, who are especially experienced in cases of unsoundness of mind.'[13] This unselfconscious avowal of professional insight met no courtroom opposition. The jury, for its part, had little trouble applying the proffered concept of deranged moral sentiments to the would-be assassin's actions. The verdict in the *Oxford* case not only introduced moral insanity as possible grounds for acquittal, but appeared to bolster medical claims to an expertise that rested on a greater familiarity with the deranged than the lay person's.

The years following the *McNaughtan* acquittal witnessed just such 'particular cases' making their way into the Old Bailey in the form of defendants alleging an array of ever-expanding aberrant mental states. Accounts of these trials are given in the *Old Bailey Sessions Papers*, verbatim transcripts of trial testimony taken down by shorthand writers and sold on the London streets the next day.[14] These *Papers* remain intact, and provide today's legal historian with contemporary courtroom testimony, cross-examination, and, in a few instances, the judge's charge to the jury. An analysis of courtroom testimony and jury verdicts over a period of ten years following the *McNaughtan* trial yields a total of ninety defendants in London's central criminal court who raised some form of mental debility in their trial.

Although certain of these states of distraction closely resembled the eighteenth-century courtroom's experience with delirium and insensibility, post-*McNaughtan* medical witnesses described behavioural states that challenged for the first time the law's assumption that individuals were *continuous* persons. Since at least the thirteenth century, the English common law had assumed that knowledge of right and wrong informed criminal intent: understanding the evil of one's acts conferred responsibility for one's subsequent actions. The common law's psychology rested on the notion that individuals were relatively continuous beings: associations learned and remembered constituted one's moral sounding board when considering future behaviour. But how was the law to respond to a defendant who was 'not himself' on the day of the crime? The fact that the accused individual *customarily* understood the difference between right and wrong was of little significance unless he could remember these lessons and realise that he was the person committing the action. Courtroom testimony alleging that 'he seemed to know no more about it, any more than it was done by another person', challenged the jury to determine *who* exactly had committed the crime. Seen against the backdrop of a defendant population increasingly 'missing' at the time of their crimes, the concept of moral insanity represents much more than a momentary courtroom diversion on the way to the McNaughtan Rules.[15] It signalled the beginning of medical testimony that would question whether intellect, cognition, and will were integrated in any meaningful way.

Post-*McNaughtan* defendants who suffered bouts of amnesia, who committed an assault while sleepwalking or experienced states of 'absence' when attacking a neighbour, or who 'disappeared' on the witness stand only to be replaced by a ranting, delirious 'double', exposed the limited utility of 'knowing right from wrong' as the standard for assessing degrees of derangement in relation to criminal responsibility. In each of the above instances, no long-standing pathology preceded the crime; no state of delirium or even delusion 'led' the accused to the crime. Rather, these defendants revealed lapses in consciousness that suggested they were 'missing' at the time of the crime. In some unaccounted-for way, these defendants were described as more bystander to than perpetrator of their own crimes.

Consideration of such states of dissociation was not unique to the courtroom. Popular entertainments demonstrating hypnotic and mesmeric trances, literary explorations of sleepwalking, and medical commentary documenting cases of 'doubled personality',[16] ensured that jurors were well familiar with the possibility of multiple planes of consciousness. After *McNaughtan*, the Old Bailey became merely the latest arena to feature *doubles*: individuals whose psyche split into several persons. But this was a forum with a difference. Literary and medical consideration of the phenomenon of splitting need only serve the genre of fiction or the medical case history: no abiding legal exigency intruded upon the analyst's formulation. The courtroom existed to determine culpability, however, not to explore human variability as a curiosity. As with the centuries-long experience with insanity, the assertion of an exaggerated medical condition *began* the inquiry, it did not end it. When the *Allnutt* jurors learned, therefore, that the juvenile poisoner suffered a 'split' in psychic integrity – that his knowledge of right and wrong need not necessarily have informed his choice of action – they had to ask what practical significance this carried for their determination of responsibility. Medical witnesses may have suggested that the youth's faculties of cognition and volition had belonged to two different people, but the judge was on hand to remind the jurors that only one defendant was facing them in the witness box.

III *Splitting* the defendant

For all the attention Victorian medical men paid to questions of 'splitting', sleepwalking, and mesmeric trances, it would be an error to assume that forensic-psychiatric witnesses were unanimously arrayed on the side of the defendant. Prison surgeon Gilbert McMurdo rarely supported a defence of insanity in any of the twenty insanity trials in which he testified, and he failed to find sufficient grounds to affirm such a plea in the trial of Allnutt.[17] In the employ of the Corporation of London to visit prisoners thought to be contemplating an insanity plea, McMurdo informed the *Allnutt* jury as follows:

'I have not observed anything about him which induces me to doubt his being of sound mind – the evidence to-day does not alter my opinion of his sanity.' McMurdo was then asked a highly unusual question, the first time in his career that he was queried about the grounds for his opinion:

> (*Cross-examination*): You have not, I believe, particularly studied matters of this sort?
>
> *Mr McMurdo*: I have been obliged to do it, in connexion with this prison, but not besides that – it has been made a branch of itself for many years, there are many distinctions and forms which insanity takes, not at all apparent to ordinary observers.[18]

This was a terribly important question because it effectively grouped McMurdo with neighbours and acquaintances who also commented on their conversations with, and observations of, the accused. The defence lawyer's question implicitly limited the weight of McMurdo's testimony because the prison surgeon could base his *opinion* on nothing more than common cultural understandings used by 'ordinary' observers. He had only the *fact* of a conversation to give the jury, not an opinion informed by schooling in this particular branch of medicine.

But of what, exactly, did this 'branch' of medicine consist? When medical witnesses commented on a *lesion of the will* or *brain fever*, was there in fact a branch of physical medicine to which they could refer? Or was insanity purely a mental disease, consisting of a derangement of the moral sensibilities? The first medical witness called by the defence immediately rooted the defendant's derangement in his chronic scrofula – establishing a critical link between physical illness and its mental consequence.

> [T]he irritation of ring-worm might have the effect of disturbing an already . . . disturbed mind. The nature and character of scrofula is calculated to affect the mind. . . . When he was suffering from [partial insanity] it would prevent him distinguishing right from wrong . . . when I saw him in prison, he spoke of a voice inducing him to do what he is charged with . . . I consider that to be a delusion . . . the brain was certainly in a diseased state . . . [and] . . . as a medical man . . . I have no hesitation in saying so.[19]

So testified the victim's brother-in-law, disclosing no obvious *animus* towards his nephew, the defendant. Still, one wonders how the boy could *not* have known that it was wrong to put arsenic in his grandfather's sugar. What else could he have thought he was doing?

The next medical witness's testimony reveals that the migration of medical testimony from fact to opinion entailed something more challenging to the law than mere claims to expertise. Six months before the alleged poisoning, Allnutt's mother had consulted Frederick Duesbury, a 'Doctor of medicine at Clapton', in hope of securing treatment for her son's scrofula. Testifying about his young patient's physical condition at the subsequent murder trial, Dr

Duesbury added a comment about the boy's sleepwalking episodes. 'I do not believe him to have been in a sane state of mind at the time [these episodes] occurred.' Under cross-examination, Duesbury was asked to specify whether he considered Allnutt 'permanently insane, or liable to accidental derangement'. Duesbury's reply engaged the law's fundamental conception of 'the person'.

> *Dr Duesbury*: My opinion is that it is the early stage of insanity, implicating the moral sentiments, the sense of right and wrong, and not as yet having reached the intellect in any marked degree, or interfering with his judgement of right and wrong.
>
> *Cross-examination*: What do you mean by a marked degree? Has it gone to a length to injure the intellect, so as not to know he was poisoning a person when he did it?
>
> *Dr Duesbury*: He might know [right from wrong] as a principle of hearsay, but not as a controlling principle of his mind – I think he would understand that he was poisoning his grandfather, if explained to him, but at the time the sense of right and wrong was not acting with sufficient power to control him. I mean a morbid state of the moral feeling, or the sense of right and wrong – I think he knew what the act was that he was doing, but that he did not feel it as being wrong – I am speaking of moral feeling.
>
> *Cross Examination*: [D]o you consider when he did this that he did not know that poisoning his grandfather was a wrong act?
>
> *Dr Duesbury*: I think he has not the moral sense of wrong distinguished from right, or right distinguished from wrong, to give him a moral sense of feeling; that it was an irresistible impulse on his part – I draw that conclusion from his having perpetrated this act without hesitation, or struggle of mind, or remorse, or compunction, and without any sensible object[ive]; and also another circumstance which I heard, leads me to believe his conscience is diseased, that he could not feel it as an influential agent to distinguish between right and wrong, although his intellect leads him to understand what others tell him.[20]

Duesbury was followed into the witness box by renowned mad-house superintendent John Conolly, who had not interviewed Allnut prior to the trial. Conolly's opinion was based on the testimony of the previous forensic medical witnesses, and on his own experience in assessing insanity generally.[21] He affirmed the image of a scrofulous boy, unmindful of his acts, prone to sleepwalking, and altogether 'imperfectly organized'.

> *Conolly*: [T]aking the word 'mind' in the sense in which it is used by all writers, I should say he is of unsound mind . . . that the future character of his insanity would be more in the derangement of his conduct than in the confusion of his intellect – that is conjecture.[22]

The physicians' testimony brought into focus the role that cognition – and hence *consciousness* – was thought to play in human functioning. Traditionally,

English common law assumed that knowledge of right and wrong necessarily informed (perhaps constrained?) the choice to commit evil. Yet the *Allnutt* court was confronted with a young defendant described as capable of understanding the difference between right and wrong, though nonetheless unrestrained when it came to his murderous deed. What level of conscious awareness attended his mixing arsenic with the family sugar? Medical opinion left the unmistakable impression that cognitive awareness of his deed was totally separate from the moral consideration of what he was doing. As Duesbury testified, although the defendant's intellect 'leads him to understand what others tell him, he could not feel [his conscience] as an influential agent to distinguish right from wrong'.

The jury did not have to wait long for guidance from the bench. Baron Rolfe advised that 'Such evidence ought to be scanned by juries with very great jealousy and suspicion, because it might tend to [justify] every crime that was committed.'[23] The use of the term 'jealousy' could not have been lost to members of the jury: it was *their* function that such medical testimony threatened to usurp. Expert opinion equating insanity with moral depravity would make it next to impossible to convict any felon of anything. In this regard, it was particularly unwise for Duesbury to cloud the issue by interjecting the term 'irresistible impulse'. Then as now, the difference between an irresistible impulse and an unresisted impulse was nowhere apparent, and once this argument could be successfully challenged, the *splitting* of cognition from volition was an easy target. '[T]he object of the law was to compel persons to control influences . . . which medical men might choose to say [the defendant] could not control.'[24] As reported in *The Times*, Baron Rolfe 'rejoiced' that the jury 'had thrown to the winds the idle sophistry [of the defence case]'. What else was crime, asked the judge, '[but the] willing indulgence in such evil vice.' As for moral insanity, it was 'only the self delusion of hardened conscience'.[25]

Although one may be tempted to see Baron Rolfe's contemptuous tone as a rather predictable instance of juridical hauteur, there is a tag line at the end of his instructions that perhaps concedes more than he intended. His rejection of medical opinion regarding moral sentiments was encased in an unequivocal avowal of physicalist theories of insanity. Indeed, his voluble rejection of moral insanity originated in its having been put forward as a disease of the *mind* . . . and he was clearly having none of this. It was the independence of moral sentiments from organic grounding that he rejected, refusing 'to assume that the mind, in its essence, is susceptible of disease which the body does not share'. Touching on the defining aspect of expert testimony, he added,

> if this theory were just, the physician or surgeon would be as incompetent as any stranger to the profession, to form an opinion on lunacy. . . . But let it be assumed that the mind is capable of disorder apart from bodily ailment, what do we know of it more than others? The mind has no pulsation . . . no dyspepsia

> . . . but though [the physician] may truly say that he has known this or that visionary idea to be prevalent in some case of mania, he will not say he has felt competent to decide on the existence of mania by the prevalence of the visionary idea alone . . . the visionary idea must be associated with irregularity of the animal functions to satisfy his mind.[26]

IV The fact of a juvenile poisoner

The debating points one hears between this resolute judge and the more cognitively ambitious medical witnesses were not those of physic versus metaphysic, lawyer versus doctor, or witness versus juror – although they were, of course, about all these things. Most particularly, however, this territorial dispute was about nothing so much as 'opinion versus fact'. Insanity as a 'fact' had long existed at the Old Bailey. Its common features of insensibility, delirium, and delusion, were familiar to, and accepted by, the courts. In the years that witnessed the quantum growth in medical participation in insanity trials (1825–43) – and not coincidentally, the growing incidence of delusion to typify the precise derangement of the accused – the rooting of delusion in organic substance figured prominently in medical testimony.[27] The physician's *opinion* about insanity's material basis nicely complemented the *fact* of delusion – transported into court by the lay witnesses' observations: hearing the ranting, seeing the behaviour, perceiving the dramatic change in behaviour whenever the delusion was touched upon. Not surprisingly, medical witnesses who spoke to the thrust of delusion – its supposed bodily origin and its presumed behavioural consequence – were neither derided nor dismissed. What the courts were *not* willing to entertain, however, was medical opinion that asserted categories of derangement divorced from physicalist renderings of functioning – even when those physicalist renderings had never been made very clear.

Baron Rolfe's remarks to the *Allnutt* jury – in which he drew such a distinction between physiologically based insanity and the free-floating notions of moral derangement – are likely to strike today's reader as not a little disingenuous. Delusion had, of course, no more organic basis in bodily disruptions than a *diseased* will could take on a 'lesion'. Once juries accepted delusion as the *sine qua non* diagnosis for a legally recognised criminal insanity, the courts were also bound to entertain the inevitable force of delusion to find its conclusion in crime. An often unspoken assumption was delusion's existence as a physical entity; inducing blood flow was sometimes mentioned as a possible remedy. The materialist basis for this psychological affliction was underlined by endowing delusion with a force all its own. Neither courtroom questioning nor the official Rules that followed the *McNaughtan* acquittal challenged the notion that delusion could 'lead the defendant to any act'. When a medical witness in the *McNaughtan* trial concluded that 'nothing but a physical force would have stopped him from the act he was compelled to do', the Crown prosecutor did not stand up to object.

In retrospect, delusion – with or without an explicit physiological basis – paved the way for questions about human agency to sit at the centre of all subsequent trials that turned on questions of suspended or *missing* consciousness. Defendants who alleged a history of sleepwalking, or being 'absent' at their crime – 'as if it had been done by another person' – or who were *replaced* by another self while on the witness stand, were supported by medical witnesses prepared to question the assumed integration of consciousness and volition that had framed similar discussions about delusion. Each of these behavioural states challenged the common law's perception of 'the person': an individual whose remembered associations informed future action, one whose continuous consciousness linked thought to action and responsibility to assault. Perhaps not as 'discontinuous' as the sleepwalker or as *absent* as the amnesiac, Allnutt's psyche, according to the medical witnesses, nonetheless revealed a failure to integrate moral feeling with cognitive awareness.

Although anathema to the law, the possibility that persons occupied varied planes of consciousness was hardly foreign to common cultural consciousness in an era awash with parlour-induced mesmeric trances and hypnotic spells. What was unique in newly professed medical opinion was the possibility that one's *criminal* behaviour could belong to *another* self or to a self that had failed to integrate disparate psychic elements. Commenting on contemporary notions of dissociation, philosopher Ian Hacking has written that persons who suffer twentieth-century multiple personality syndrome do not experience a multitude of personalities, they rather lack one coherent personality.[28] Medical testimony offered in the *Allnutt* case held out just such a possibility to the nineteenth-century court: the William Newton Allnutt who poisoned his grandfather was not the William Newton Allnutt who understood the difference between right and wrong. Perhaps the reason this understanding failed, in the words of Dr Duesbury, to 'control' him, was that *he* who understood was not *he* who poisoned.

Although it was the medical witness whose opinion affirmed the possibility of multiple states of being, one should not lose sight of the legal forces that framed this debate. Earlier work on the origins of forensic-psychiatric testimony has highlighted the observation that while professional motives did indeed animate an enhanced role for medical witnesses in the courtroom, the professional most active in the proffering of medical opinion was the defence counsel. In the *Allnutt* trial he was the one who minimised Prison Surgeon McMurdo's basis of expertise; he was the one who called the victim's own brother-in-law to speak on behalf of the defendant's scrofula. Medical witnesses, then as now, did not flock to the courtroom in search of professional aggrandisement since they were likely to encounter the hostile comments of the judiciary. They were in court, quite simply, because they had received a subpoena.[29] The courtroom served as a critical forum to find a professional voice, however, and in trials such as Allnutt's, medical men engaged legal questions directly, offering opinions where the court might have preferred they cleave closer to *materialist* fact.

The adversary process was prepared to accept – indeed, it appeared eager to solicit – medical opinion that spoke to the 'fact' of insanity, or in the words of Baron Rolfe in *Allnutt*, an insanity 'physiologically based'. It is endlessly curious to speculate about what was behind this concession – for that is indeed what it was. Easy traffic between the body and the mind had long embraced the notion of a materialist basis for psychological distress. In reifying this connection, however, it seems that judges were ceding more territory to the medical witness than they were gaining. It now appears that the decision to embrace materialism – and by extension medical testimony – was a strategic decision that allowed judges to repel notions of moral insanity, lesion of the will, and monomania.[30] The basis for rejecting these states was not the lack of *agency* such states connoted, because compulsion had already been admitted as the likely result of delusion. It seems more to reflect the judges' belief that they could circumscribe the range of forensic-psychiatric opinion by restricting the type of insanity that medical witnesses could introduce as 'fact'.

There is a further way to consider the obstacle medical witnesses faced with concepts embracing a moral rather than a cognitive basis for insanity, which has little to do with a judge's penchant for physicalist renderings of insanity. A recent text on science and the law depicts the struggle between the two professions originating in their rather particularist 'job descriptions'. Law is said to be prescriptive; science, descriptive.[31] Naturally these two characterisations need considerable parsing, but at the level of the forensic-psychiatric testimony in this particular trial, there may be something instructive in this rendering. Insanity as *fact* is a descriptive category; medical witnesses might be employed to detect its more recondite characteristics – and its more dexterous circumnavigations – but no one had to be convinced that bizarre, *uncharacteristic* behaviour flowed from delusory perception. In the evolving opinion of the *Oxford* medical witnesses, however, insanity was an aberration in how one ought to feel. Nothing could be more prescriptive than this. Perhaps one way to appreciate Baron Rolfe's vituperative reaction to the *Allnutt* medical testimony is to consider the perceived assault on the law's prescriptive function: the normative standard of behaviour that law alone was charged to defend.

Although this separation of law and medicine into sovereign territories is meant to be a contemporary historical idea, it was not lost on nineteenth-century medical men that they were entering a forum fraught with potential professional assault. Then, as now, forensic-psychiatric witnesses faced questioning that not only aimed to expose differences in professional opinion, but differences regarding whether such opinion should even be seen as creditable. Assuming that these medical men were not self-selected masochists, one would have to wonder why forensic-psychiatric witnesses answered as they did. Although their appearance in court may have been prompted by a subpoena, their testimony does not reveal a diffident posture when asserting their claims to asylum-based professional knowledge. At times the arrogation of a privileged gaze was made in response to a defence counsel's clear prompting; at other times it was uttered in response to judicially assaultive questions, as seen in the *Oxford* trial. In either case, medical men such as prison-surgeon Gilbert McMurdo and Dr Duesbury found themselves called into court – and often on opposite sides – precisely because the Crown prosecutor and the defence counsel believed they could win their case by enlisting, shaping, and eliciting forensic-psychiatric opinion touching on the *facts* of the case. That medical men were at the Old Bailey at the law's behest was clear, but it was much less apparent that they were bound to respect the division of labour they found there. Once the lawyers opened the door to opinion-based testimony, they could hardly control the direction such testimony would take.

Courtroom narratives have therefore proven an invaluable resource for capturing the process by which medical facts became courtroom opinion – and for reasons that had little to do with medical plans for enhancing its courtroom role. The law has its own designs, and by employing medical testimony to advance either side of the case, the courts lent their considerable cultural authority to various claims of 'splitting'. In its effort to exclude the notion of autonomous psychological faculties, the courts also explicitly embraced materialist conceptions of derangement that further affirmed medicine's assertions to greater means of 'forming an opinion on insanity than other persons'. It would not be the first time in the history of forensic medicine that the needs of law would serve to reify, however inadvertently, the clinical practitioner's claims to expertise.

Notes

1 For a comprehensive study of the *McNaughtan* trial and its political context, see Richard Moran, *Knowing Right From Wrong: the Insanity Defense of Daniel McNaughtan* (New York: Free Press, 1981).
2 Nigel D. Walker, *Crime and Insanity in England, vol. 1: the Historical Perspective* (Edinburgh: Edinburgh University Press, 1968).
3 According to John Henry Wigmore, the witness must speak as a knower, not a guesser. He must see an action, not merely believe it took place. *Evidence in Trials at Common Law*, vol. 7 (Boston: Little, Brown, 1985), p. 2.
4 For a discussion of the legal provisions for opinion-based testimony, see Learned Hand, 'Historical and practical considerations regarding expert testimony', *Harvard Law Review*, 15 (1901), 40–58, 45; and James Bradley Thayer, *A Preliminary Treatise on Evidence at the Common Law* (Boston: Little Brown, 1898).
5 *Old Bailey Sessions Papers* (hereafter *OBSP*), 1876–7, case 246, 4th session, p. 456.
6 Walker, *Crime and Insanity*, pp. 60–2.
7 Roy Porter, *Mind-Forg'd Manacles: a History of Madness in England from the Restoration to the Regency* (London: Athlone Press, 1987), p. 35.
8 Joel Peter Eigen, 'Intentionality and insanity: what the eighteenth-century juror heard', in William F. Bynum, Roy Porter, and Michael Shepherd (eds), *The Anatomy of Madness*, vol. 2: *Institutions and Society* (London: Tavistock, 1985), pp. 34–51.

9 Joel Peter Eigen, 'Delusion in the courtroom: the role of partial insanity in early forensic testimony', *Medical History*, 35 (1991), 25–49.

10 *OBSP*, 1842–3, case 874, 5th session, pp. 760–3.

11 *Ibid.*, 1840, case 1877, 9th session, p. 506.

12 *Ibid.*, 1840, case 1877, 9th session, pp. 505–10. Analysis of the *Oxford* trial can be found in Walker, *Crime and Insanity*, pp. 186–7; and Richard Moran, 'The punitive uses of the insanity defense: the trial for treason of Edward Oxford (1840)', *International Journal of Law and Psychiatry*, 9 (1986), 171–90. A discussion of the origins of moral insanity in the courtroom can be found in Joel Peter Eigen, *Witnessing Insanity: Madness and Mad-doctors in the English Court* (New Haven and London: Yale University Press, 1995), pp. 76–9 and 150–2.

13 *OBSP*, 1840, case 1877, 9th session, p. 505.

14 The utility of the *OBSP* to historical reconstruction of the day-to-day workings of London's central criminal court is comprehensively described by John H. Langbein in 'The criminal trial before the lawyers', *University of Chicago Law Review*, 45 (Winter 1978), 263–316.

15 Following the acquittal of Robert Peel's would-be assassin, the McNaughtan Rules were fashioned to provide jurors with criteria with which to assess the legal significance of a defendant's alleged mental derangement. These guidelines restricted the jurors' consideration of the defendant's cognitive faculties: *knowing* the difference between right and wrong; *knowing* the nature and likely consequences of an act. The Rules conspicuously limit insanity to matters of intellectual incoherence, excluding states of autonomous behavioural chaos. The latter would encompass 'moral insanity' or 'lesion of the will', which left the afflicted fully aware of his or her act, yet either indifferent to the outcome or incapable of resisting a compelling impulse.

16 Early nineteenth-century medical tracts that explored this phenomenon include Samuel L. Mitchill, Felix Pascaslis, and Samuel Akerly, *The Medical Repository of Original Essays and Intelligence Relative to Physic, Surgery, Chemistry and Natural History* (New York: T. J. Swords, 1817); and H. Dewar, 'Report on a communication from Dr Dyce', *Transactions of the Royal Society of Edinburgh, 9* (Edinburgh: William and Charles Tait, 1823). Historical appraisal of the 'doubling' phenomenon can be found in Henri F. Ellenberger, *The Discovery of the Unconscious: the History and Evolution of Dynamic Psychiatry* (New York: Basic books, 1970), see esp. pp. 127–48; and Ian Hacking, 'Double consciousness in Britain 1815–75', *Dissociation*, 4: 3 (September 1991), 134–46. The history of the array of mesmeric and somnambulist states in the 1800s is the subject of Alison Winter's *Mesmerized: Powers of Mind in Victorian Britain* (Chicago: University of Chicago Press, 1998).

17 McMurdo's contributions to the history of medical testimony bearing on insanity is discussed in Eigen, *Witnessing Insanity*, see especially pp. 129–30.

18 *OBSP*, 1847–8, case 290, 2nd session, p. 289.

19 *Ibid.*, pp. 291–2.

20 *Ibid.*, p. 293.

21 Assessing Allnutt from this particular vantage point was not unusual for Conolly. He had been prominent among members of the first generation of asylum superintendents cum expert witnesses who claimed a familiarity with insanity 'in the general case' by virtue of their experience with 'many hundreds'. Given their unique work-related experience – *the* critical element that permitted mad-doctors to claim

expertise and thus to offer opinions – these first forensic-psychiatric witnesses commented not only on the probable origins of the mental derangement, but the likely consequences this condition would auger for subsequent behaviour.

22 *OBSP*, 1847, case 290, 2nd session, p. 294.
23 *Times* (16 December 1847), p. 8.
24 *Ibid.*
25 'Analytical reviews: Baron Rolfe's charge to the jury', *Journal of Psychological Medicine and Mental Pathology*, 1 April 1848, p. 201.
26 *Ibid.*, p. 215.
27 Eigen, *Witnessing Insanity*, see especially pp. 145–9.
28 Ian Hacking, *Rewriting the Soul: Multiple Personality and the Sciences of Memory* (Princeton: Princeton University Press, 1995).
29 The various professional and affiliational paths medical witnesses took into the courtroom are examined in Eigen, *Witnessing Insanity*, pp. 122–30.
30 Baron Rolfe's complete charge to the jury can be found in the 1 April 1848 *Journal of Psychological Medicine and Mental Pathology*, pp. 193–219.
31 Sheila Jasanoff, *Science at the Bar: Law, Science, and Technology in America* (Cambridge, Mass.: Harvard University Press, 1995).

3

Trials of character: the use of character evidence in Victorian sodomy trials

H. G. Cocks

On 31 July 1854, a man who gave the name George Campbell appeared at the Guildhall magistrates court in the City of London. He had been arrested a few days previously at an unlicensed dancing place and charged, along with one other man, with conducting himself 'in a manner to excite others to commit an unnatural offence'.[1] He and his partner had both been dressed in women's clothes. While his companion, a man of 60, had been 'dressed in the pastoral garb of a shepherdess of the golden age', Campbell had been 'completely equipped in [the] female attire of the present day'.[2] The police alleged that the defendants had been dancing together in the company of several other men, and that their actions constituted an incitement to commit a homosexual act. Campbell's defence was that he had done nothing immoral, but had dressed as a woman merely in order to disguise himself and 'see a little of London life, without mixing with its abominations'.[3]

Conclusive evidence that Campbell had committed any indecent acts was lacking. In fact the principal evidence comprised the competing testimonies of the police and a few conveniently myopic bystanders. Neither were Campbell's intentions judged by the nature of his attire. Effeminacy, which might have been inferred from his dress, was not considered an inevitable sign of homosexual desire.[4] In fact, Campbell's explanation of his clothing as a form of disguise was accepted without murmur by the court. In the absence of a clear description of the defendant's actions or a recognised interpretation of his general demeanour, evidence of the defendant's good character took on a disproportionate importance. The chief magistrate at the Guildhall, Sir Richard Carden, told Campbell that the case was 'entirely a question of character, and if you can show me that you are a respectable person, it will have more weight in my mind than anything you can elicit from the [police] officers.'[5]

Campbell's trial was not unique among nineteenth-century trials for sodomy and homosexual offences in its emphasis on character. While the numbers of reported cases are small, the evidence which emerges from law reports, newspaper accounts, and other sources suggests that the character of the defendant, prosecutor, and witnesses were central to this type of criminal litigation. A sample of forty-eight criminal petitions between 1829 and 1877 shows that in almost all of these cases where character evidence was presented, the good character of the defendant and the bad character of his accusers had been a principal issue at the trial and was repeated in almost every petition for re-hearing or clemency.[6] There were two principal reasons why character evidence achieved such prominence in trials for homosexual offences: one practical and one legal. First, the 'secret' nature of these offences meant that the facts were often in dispute and not subject to verification by independent witnesses. Second, but related to the first, the rules of evidence in sexual offences stressed the significance of the respective characters of the persons involved.[7] For both of these reasons, a defendant charged with homosexual offences often found that the best means of gaining an acquittal was to demonstrate that he was not the sort of man capable of committing this sort of offence and, if possible, to demonstrate that his accusers were the sorts of persons whose accusations could not be trusted.

Character evidence had a protean nature – it might speak either to the individual's reputation or to his mental state. In the context of trials for homosexual offences during the nineteenth century, however, character evidence did not perform the same function for the prosecution and the defence. Evidence of 'bad character' could discredit an accuser, by suggesting that he was morally or mentally suspect. Only evidence of 'good character', however, was admissible as regards a defendant. Moreover, it was settled in 1864 that evidence of the defendant's character – whether offered for or against him – must speak to reputation, and not mentality.

Homosexual offences therefore provide a contrast to the increasing willingness of the English judicial system to examine directly a defendant's mental state. Joel Peter Eigen has shown that in trials of murder and other offences against the person and property it was increasingly common to investigate states of partial or total derangement through expert testimony.[8] 'Sodomitic acts' were often thought of outside the court as a species of derangement, but expert testimony rarely figured in the outcome of trials for these offences. Moreover, the other likely means by which an analysis of the defendant's mental state might have been explored – character evidence – was so hemmed in by restrictions as to render it largely useless for this purpose.

I Homosexual offences and their interpretation

The number of prosecutions for homosexual offences increased enormously during the late eighteenth century and continued to grow throughout the nineteenth century. Yet there has generally been a lack of clarity among historians as to what counted as a homosexual offence in this period. It has often been assumed that male homosexual behaviour was only generally

Figure 3.1 *Indictments for sodomy, indecent assault, and other homosexual offences presented at the Old Bailey, 1750–1830*[9]

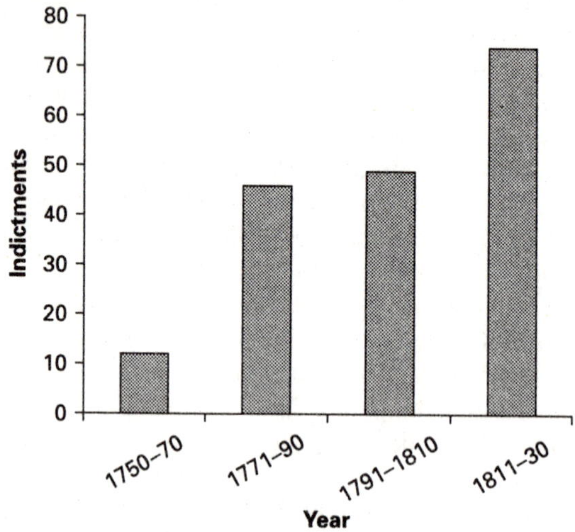

criminalised in 1885, when the Criminal Law Amendment Act outlawed acts of 'gross indecency' between men in public and in private.[10] However, it is clear that all male homosexual acts, whether committed in public or private, were already liable to prosecution under the medieval law against sodomy, which was defined as anal penetration or bestiality. By the eighteenth century, the common law principle that any attempt to commit a crime was in itself a crime had begun to be applied to the crime of sodomy. Most eighteenth- and nineteenth-century trials, therefore, proceeded under the formal legal assumption that any homosexual act was an attempt to commit sodomy. Any act which stopped short of sodomy therefore began to be described as an 'assault with intent to commit sodomy'.[11] All kinds of homosexual acts, including indecent assaults, verbal or written invitations, consenting acts including kisses, touches, and other intimacies were therefore criminal, and susceptible to prosecution.[12]

In London, where homosexual offences were prosecuted most frequently, there is a clear increase in the numbers of sodomy/indecent assault cases, as Figure 3.1 demonstrates. This pattern of increase is repeated throughout the nineteenth century. Between 1806 and 1900, a total of 8,497 men were committed for trial, of whom 56 were executed.[13]

The rise in numbers of indictments does not seem to have spurred a discussion of homosexuality in legal circles. Transcripts of sodomy and indecent assault cases – other than the verdict and the name of the defendant – were not recorded in the *Old Bailey Sessions Papers* and detailed accounts rarely figured in other legal documents.[14] Scientific opinions on the nature of homosexuality were rarely given in court. Judges and barristers celebrated their ignorance as a sign of the moral rectitude of the British legal system. Sir John Duke Coleridge, who was Attorney General at the time, remarked in 1871 that such knowledge might be suitable for foreign scientists, but it had no place in British justice. It was fortunate, he argued, 'that there is very little learning or knowledge upon this subject in this country; there are other countries in which I am told learned treatises are written . . . [but] fortunately doctors in England know very little about this matter.'[15]

In spite of this legal rebuff, the increasing numbers of cases meant that some public discussion of 'abominable crimes' could hardly be avoided. Significant scientific investigations of the nature of homosexuality did not begin until the rise of sexology in the 1890s. Nevertheless, several explanations for homosexual desire and behaviour did emerge in the course of the century. The eighteenth-century idea of the 'molly', an effeminate, usually lower-class, man who lived his life in imitation of the female sex was rarely employed in the nineteenth century.[16] Instead, interpretations of homosexual acts tended to focus on the defendant's moral behaviour and intellect, rather than immediately assuming that a homosexual act was the equivalent of gender inversion or of a homosexual 'identity'.

Homosexual behaviour was interpreted in roughly three ways. Firstly, it was possible for 'sodomites' to form part of a 'detestable race' who might be 'addicted to bestial propensities'.[17] Such a 'race' might commit the crime over and over, unable to escape from its compelling hold. These men might be known for their 'effeminate air' but this was not always a telling sign.[18] This idea that homosexuals might form a kind of sub-species of humanity, however, was not widely expressed. More important was the view that sodomy might result from progressive moral decay, which led the sufferer into ever-greater depths of depravity. One of the more notorious accounts of this type comes from William Acton's *The Functions and Disorders of the Reproductive Organs*, published in 1865. He presents sensuality as a gradual decay from the moral state, through a series of almost imperceptible stages, until ever-increasing perversions are required to excite a physically tired and emotionally jaded lust. The search for stimulus leads the debauché through the full repertoire of immorality, until 'as a last resource, unnatural excitement is brought to bear, and we probably find that the first check to the lust of the opulent satyr, is his finding himself the hero of some filthy police case – then, maybe, a convict or a voluntary exile'.[19]

Acton shares with John Frost an attention to the degenerative nature of a sodomite's character. Frost, the leader of the Chartist Newport rising of 1839, described his experiences as a transported convict in Van Diemen's Land in an attempt to attack the government of Lord Palmerston. In a series of speeches made on his return from the penal colonies in August 1856, he claimed to have witnessed the effects of the cruel and unjust penal system, which was the natural consequence of the corrupt English political system. The former denied men generally their moral rights, but the impact of the latter upon convicts was to destroy their moral sensibility, and this made them prey to their lowest inclinations, including the widespread commission of sodomy and other homosexual acts. Frost explained,

> It is said by the philosophers, and I believe the saying is a true one, that injustice and cruelty destroy the reflecting faculties and leave no thought or wish but for the immediate gratification of the sensual. In such cases no moral feelings can restrain men from the commission of the very worst acts that can be committed, and these results I have witnessed in Port Arthur to an extent probably not equalled in the world.[20]

Thirdly, if not a product of moral decay, homosexual acts might be a sign of mental derangement. This seems to be the reason why Joseph Pritchard, convicted of sodomy in 1836, was committed to an institution, even though the parish overseers discovered in 1851 that he was 'perfectly sane and not in any sense a proper person to be confined in a lunatic asylum'.[21] Even in 1813 it appeared to the London lawyer Robert Holloway that the apparently overpowering nature of homosexual desire meant that it was a 'dreadful malignant malady'.[22] In 1838 the Scottish alienist Alexander Morison confidently concluded that homosexual acts were not always the result of 'moral depravity' but might actually be a species of insanity. Morison argued that 'monomania with unnatural lust' was 'a well marked variety of insanity of not unfrequent [*sic*] occurrence'. In Morison's experience 'the existence of this disease was rendered more certain by other marks of disordered mind being combined with [the] unnatural propensity'.[23] This interpretation was especially useful in considering those 'men of wealth and talents' who were convicted of such offences. If not actually insane, the sodomite could also be explained as ignorant or incompetent. Those who tried to save young offenders from the gallows by petitioning the Home Office often argued that the criminals' youth or 'extreme ignorance' rendered them incapable of recognising the illegality or sinfulness of the act.[24]

Outside the courtroom, homosexuality was explained by a man's mental state – his depravity, insanity, or ignorance. Hence his mental 'propensity' to commit homosexual acts was relevant to a 'common sense' decision about whether he was a sodomite. In order to determine whether an individual's mental state was legally relevant to a homosexual offence, however, we must turn to a more particular examination of how such offences were prosecuted.

II Character and criminal evidence

In 1854 the Guildhall magistrate Sir Richard Carden, gave it as his opinion that in cases involving 'one of the most loathsome offences a man could commit', character was 'most at stake and most required'.[25] Character, in this context, might mean an individual's general reputation within the community, or it might mean a hypothesis about an individual's mentality that rested on his known conduct or circumstances. There were important practical and legal reasons why character evidence achieved such prominence in trials for homosexual offences. Crimes of this nature were frequently committed in private, and the facts were almost always in dispute because the defendant would usually deny that the alleged acts had taken place. Since evidence of an indecent assault often consisted of touching or other advances which left no evidential trace, such an allegation was easily contested if there were no independent witnesses. Such witnesses, moreover, were rarely found, with the result that only those who had participated in the alleged acts were able to give evidence about them. In addition, as the century progressed it became less common for defendants to make statements to the court, especially after the Prisoners' Counsel Act of 1836 enabled the defence to be put by a barrister.[26] These circumstances placed particular emphasis on the prosecutor's credibility, which was effectively decided by reference to his 'character' for truthfulness. Similarly, in the absence of any other means of refuting the prosecutor's factual account, the defendant would tend to produce witnesses who could speak to the defendant's own 'character' for morality, regularity, and integrity.

In addition to these practical considerations, several particular legal assumptions about character brought character evidence to the fore in trials for homosexual offences. As a general matter, where it was not possible to prove that an offence had been committed, character evidence was relevant to show that it was more or less likely to have been committed.[27] As one judge explained in a case of indecent assault in 1829, 'altho' character cannot answer a specific charge on oath . . . something must depend on the probability.'[28] More specifically, the rules of evidence relating to homosexual and heterosexual offences emphasised the role of character evidence. Presumably because they were similar offences, with similar standards and requirements of proof,[29] the rules of evidence in sodomy appear to have been modelled on the law of rape. Certainly the dictum of the great seventeenth-century jurist and judge Sir Matthew Hale that an accusation of rape was 'easily to be made and hard to be proved, and harder to be defended by the party accused, tho never so innocent' was endlessly quoted in sodomy trials.[30] To provide 'greater probability to her testimony', Hale had argued that the alleged rape victim should be 'of good fame'.[31] Hale had provided further indicia of probability,[32] but many trials for homosexual assaults turned particularly on the relative reputations of accusers and accused.

The issue that was particularly relevant to a prosecutor or prosecution witness in a case of sodomy or indecent assault was whether he had ever committed such acts himself. If he had committed them in the past, this raised doubt about the reliability of his testimony. In this context, character evidence seems to have been linked to the general perception that homosexual acts were evidence of a mental or moral aberration. A man who was known to have indulged in homosexual conduct was immoral or deranged; in either case he was unlikely to tell the truth. A further practical objection to testimony by a known sodomite was that extortion might lie behind the accusation. Baron Gurney observed in 1835 that charges of indecent assault were often used as a means of extortion, and that it was 'the melancholy experience of those tribunals before whom guilty individuals of this description [extortionists] have been convicted, to discover that such charges are rarely, if ever made except by those debased beings who are conscious of the horrid offence in their own bosom.'[33] If the accuser had consented to the acts alleged in the present case, this created a further evidential problem. Anyone over the age of 14 who consented to the acts was a principal in the crime, and therefore regarded in law as an accomplice. Rules that developed at the beginning of the nineteenth century stated that the testimony of an accomplice must be corroborated in order for a conviction to be secured.[34]

Corroboration was not always required by the court. James Smith was convicted in 1877 of committing sodomy with a telegraph boy, who had allegedly been following the common practice of boys so employed of operating a lucrative sideline in prostitution. Smith protested that 'the evidences of at least two independent witnesses of the actual perpetration of the alleged crime were indispensably necessary before the case could be legally left to the Jury.'[35] He added that 'the crime for which I am sentenced has been very prevalent amongst the Telegraph lads', and that the case against him rested upon the 'unsupported testimony of lads who admitted having allowed themselves to be defiled for five shillings'.[36] However, the fact that the character of accusers was *likely* to be heavily scrutinised at trial meant that their character was probably central to the prosecution's decision to bring the case to trial in the first place. This question was at the centre of the difficulties encountered by the British government over the Cleveland Street scandal of 1889–90.[37] This scandal followed the discovery that a male brothel in the West End of London was being frequented by members of the aristocracy and perhaps even by members of the royal family. The principal suspects in the case absconded while the government and the police debated what to do, thereby enabling the radical Liberal MP Henry Labouchere to denounce the delay as part of a cover-up designed to allow the high-born and Tory culprits to escape abroad.

The relevant files show another side to this affair. In particular, they show that the government did not want to proceed with a case that might collapse because most of the witnesses were youths who had willingly participated in 'unnatural acts' and had even earned their living in this way. The Attorney General, Sir Richard Webster, expressed the view that the principal witness, a professional 'Mary Anne' called John Saul, was 'in my judgement utterly unworthy of credit'. The Home Secretary, Henry Matthews, agreed, telling his officials that 'the evidence of a participator in the offence . . . would not be sufficient in law to warrant a conviction.' The evidence in this case, he concluded, 'stands peculiarly in need of corroboration'.[38] Saul's evidence in a failed libel case connected with some of the Cleveland Street allegations had also been utterly discredited. *The Times* commented that the fate of Saul's evidence in that case 'showed beyond all doubt that the law officers were fully justified in declining to institute further prosecutions upon evidence which appeared in the witness box to be not only tainted in its origin, but absolutely untrustworthy from beginning to end.'[39]

Even where the sexual behaviour of a prosecutor or prosecution witness was not in doubt, his character – in the sense of an assessment of his reliability based on his conduct or circumstances – could still discredit the prosecution. When John Avis was convicted of indecently assaulting a man named Hugh Johnson in 1829, he protested in his petition to the Home Office that the character of his accuser had not been sufficiently examined in court. If it had been, he argued, the outcome of the trial would have been different. According to Avis, he had gone to obey a call of nature in a side street near Mayfair when Johnson had seized him and accused him of attempting to commit an indecent assault. Avis pointed out that his accuser was a servant who had been out of place for ten months, and that he lived in a coffee shop 'of the lowest description in a narrow passage in the neighbourhood of Oxford Street and the resort of low characters'.

Avis complained that his defence had been 'grossly neglected' by his barrister 'inasmuch as he took no trouble to ascertain the character of the prosecutor although particularly requested to do so . . . though by showing which he might have shown that the Prosecutor was not to be believed on his oath'.[40] In response to Avis's complaints, the trial judge said that he had pointed out to the jury that character could carry weight in circumstances like these where there were no independent witnesses to the alleged assault. He had also told the jury that the prosecutor was a servant out of place 'which though it was not necessarily an inference of immorality left him in an equivocal situation, in establishing a charge which a bad man might easily make'.[41] Avis's arguments appear to have held sway, and the case was referred back to the chairman of the Middlesex Sessions.[42]

While clearly relevant to proving the (in)credibility of the prosecutor and prosecution witnesses, character could also be directly relevant to establishing the defendant's innocence. In this context, however, character evidence spoke to the defendant's 'good character'. This was established by showing the defendant's status, habits, and his general reputation for morality and integrity. A man of that *character*, it was argued, was hardly likely to engage in homosexual behaviour. In the case of William Dorrien, a 'young gentleman of high connexions in the city', who was accused of an indecent assault in 1825, evidence of his status and habits secured an immediate acquittal. Mr Adolphus for the defence pointed out that if the jury considered the defendant's station in life, and

> heard from the host of honourable persons he would call before them, who were his intimate acquaintances that his whole conduct, that all the habits of his life, were in strict conformity to the respectability of his situation and prospects, they could not believe that he could have plunged headlong into an abyss of infamy by a publicity of depravity from which the most habitually hardened would have shrunk.[43]

Dorrien's character witnesses, including the governor of the Bank of Ireland, then paraded through the court and testified to his good conduct, 'his attention to religious duties', and devotion to his family. The Recorder, suitably impressed, pointed out the 'improbability that a person of the defendant's character – for it was impossible that any man could have a higher character – should forfeit that character by any act that would forever consign him to infamy'.[44]

The defendant's general good reputation could also show that he was unlikely to commit homosexual acts.[45] William Elder, a man of 'gentlemanly appearance' employed in the ordnance department of the Tower of London was accused of indecently assaulting a soldier in 1842. His chief character witness told the court that he had known the defendant for thirty-five years and 'had always considered him to be a strictly moral and gentlemanly man, and he believed him to be quite incapable of conduct such as that imputed to him'. The witness added that 'he had never observed the slightest tendency on his part to impropriety of any sort'. The judge committed Elder for trial but only because he felt it necessary in order for Elder to be completely vindicated. It was, he said 'quite impossible that anything short of a most searching investigation and an acquittal by a jury, could free the accused's character from the most serious imputation cast upon it'.[46] Similarly, in the 1867 case of an unnamed 'gentleman' arrested for an indecent assault on a policeman in a Vine Street urinal, John Duke Coleridge, 'rested the defence on the improbability of the defendant, who would be proved to have borne the character of a moral, pure-minded man, suddenly committing such an offence upon an officer of the police, who would certainly apprehend him'.[47]

Evidence of character – of prosecutors, prosecution witnesses, and defendants – was clearly relevant and important in cases of sodomy and indecent assault. The role played by such evidence, however, differed according to whether it was applied to the accusers or the defendant. With regard to the former, evidence of prior illegal, immoral, or socially undesirable acts undermined the accuser's credibility in the present case. With regard to the latter, evidence of the defendant's gentlemanly status, respectable habits, and general reputation for morality suggested that he was unlikely to have committed the offence in question. In both contexts evidence of character related, indirectly, to the individual's supposed mental state, but the evidence pointed in different directions. The accuser's 'bad' character implied a defective moral or intellectual nature, while the defendant's 'good' character implied a healthy one. But could the law inquire no further into the defendant's mentality? Was it possible to use character evidence, or some other investigative tool, to prove that the defendant *was* likely to commit homosexual acts?

III Character evidence and the investigation of 'propensity'

That a defendant was likely to commit homosexual acts might have been relevant to the defendant's or prosecution's case. A defendant, conceivably, might wish to argue that his predisposition towards homosexuality excused or mitigated his unlawful conduct, while a prosecutor who could not prove that the defendant had committed the offence would wish to argue that the defendant was so inclined to conduct of this type that he had *probably* committed the offence on this occasion. In fact, however, the first rarely happened, and the second was not permitted.

To bring before the court evidence of a general predisposition towards homosexuality, a defendant had to admit his guilt and offer a plea of mitigation. This seems rarely to have happened in the nineteenth century.[48] However, in isolated cases where a guilty plea was entered, defendants relied on the contemporary assessment of homosexuality as a form of mental illness. Sergeant Ballantine told the Old Bailey in 1851 that his client, a Greenwich schoolmaster named Samuel Miller, had succumbed to a 'sudden impulse he could not account for'.[49] Similarly, in the 1870 trial of Edward Park it was argued by the defence that

> Many persons were of the opinion that the perpetration of such offences in itself showed something wanting in mind and feeling which indicated that the offender was not in full possession of his faculties and that such cases would be far better treated in a lunatic asylum than in a court of justice.[50]

Whatever defendants might or might not wish to admit, prosecution counsel would have been keen to use evidence of the defendant's 'bad' character to undermine the defendant's credibility in the same way that an accuser's credibility could be impugned. Evidence of the prior commission of homosexual acts would have been particularly helpful to show that the defendant was very likely guilty of the crime with which he was charged. Such evidence, however, was out of bounds for the prosecution. In 1810 it was decided that previous unnatural offences, or a disposition of character to commit such offences, were inadmissible. *R.* v. *Cole*, a case from the Buckingham Assizes, applied the principle that 'an admission by the prisoner that he had committed such an offence at another time and with another person, and that his natural inclination was towards such practices, ought not to be received in evidence'.[51] This rule was adhered to in 1851 in *R.* v. *Burt* where, although witnesses had been called to prove the defendant's good character, the prosecution was not entitled to call witnesses to give evidence of his bad character.[52]

Occasionally, however, some barristers did test the boundaries of these decisions by attempting to make the defendant's 'bad' character, and hence his mental 'propensity' to commit homosexual acts, relevant to the outcome of a case. Such a challenge consisted of calling witnesses to testify to the previous bad acts or propensities of the defendant, rather than to his good conduct, gentlemanly status, or reputation for morality. The rule expressed in *R.* v. *Cole* and *R.* v. *Burt* usually prevented such evidence from coming forward, but in two cases at least, the prosecution succeeded in having it admitted. In doing so, the prosecution counsel exposed the contradictory nature of character evidence when applied to defendants. While it could be used to suggest the defendant's healthy mentality – it could not be used to suggest that he suffered from mental or moral infirmity.

The first of these challenges occurred in 1846, when William French, 'a very respectable-looking' pawnbroker and dissenting minister, whose 'connections are of the utmost respectability', was charged with an indecent assault on a 15-year-old youth. At the committal hearing, witnesses were called to show that the defendant was in fact a sodomite according to most available definitions. Not only had his employer conducted an investigation which had led to his dismissal, but French had also, according to the prosecution, 'been committing most abominable practices for many years'. The defence objected, saying that such evidence 'would only raise a prejudice against the unhappy man by going into other cases, said to have occurred many years ago', and that it was in any event inadmissible. However, the magistrate disagreed and said that he would hear evidence 'as to the defendant's general pursuits and whether he had indulged in immoral practices before, and he [the magistrate] had as much right to do so, as the defence had to call evidence to his [good] character'. Four men then 'deposed to the abominable practices of the prisoner', and French was committed for trial.[53]

A more significant challenge was made in the case of *R.* v. *Rowton*. In September 1864, James Rowton, a clerk in holy orders, was accused of indecently assaulting an office boy named George Low at Chalk Farm railway station in north London. At the trial on 30 September Rowton's counsel, Mr Sleigh, produced a number of 'reverend gentlemen' to testify to the defendant's good character. In reply, Mr Tayler for the prosecution announced his intention to call a number of witnesses to rebut this evidence. Tayler called one Rowland Bateman, who had been taught by the defendant, and asked him if he 'could tell us of any acts done by the prisoner?' Sleigh protested, arguing that it was not correct for the prosecution to be trying his client for anything but the present alleged offence, and citing *R.* v. *Burt* to the effect that no evidence of bad character could be admitted. However, despite these objections, the chairman of the sessions allowed Tayler to pursue his line of questioning, asking the witness what he thought of the defendant's character 'as to purity and decency?' Bateman replied that he thought Rowton 'capable of being guilty of the grossest indecency and the gravest immorality', all of which contributed to his immediate conviction. Sleigh protested that he could not 'sit here and hear the rules of law violated by the bench' and asked that the point of law be put aside for consideration by the Court for Crown Cases Reserved (the precursor of the Court of Appeal).[54]

The argument was, in effect, over whether the previous bad acts of the defendant could be considered, and whether they could be used to show that he had an inherent tendency to commit such acts. These questions went to the heart of the case and to the nature of character evidence when applied to a defendant. The prosecution argued that prior homosexual conduct created a presumption that the defendant had a predisposition to such conduct. 'It was a question of the mind; the inference to be drawn from a course of conduct [which] was accepted as assisting to solve the question, and that necessarily involved the mental condition of the individual.'[55] The defence did not object to all 'bad' character evidence employed against a defendant, but specifically to evidence of a defendant's 'bad' acts. The defence argued that if character evidence was admitted, it had to have reference to the defendant's general reputation, and not to specific acts or tendencies of the mind. With regard to a defendant, character consisted in the approbation of others, whether an employer's testimonial written for a domestic servant, or the oral testimony provided by the businessman's respectable connections. Sleigh argued that the court should, like Lord Erskine, define character as 'the slow-spreading influence of opinion arising from the deportment of a man in society', which 'necessarily produced one circle without another, and so extends itself till it unites in one general opinion'. Sleigh also cited Lord Ellenborough for the proposition that 'It is reputation . . . [only] that is admissible in evidence.'[56]

Speaking for the majority, Sir Alexander Cockburn, the Lord Chief Justice of the Queen's Bench, noted the principal difficulties of using character evidence. On the one hand, the case could not be decided unless the inner disposition of the defendant was interpreted, but evidence to general reputation was the only means by which to interpret these private propensities. The central point of the case, Cockburn argued, 'bearing materially on the probability or improbability of the prisoner's guilt' was 'the tendency or disposition of the prisoner's mind to commit the particular offence with which he stands charged'. However, questions relating specifically to disposition were never put, and 'the only way the law allows of your getting at the disposition and tendency of his mind, is by the evidence as to his general character founded upon the knowledge of those who know anything about him and his general conduct'.[57] Bateman's testimony, since it had been the opinion of an individual and not evidence of Rowton's general reputation, was inadmissible, and the conviction was quashed.[58]

IV Conclusions

'Character' was central to many trials of sodomy and indecent assault in the nineteenth century, and the rules determining the kind of character evidence that could be produced with respect to the defendant had important consequences for the trials themselves, and also for the wider understanding of homosexuality. Evidence of the defendant's 'good' character helped to establish that he was unlikely to have committed the acts with which he had been charged, but evidence of 'bad' character – which might have suggested a propensity towards homosexuality – was not admissible. This rule did not prevent a mid-Victorian debate over precisely which aspects of character could be admitted and what kind of testimony about character was appropriate. The debate reflected the fact that mental and moral states were directly relevant in these cases. It was commonly assumed that homosexual acts reflected an individual's moral or intellectual degeneration. It was important, therefore, to understand the defendant's mentality, particularly when the charge could not be proved or disproved on the basis of direct evidence. The decision in *R.* v. *Rowton* affirmed the importance of inquiring into the defendant's mental state, but also affirmed that this inquiry must be limited. Only those who knew the defendant's general reputation over a long period could testify to his mental state. A more specific inquiry into the defendant's past homosexual conduct, therefore, was prevented. Homosexual acts had to be considered as separate, isolated occurrences, and not as a reflection of the defendant's mentality. Interestingly, previous homosexual conduct *was* admissible as regards the mentality of prosecutors and prosecution witnesses. A personal history of this sort helped to prove that the accuser was a liar and possibly an extortionist. It could not, however, help to prove that a defendant had a homosexual 'character'.

There is an obvious affinity between the legal discourse of character and its wider meaning in Victorian society.[59] Character evidence could indicate an individual's mental state through the investigation of his conduct and reputation. Similarly, an individual with a 'good character', as agreed by writers as diverse as Samuel Smiles and the psychologist W. B. Carpenter, had developed regular moral habits, exhibited self-command, and established the control of his will over his passions.[60] Good character, in Carpenter's sense of the term, was a form of 'drilling' of the mind to maintain an automatic and involuntary dominion over the body. In popular texts like his best-selling *Self-Help* (1859) and *Character* (1871), Smiles exhorted his readers to 'build up' character on a sound footing through regular habits, moral behaviour, and dutiful purpose.[61] There are clear echoes of this understanding of character as founded on morality imposed by the will in the testimony of character witnesses as to the 'pure minded' or morally constant nature of a defendant's conduct.

Sodomy and indecent assault trials therefore provide a curious example of cases in which the defendant's mental state was recognised as relevant, but in which the particular rules about character evidence actually hid the defendant's mentality from view. Moreover, because character evidence appears to have been the only means by which the defendant's mentality could be approached, the consequences of this limitation were significant. The issues raised in *R.* v. *Rowton* were germane to the understanding of homosexual acts within a legal context: they questioned whether 'unnatural lusts' should be viewed as isolated acts, and instead tried to put forward the view that 'habitual' indulgence in immoral conduct should be made relevant to the case. The issues also had a wider resonance. Evidence of a defendant's propensity to homosexual conduct might have contributed to a more sophisticated analysis of such conduct within the legal system. Such an analysis would have had inevitable consequences for defendants, as well as influencing the scientific and popular assessments of homosexuality. Thanks to the law of evidence, however, such an analysis was prevented. The 'sodomite' remained, in Michel Foucault's famous terms, a 'juridical subject'. He was yet to become a 'case history . . . a type of life', a man 'with an indiscreet anatomy, and a possibly mysterious physiology'.[62]

Notes

1 *Morning Chronicle* (1 August 1854). 'Unnatural offences' was the principal legal term used throughout the nineteenth century to describe a group of different homosexual offences. In official statistics, these generally included sodomy (both between men and bestiality), indecent assaults, consenting sexual behaviour, incitements and invitations to commit the offence, and some indecent exposures. Anything not included in these descriptions (and there were almost no homosexual acts which could not be so described) was described as 'other unnatural misdemeanours'. See Parliamentary Papers, Judicial Statistics, various volumes.

2 Private cuttings collection of William Bell Macdonald, 'Various trials cut from newspapers' (not dated), quoted in Thomas Boyle, *Black Swine in the Sewers of Hampstead: Beneath the Surface of Victorian Sensationalism* (New York: Viking, 1989), p. 11.

3 *Morning Chronicle* (2 August 1854).

4 On the demonstration of this fact in the 1871 case of Ernest Boulton and Frederick Park, see Jeffrey Weeks, *Sex, Politics and Society: the Regulation of Sexuality in Britain Since 1800* (London: Longmans, 1989); Alan Sinfield, *The Wilde Century: Oscar Wilde, Effeminacy and the Queer Moment* (New York: Cassell, 1994); Neil Bartlett, *Who Was That Man: a Present for Mr Oscar Wilde* (London: Penguin, 1987).

5 *Morning Chronicle* (1 August 1854). Campbell was conducting his own defence. He was neither sent for trial nor fined, his respectability and status having been adequately proved.

6 See Public Record Office, Kew (hereafter PRO) HO 17–19, register of criminal petitions. See H. G. Cocks, '"Abominable crimes": sodomy trials in English law and culture, 1830–1889', (Ph.D. dissertation, University of Manchester, 1998), pp. 260–1 for a list of the petitions.

7 Character evidence was very important in other forms of sexual assault as well. Carolyn Conley has noted its prominence in Victorian rape trials, where the 'fundamental consideration' was 'the perceived character of the accused'. Carolyn Conley, 'Rape and justice in Victorian England', *Victorian Studies*, 29: 4 (Summer 1986), 519–36, 530.

8 In addition to his chapter in the present volume, see Joel Peter Eigen, 'Intentionality and insanity: what the eighteenth century juror heard', in William F. Bynum, Roy

Porter, and Michael Shepherd (eds), *The Anatomy of Madness, vol. 2: Institutions and Society* (London: Tavistock, 1985), pp. 34–51; Joel Peter Eigen, 'Delusion in the courtroom: the role of partial insanity in early forensic testimony', *Medical History*, 35 (1991), 25–49.

9 Corporation of London Record Office (hereafter CLRO), calendar of prisoners, 1756–1822.

10 On this see, F. B. Smith, 'Labouchere's amendment to the Criminal Law Amendment Bill', *Historical Studies*, 67: 17 (October 1976), 165–73. Lesbianism has never been a crime in Britain, although one or two women were charged with sodomy (bestiality) in the course of the nineteenth century. See, for example, Cocks, '"Abominable crimes"', p. 258.

11 See Parliamentary Papers, various volumes.

12 The development of these offences is dealt with in Cocks, '"Abominable crimes"', chs 1 and 2.

13 Reliable figures in the form of Parliamentary returns begin in 1806. For these statistics see Cocks, '"Abominable crimes"', pp. 254–5. The last two men to be executed were James Pratt and John Smith, dispatched together for consensual sodomy in 1835. For this case, see *The Times* (28, 29 September 1835; 28 November 1835). For efforts to save the men from the gallows via petitions for mercy see PRO, HO 17/120 Xv 13.

14 A few records have survived, including the seventy-seven petitions of those convicted of sodomy and related offences in the first half of the century. But no systematic record remains. On this, see Cocks, '"Abominable crimes"', pp. 260–1, and PRO HO 19/5, 6–10, 12, register of criminal petitions.

15 PRO, DPP 4/6, p. 44, *The Trial of Boulton and Park and others for Unnatural Offences*.

16 On the idea of the molly, see Randolph Trumbach, *Sex and the Gender Revolution: Heterosexuality and the Third Gender in Enlightenment London* (Chicago: University of Chicago Press, 1998); Randolph Trumbach, 'Sex, gender and sexual identity in modern culture: male sodomy and female prostitution in enlightenment London', in John C. Fout (ed.), *Forbidden History: the State, Society and the Regulation of Sexuality in Modern Europe* (Chicago: University of Chicago Press, 1992), pp. 89–106; Randolph Trumbach, 'London's sodomites: homosexual behaviour and western culture in the eighteenth century', *Journal of Social History*, 10 (Fall, 1977), 1–33; Rictor Norton, *Mother Clap's Molly House: the Gay Subculture in London, 1700–1830* (London: Gay Men's Press, 1994); Tim Hitchcock, *English Sexualities, 1700–1800* (Basingstoke: Macmillan, 1997).

17 Anon., *Hints to the Public and to the Legislature on the Prevalence of Vice and on the Dangerous Effects of Seduction* (London: E. Wilson, 1811), p. 101; *R.* v. *Morgan* (1832), quoted in Anthony Simpson, 'Masculinity and control: the prosecution of sex offences in eighteenth century London' (Ph.D. dissertation, University of Michigan, 1984), p. 875.

18 On this see *The Yokel's Preceptor; or, More Sprees in London! Being a Regular and Curious Show-up of all the Rigs and Doings of the Flash Cribs in this Great Metropolis*, quoted in Pisanus Fraxi (Henry Spencer Ashbee), *Index Librorum Prohibitorum*, vol. 1 (London: privately printed, 1877).

19 William Acton, *The Functions and Disorders of the Reproductive Organs* (London: John Churchill and Sons, 1865), p. 219.

20 John Frost, *The Horrors of Convict Life* (1856, repr. Hobart, 1973), p. 38.

21 PRO, HO 17/100 Part 2 Sw 43, petition of the overseers of the poor in the parish of St Mary in Shrewsbury to the Home Office, 1851.
22 Robert Holloway, *The Phoenix of Sodom; or, The Vere Street Coterie: Being an Exhibition of the Gambols Practised by the Ancient Lechers of Sodom and Gomorrah, Embellished and Improved with Modern Refinements in Sodomitical Practices, by Members of the Vere Street Coterie of Detestable Memory* (London, Cook, 1813), p. 17.
23 Sir Alexander Morison, *The Physiognomy of Mental Diseases* (London, 1838), quoted in Richard Hunter and Ida Macalpine, *Three Hundred Years of Psychiatry, 1535–1860* (Oxford, 1963), p. 773.
24 See, for example, the petition of Joseph and Mary Gibson to Lord Melbourne, which argued that 'from weakness of mind', their son Jesse 'knew not, nor understood the nature, nor extent of the guilt and depravity of the offence to which he then pleaded guilty'. PRO, HO 17/47 Part 2 Gt 39, petition to Lord Melbourne, March 1834.
25 *Morning Chronicle* (1 August 1854).
26 Even when such statements were made, they tended to be truncated and of little assistance to the defence, as they did not have the same authority as other evidence. Until the passage of the Criminal Evidence Act (1898), a defendant could only make an unsworn statement. For an example of such a statement, see Anon., *The Trial of David Robertson of the Jerusalem Hotel . . . for an Unnatural Crime with George Foulston* (London: J. Day, 1806). On the Prisoner's Counsel Act, see J. M. Beattie, 'Scales of justice: defense counsel and the English criminal trial in the eighteenth and nineteenth centuries', *Law and History Review* 9: 2 (Fall, 1991), 221–67. For an overview on the law of evidence see Christopher Allen, *The Law of Evidence in Victorian England* (Cambridge: Cambridge University Press, 1997), ch. 5.
27 In 1862 Sir George Grey argued that in cases of murder character was irrelevant because 'Character may be entitled to much weight where doubt exists as to the facts but not so where the crime is clearly proved to have been committed.' Quoted in Martin Wiener, *Reconstructing the Criminal: Culture, Law and Policy in England 1830–1914* (Cambridge: Cambridge University Press, 1994), p. 90.
28 PRO, HO 47/75, Judges' reports on the petition of John Avis, 22 December 1829.
29 After 1828, anal penetration was the required proof of sodomy. Previously emission in the body had also been required.
30 Mathew Hale, *Historia Placitorum Coronae: the History of the Pleas of the Crown* (2 vols, 1736, repr. London: Professional Books, 1971), p. 635. Similar rules to those laid down by Hale regarding the credibility of witnesses were also applied in a modified form in sodomy trials.
31 Hale, *Historia*, p. 633.
32 These included whether the alleged victim had 'presently discovered the offence and made pursuit of the offender, [and] shewed circumstances and signs of the injury', whether the alleged attack had occurred somewhere 'remote from people, inhabitants or passengers', or 'if the offender fled for it'. Hale, *Historia*, p. 633.
33 *The Times* (29 September 1835).
34 On this, see Douglas Hay, 'Controlling the English prosecutor', *Osgood Hall Law Journal*, 21 (1993), 165–86. The case law relates to *R.* v. *Attwood* and *R.* v. *Hervey and Fordham*, for which see *Annual Register*, 49 (1807), pp. 356–7, in which the judge commented that a conviction on the evidence of an accomplice was unsafe.

See also Simpson, 'Masculinity and Control', p. 53. On the situation just before these rules developed see Valentine Jackson, *The Remarkable Trials at the Lancashire Assizes, held August 1806 at Lancaster Before Sir Robt Graham Knight* (London: T. Day, 1806), which details a series of cases arising from the investigation of a group of men in Warrington in 1805. In these trials, evidence was provided mainly by those who admitted having committed sodomy with others in the past. The judge wished 'sincerely that the prisoner had brought some witnesses to his character' since 'this was one of those cases in which satisfactory testimony to character would have greatly increased' his doubt about the principal evidence. Jackson, *Remarkable Trials*, p. 54.

35 PRO, HO 144/20/58480, petition of James Smith to the Home Office (July 1890).

36 PRO, HO 144/20/58480, first petition of James Smith to the Home Office (April 1877). On the question of corroboration see also H. Montgomery Hyde, *Famous Trials: Oscar Wilde* (London: Penguin, 1970), pp. 214–15. For another conviction on the unsupported evidence of one person see the case of John Goode, PRO, HO 19/114 Wq–Ws, criminal petitions.

37 For accounts of the Cleveland Street Scandal, see H. Montgomery Hyde, *The Cleveland Street Scandal* (London: W. H. Allen, 1976); Lewis Chester, David Leitch, and Colin Simpson, *The Cleveland Street Affair* (Boston: Little Brown, 1976); Theo Aronson, *Prince Eddy and the Homosexual Underworld* (London: Murray, 1994); Morris Kaplan, 'Did "My Lord Gommorrah" smile: homosexuality, class, and prostitution in the Cleveland Street Affair', in Nancy Erber and George Robb (eds), *Disorder in the Court: Trials and Sexual Conflict at the Turn of the Century* (New York, New York University Press, 1999), pp. 78–99; Morris Kaplan, 'Who's afraid of John Saul?: urban culture and the politics of desire in late Victorian London', *GLQ: A Journal of Gay and Lesbian Studies*, 5: 3 (1999), 267–314; Jeffrey Weeks, 'Inverts, perverts and Mary Annes: male prostitution and the regulation of homosexuality in the nineteenth and early twentieth centuries', in Martin Duberman, George Chauncey, and Martha Vicinus (eds), *Hidden From History: Reclaiming the Gay and Lesbian Past* (London: Penguin, 1991), pp. 195–211.

38 PRO, DPP 1/95/1, letter from Henry Matthews to Sir Augustus Stephenson, 26 August 1889.

39 *The Times* (1 March 1890).

40 PRO, HO 47/75, petition of John Avis to Robert Peel, attached Judge's Reports, not dated (1829).

41 PRO, HO 47/75, letter from trial judge to Robert Peel, 22 December 1829.

42 See also PRO, HO 19/114 Wq–Ws, petition of John Goode, March 1834.

43 *The Times* (7 November 1825).

44 *Ibid.*

45 On the importance of character in rape cases, see Carolyn Conley, *The Unwritten Law: Criminal Justice in Victorian Kent* (Oxford: Oxford University Press, 1991), p. 173.

46 *The Times* (11 July 1842).

47 *The Times* (4 April 1867). For similar cases see *Weekly Dispatch* (3 October 1847); *The Times* (13 May 1833); PRO, HO 17/60 Kt 3, petition of Joseph Peveril to Lord Melbourne, undated (1833); *The Times* (5 August 1835, 5 April 1847, 27 October 1847, 15 June 1850, 14 August 1862).

48 On successful challenges to medical evidence see PRO, DPP 4/6, *R.* v. *Boulton* (1871). In the twentieth century, defendants were much more likely to throw

themselves on the mercy of court psychiatrists, especially since such treatment was an alternative to prison. On this, see Patrick Higgins, *Heterosexual Dictatorship: Male Homosexuality in Post War Britain* (London: Fourth Estate, 1994).

49 *The Times*, 20 June 1851.

50 *The Times*, 26 July 1870. The defendant was Edward Park, whose more famous brother Frederick had been arrested two months before while wearing women's clothes in the West End in company with Ernest Boulton. On this case see *Queen* v. *Boulton and Others* . . . PRO, DPP 4/6.

51 J. W. Cecil Turner, *Russell on Crime* 12th edn, 2 vols (London: Stevens & Sons, 1964), vol. 1, p. 737.

52 *R.* v. *Burt* (1851) 5 Cox C.C. 284.

53 *The Times*, 27 June 1846.

54 *The Times* (1 October 1864). *R.* v. *Rowton* (1865) is reported at 13 W.L.R. 436; 34.3 L.J.R. (n. s.) 57; 10 Cox C.C. 25.

55 *The Times* (23 January 1865).

56 (1865) 34.3 L.J.R. (n. s.) 58. For Erskine's remarks, see *R.* v. *Hardy* (1794) 24 S.T. 1079; for Ellenborough's remarks, see *R.* v. *Jones*, (1809) 31 S.T. 310.

57 34.3 L.J.R. (n. s.) 60–1.

58 *The Times* (28 January 1865).

59 This has been remarked upon by Martin Weiner, *Reconstructing the Criminal*, pp. 38–43.

60 See, for example, Samuel Smiles, *Self-Help, with Illustrations of Conduct and Perseverance* (London: John Murray, 1859). Carpenter argued that the chief 'motive power' of the mind was 'previously acquired habits, which automatically incite us to do as we have been before accustomed to do under the like circumstances, without the idea of prospective pleasure or pain, or of right or wrong being at all present to our mind.' W. B. Carpenter, *Principles of Mental Physiology* (London: Kegan Paul & Co., 1874), p. 414. On the idea of character and its absorption into a variety of discourses, see Stefan Collini, *Public Moralists: Political Thought and Intellectual Life in Britain, 1850–1930* (Oxford: Clarendon Press, 1991); Nathan Roberts, 'Investigating character in England, *c.* 1890–1914', Ph.D. dissertation, University of Manchester, (forthcoming 2002).

61 On the pervasiveness of character across a variety of discourses, see Roberts, 'Investigating character'.

62 Michel Foucault, *The History of Sexuality*, 3 vols, vol. 1 (London: Penguin, 1984), p. 43.

4

Pains and penalties procedure: how the House of Lords 'tried' Queen Caroline

R. A. Melikan

In the summer of 1820, King George IV demanded that his government secure the punishment of his estranged wife, Caroline, for her allegedly adulterous behaviour. Ministers acquiesced, and introduced a bill of pains and penalties to deprive the Queen of all royal titles and privileges, and to affect a divorce. After lengthy consideration by the House of Lords the bill was withdrawn, to the King's annoyance and the embarrassment of his government. This incident is well known to historians of early nineteenth-century social and political history.[1] The actual process undertaken against the Queen is less so. Nor was it generally understood at the time. Writing to her brother in August of 1820, Lady Cowper complained, 'A bill of Pains and Penalties is an awkward name, it sounds to the ignorant as if she was going to be fried or tortured in some way.'[2] It is the aim of this chapter to examine in some detail the bill procedure as a parliamentary phenomenon. It conferred on Parliament considerable authority, but its unusual process also subjected the legislature to considerable strain. In the Queen's case this strain fell upon the House of Lords, and it is enlightening to consider how this was borne by a group described by one observer as notable for its education and experience of public affairs,[3] and by a member as 'by far the stupidest and most obstinate collection of men that could be selected from all England'.[4]

It is appropriate to begin with a brief chronology of the Queen's domestic problems. On 8 April 1795 Caroline of Brunswick married her cousin George, the Prince of Wales. Despite the birth of their daughter, Charlotte, on 7 January 1796, the marriage was a failure. As early as May of that year the Prince submitted a request to George III for a formal separation. While this was refused, a separate establishment was purchased for the Princess, and the Prince avoided any unnecessary contact with her. The Prince's conduct towards his wife, together with his dissolute lifestyle, resulted in considerable public sympathy for Caroline. This state of affairs was not to last, however. Stories spread about her eccentric, indecorous, and improper behaviour, and in the spring of

1806 the Prince prevailed upon ministers to appoint a commission of inquiry.[5] In their report of 14 July the commissioners acquitted the Princess of the specific charge of adultery, but expressed concern about other evidence of indelicate behaviour.[6]

Following this cautious vindication, Caroline's public reputation improved somewhat. Her situation became more precarious, however, following the creation of the Regency, in 1811. In 1813 the Regent's determination further to limit his wife's access to their daughter led to the re-publication of the old charges and counter-charges.[7] In the following year she was barred from the celebrations marking the defeat of Napoleon, and shunned by the visiting Allied dignitaries. Shortly after this she indicated a wish to leave England. Far from voicing any objection, the government hurriedly took the necessary steps to assist the departure of this embarrassing individual. Legislation was enacted, recognising her separation from the Regent, and providing for her establishment abroad.[8] She returned to Brunswick, and then embarked upon an extensive tour of the eastern Mediterranean. In 1816 she purchased an estate on Lake Como, and thereafter divided her time between northern Italy and Austria.

The Princess may have been gone, but she was not forgotten. The Regent received unfavourable reports of her conduct from the Austrian court, particularly of her relationship with one Bartolommeo Bergami. In 1816 this information was placed before the Cabinet. Buttressed by discouraging opinions from the law officers, ministers advised inaction.[9] Not content, in 1817 the Regent turned to his friend Sir John Leach. Leach considered an investigation of the Princess's travels in Italy and beyond as likely to produce more compelling evidence of misbehaviour. While unwilling to sanction an official inquiry, ministers agreed to fund the three-member commission that Leach assembled. This panel was despatched to Milan in September 1818.[10] The appointment of the Milan Commission also inspired those who wished to support Caroline if the Regent attempted to divorce her.[11] One of these, Henry Brougham, sent his brother to Italy in the spring of 1819 to discuss with her the possibility of a permanent separation. For their part, ministers looked favourably on this plan, provided it was seen to originate with the Princess.[12] Efforts to secure a separation, however, were unsuccessful.

The death of George III, on 29 January 1820, threatened to upset the status quo. The Regent became George IV, and his wife's position also required reconsideration. As a practical matter, the settlement arranged in 1814 had determined on the demise of the old king, and it remained for the government to recommend a new one. Ministers found themselves awkwardly placed between the King, who felt that his wife's outrageous behaviour merited little sympathy, and the likely public preference for a woman cruelly treated by a dissolute husband. In February 1820, the Cabinet acquiesced to the King's demand that Caroline be excluded from that part of the Anglican liturgy in which prayers are said for the royal family, and denied the honour of coronation.[13] They strongly advised, however, that he content himself with a re-negotiated separation, which could tie her financial support to her continued exile abroad.[14] The King grudgingly accepted what he called 'this mitigated measure'.[15]

Exclusion from the liturgy, and the unfriendly treatment accorded her by foreign dignitaries, seems to have provoked the Queen to just the sort of action that ministers wanted to prevent – her return to England. On 3 June she rejected the government's proposals, and two days later she arrived at Dover. Her progress to London was marked by large demonstrations of popular support. In no way dismayed, on 6 June the King deposited with Parliament the evidence compiled by the Milan Commission, and ministers re-opened negotiations with Brougham. The liturgy again proved an insurmountable obstacle,[16] and on 23 June she rejected the compromise urged by a Commons delegation.[17] Ministers then put in train the process that would result in the Queen's trial. On 26 June the Commons adjourned in deference to the Upper House, which had previously named a Secret Committee of Inquiry. On 28 June this committee met, and six days later it reported that, so serious were the accusations against the Queen, 'it is indispensable that they should become the subject of a solemn Inquiry'.[18] On 5 July the Prime Minister, Lord Liverpool, introduced a bill of pains and penalties.

While the necessity of the government's taking some action against the Queen thus becomes clear, the decision to proceed by a bill of pains and penalties requires further explanation. Canon law did not recognise the possibility of divorce in the sense of dissolving a valid marriage and enabling the parties to remarry. The church could determine that a couple had never *been* married, and it could separate a lawfully married couple, where there had been serious misconduct during the marriage such as adultery or cruelty. At the end of the seventeenth century, however, it had become possible to end a valid marriage by act of Parliament, where the wife had committed adultery. It was usual, and then obligatory, for the petitioning husband first to obtain a separation in an ecclesiastical court, and a verdict at common law for criminal conversation, in which the adultery was considered a trespass by the wife's lover.[19]

The obvious means by which George IV could divorce Caroline, therefore, was by establishing her adultery, obtaining a decree of separation and a verdict for damages, and winning approval for a bill of divorce in both Houses of Parliament. Unfortunately, however, compelling legal and practical objections existed against such a course of action. Leaving to one side, for a moment, the question of her guilt, litigation against Caroline would prove difficult. A husband was not deemed to suffer an injury at common law when his wife committed adultery while they were living apart.[20] This would conceivably have barred any action based on Caroline's conduct after 1796, and certainly after 1814. Moreover, an ecclesiastical court would not grant a separation on the grounds of adultery by the wife where the husband had committed the same offence. That the King had conducted liaisons with a number of women since his marriage was notorious, and any accusation against the Queen invited the production of damaging and embarrassing 'recrimination evidence'.

It was because the usual means of proving wrongdoing on the Queen's part were thus unavailable that ministers considered less-obvious alternatives. One idea, likewise rejected, was a prosecution for treason as a proper foundation for a bill of divorce – always assuming that the King did not terminate his marriage by enforcing the criminal sanction. The Treason Act of Edward III addressed the illicit sexual activities of 'the King's companion, or the King's eldest daughter unmarried, or the wife of the King's eldest son and heir'.[21] The statute, however, was directed at the man who had violated the royal spouse, daughter, or daughter-in-law. *Her* liability rested in consenting to the treasonable act. In Queen Caroline's case, however, the alleged adultery had taken place abroad with the man Bergami, who owed no allegiance to the King of Great Britain. Bergami's conduct, therefore, could not constitute treason, nor could Caroline abet that act.[22]

The failure of this expedient naturally turned royal and ministerial attention to the question whether a bill of divorce need necessarily be founded on a separate judicial determination of fault. Certainly Parliament could impose sanctions by procedures that combined legislative and judicial functions. Where objectionable conduct would constitute a crime under English law, Parliament could conduct an impeachment. Where the conduct would not constitute a crime, Parliament could enact legislation to criminalise it retrospectively. A bill of attainder, which rendered conduct treasonable or felonious, or a bill to inflict pains and penalties, which affected less-serious conduct, proceeded through each House in the usual stages. At the second reading stage, however, the process assumed a judicial character. Counsel were heard for and against the bill, witnesses were called, and peers and MPs could participate in cross-examination. This 'trial' would effectively determine whether the bill succeeded.

The circumstances of the Queen's alleged misconduct made an impeachment for treason impossible. There were also practical objections to either a bill of attainder or of pains and penalties. In their opinion of January 1820 the law officers strongly advised against a bill of attainder *because* it would inflict such severe punishment for an act which English law would not so punish,[23] and indeed attainder does not seem ever to have been seriously considered by the government. A bill of pains and penalties, which merely found the Queen guilty of adultery and dissolved her marriage, would still bear the odium of an *ex post facto* law, but was less likely to upset public sensibilities. The law officers considered it the least objectionable option.[24] Ministers, however, did not warm to it. They did not doubt that the Queen would produce or attempt to produce all information embarrassing to the King, and they worried that Parliament would rely on such information to defeat the bill in the same way that an ecclesiastical court's decision would be affected by recrimination evidence.[25]

Even if it had not this effect, the use of such information by opposition politicians and the radical press would be harmful to the interests of the kingdom.[26] These objections, moreover, were based on the assumption that an accusation of adultery could be sustained, and ministers were far from convinced on this point. They repeatedly warned against relying on the testimony of foreigners, 'most of them not above the rank of menial servants, or that of masters and attendants in hotels, wholly unacquainted with the English language'.[27]

The Queen's return to England in June 1820, and her refusal to accept the government's compromise, forced ministers to overcome these qualms. In a letter to Lord Kenyon, Liverpool explained what had become the government's position by July.[28] This was, as much as possible, to remove all personal interest from the case and focus upon the needs of the state, Parliament, and the Crown. Liverpool argued that even if the circumstances made prosecution for treason impossible, adultery by a queen was a crime against the state. It was, therefore, an appropriate object for a bill of pains and penalties. Having recognised the criminality of that conduct, Parliament could impose an appropriate sanction, including the forfeiture of her royal status and severance of her ties with the British Crown. This would, of necessity, include the termination of her marriage. The fact that it would afford relief to the King in his individual capacity was irrelevant. He had brought the matter to Parliament's attention as a public accusation, and not as a measure of personal relief. His entitlement to such relief, therefore, was also irrelevant.[29] Whether such expressions of disinterestedness would convince Parliament, however, remained to be seen.

It only remained for the government to decide in which House of Parliament the bill should originate. The House of Lords was the obvious choice for several reasons. It was superior to the House of Commons as a judicial forum in that witnesses appearing before it could be sworn, and litigation of various kinds regularly occurred there. Bills of divorce, moreover, inevitably originated in the House of Lords, and the rank and situation of the individuals concerned in this action made the Lords particularly appropriate.[30] The government also preferred the Upper House for tactical reasons. In that generally tranquil and less-partisan setting responsibility for the bill could rest on the Prime Minister and the majority of the Cabinet, while presiding over the debates would be Lord Eldon, the Chancellor. In the more raucous, stormy Commons, by contrast, debates were regulated by a non-partisan Speaker, and the government's burden must be borne almost exclusively by the Foreign Secretary, Lord Castlereagh. On 20 July the Queen's lawyers firmly advised against reserving her defence until the bill reached the Commons. They felt that avoiding a forum where witnesses were sworn, and favouring one where they were not, would both 'raise considerable prejudice' in the minds of peers and MPs, and create real difficulties for the presentation of her case.[31]

The trial began on 17 August, the date designated for the second reading of the bill, and concluded on 6 November, when the vote on the second reading was taken. It is not the intention of this chapter to trace the substantive

Table 4.1 *Non-attendance on the first day of the Queen's trial*

Reason for non-attendance	*Numbers*
Out of the realm	25
Illness	22
Over 70 years of age	31
Absent on royal service	2
Death of family member	1
Excused attendance	3
Not summoned	3
No response	1

Source: *House of Lords Journal*, vol. 53, p. 371.

arguments made for and against the Queen, but rather to examine how the House of Lords struggled to use this complex and unfamiliar hybrid process. The judicial nature of the proceedings was certainly evident during the forty-nine days in which the House was in session. The differences between this proceeding and one conducted in a regular court of law, however, were very significant. The venue of the House of Lords, and the peculiar qualities of the personnel involved, rendered this 'trial' a strange combination of the judicial, the legislative, and the political.

There was nothing odd about the House of Lords as a setting for judicial proceedings. Appeals from English, Scottish, and Irish common law and equity decisions were regularly heard in the House of Lords. While less-frequently invoked, the Lords' original jurisdiction concerned both civil and criminal matters. It was the forum for impeachments and trials of peers. As a Committee of Privileges it decided peerage claims and could undertake advisory proceedings on private bills before they went to the floor of the House. Most of its judicial work, however, provoked scant general interest, and attendance was consequently modest. For the Queen's trial, however, the chamber was packed. The Chancellor had been charged to inform every peer and lord of Parliament of the obligation to attend. The only valid excuses for non-attendance had been advanced age, sickness, absence abroad, or the death of a close family member.[32] Unexcused absence resulted in a heavy fine: £100 for each of the first three days of the proceedings, and £50 per day thereafter.[33] Whether prompted by personal financial interest, public duty, or simply curiosity as to the details of the case, attendance was very good: 256 attended on the first day,[34] and in succeeding days attendance averaged 231.[35] This was in contrast to a regular average attendance of about fifty.[36] In addition to the lords, the high court judges were summoned to provide expert assistance to the House. Lawyers for and against the bill constituted the other significant group of participants. Appearing chiefly for the bill were Sir Robert Gifford, the Attorney General, and Sir John Singleton Copley, the Solicitor General.

Table 4.2 *Attendance in the House of Lords, 1815–25*

Year	*Days House in session*	*Average attendance*	*Range*
1815	99	41.30	3–139
1820 (excluding the trial)	86	65.10	5–222
1820 (the trial)	49	231.92	213–58
1825	101	51.76	3–199

Source: House of Lords Journal, vols 50, 53, 57.

Appearing against the bill were the Queen's law officers: Henry Brougham, Thomas Denman, and Stephen Lushington. The legal ranks on both sides were swelled by junior counsel, solicitors, and clerks. Sir Christopher Robinson, the Advocate General, Dr William Adams, and James Park assisted Gifford and Copley, together with George Maule, the Treasury Solicitor. John Williams, Nicholas Tindal, and Thomas Wilde served as junior defence counsel, and the solicitor for the Queen was William Vizard.

The attendance of all these people created a serious practical problem: accommodation. Seating in the chamber was formally allocated according to rank and office. In order to accommodate the larger than usual numbers during the trial, a gallery was erected above the benches on both sides. The judges sat beside the Chancellor, and counsel were accommodated at the bar. Provision was also made for the Queen and her attendants. When present in the chamber she was afforded a chair close to her counsel, but within the bar of the House. The trial was also well attended by spectators.[37] MPs and distinguished visitors, like Richard Rush, the American Secretary of State, were seated near the throne.[38] The less exalted were huddled below the bar.

This crowding had definite consequences for the conduct of the trial. Most notably, the noise in the chamber made it very difficult to hear.[39] This was a frequent cause of complaint, and must have increased the likelihood that peers would rely more on written accounts of the trial than they would upon what they had actually heard. The newspapers provided lengthy coverage of the trial, and journalists were among those in daily attendance during the proceedings. Nevertheless, the Chancellor adopted the usual attitude in the House towards the newspaper reporters present on important occasions – he affected not to notice them. He did warn, however, that 'if any persons answering that description had found their way below the bar, and were, in breach of their Lordships' privileges, to publish any occurrence that took place in that house, which their Lordships had particularly signified their intention ought not to be published, such persons would do so at their peril'.[40] On 23 August the Earl of Darlington requested that copies of the printed evidence be produced on a daily basis. This was opposed on the grounds that the official record of the House could not be produced both quickly and accurately.[41] Nevertheless,

Darlington's request was granted. The attempt to comply caused problems only a week later when it was found not possible to challenge a witness's prior testimony because the transcript was at the printer's.[42]

Crowding also meant that onlookers had a surprising degree of access to the lawyers. Charles Greville mentioned the opportunities for eavesdropping that such proximity afforded him. 'I cannot help hearing all their conversation, their remarks, and learning what witnesses they are going to examine, and many other things which are interesting and amusing.'[43] Others were not content with a merely passive role. Spencer Perceval, the son of the late prime minister, was standing close enough to Brougham to whisper a quotation from *Paradise Lost*, which Brougham incorporated into his interrogation of one of the Milan Commissioners.[44] When the Duke of Wellington realised that a defence witness was lying, he communicated his suspicions to the Solicitor General, whose subsequent cross-examination reduced the witness to incomprehensibility.[45]

The various personnel involved in the trial also distinguished it from the usual judicial proceeding. Most notable in this respect were the lords themselves. They were authorised to examine witnesses, and to resolve all questions regarding their own procedure. Nor did they play an insignificant part in these matters. Of the fifty-eight prosecution and defence witnesses called, only thirteen were not questioned by the lords. While the most frequent participants were those with professional experience or political precedence, cross-examination was not a task left to a few. Sixty-two different peers posed questions to witnesses, and most of these spoke on more than one occasion.[46] While the usefulness of such questions naturally varied, it should not be assumed that this phase of the proceedings was less important than the examination by counsel.

Lords' contributions, it should be noted, did not always have an obviously salutary effect on the proceedings. In the chamber their conduct could be awkward in the extreme. They failed to keep quiet – murmuring to express disapproval, laughing at humorous statements, such as an interpreter's admission that there was no word for 'gentle woman' in the French language, and generally contributing to an unsettled atmosphere.[47] Those lords who did not understand regular judicial procedure frequently asked questions and made suggestions that seemed strange to the experienced practitioner. Liverpool, for example, thought that a witness should be permitted to answer a question before counsel could object to it.[48] Those lords with professional experience offered helpful explanations to their colleagues, but their interjections were also disruptive. Lords Erskine and Lauderdale were the worst offenders in this respect. A former chancellor and distinguished advocate, Erskine could not resist indulging in reminiscences of his own courtroom experiences. For example, during the discussion of whether an Italian witness could be asked if there was a form of oath more binding upon his conscience than that used in English courts, Erskine related the story of a witness at the assizes who had objected to kissing the Bible, but had wished to hold up his hand because the Book of Revelations described an angel standing upon the sea and holding up his hand. Erskine explained, 'I said this does not apply to your case, for, in the first place, you are no angel, secondly, you cannot tell how the Angel would have sworn if he had been on shore.'[49] Lauderdale frequently complained about the irregularity of this or that line of questioning. Peers were also happy to suggest – though rarely to agree upon – improvements for their own procedure. Lord Holland suggested that the several high court judges would be better confined in an adjoining chamber so as to insulate them from the evidence.[50] Erskine wanted to permit questioning in a manner that he acknowledged was contrary to the rules of evidence, on the grounds that he had never approved of the rule in question.[51]

The degree to which the lords let political allegiances overwhelm their judicial responsibilities is questionable. During the trial there were significant demonstrations of political independence, though Wellington complained of 'a great deal of *caballing*' along party lines as the proceedings drew to a close.[52] Moreover, while the desire to score political points cannot be ignored when assessing some contributions, the tendency of the lords' examination to address details of matters raised by counsel suggests that the lords were affected by what was being said and not merely to what they wanted to hear. Outside the House, however, lords seem to have exercised very little restraint. Not only did their dinner party conversations seem to have consisted of little but the trial, they also opened their minds to counsel. Brougham and Denman were invited to spend weekends at Holland House in August and September, and Brougham confided in his memoirs, 'I went among the members of both Houses, both at Brooke's and in the families which I knew they frequented. This gave me the means of ascertaining, as we proceeded, the effects of the evidence and the arguments on both sides.'[53]

The two most important government peers were far more discreet. Liverpool and Eldon avoided discussions of the trial away from the House, and conducted themselves with propriety inside the chamber.[54] In Liverpool's case the explanation for this conduct is a straightforward one. He had been obliged to institute proceedings contrary to his wishes, and he carried out his duties conscientiously, but with little enthusiasm. For Eldon's conduct the explanation is more complex. As Speaker of the House of Lords, Eldon's role was to help members regulate their debates rather than to impose regulations upon them. This established practice, coupled with Eldon's own dislike of appearing to act other than according to clear legal principles, made him a very mild-mannered presiding officer. Consequently, he referred questions of law and procedure to the judges, despite the fact that time after time they merely confirmed his assessment. He also allowed counsel, particularly the defence counsel, considerable latitude in the manner in which they stated their case.[55]

The fact that much of the case against the Queen involved the testimony of foreigners also set it apart from regular English trials. Prosecution and defence each provided an interpreter, and the practice of interpretation contributed much to the complexity of the proceedings. The interpreters complained when witnesses interrupted, or did not understand what was being asked, while the interpreters were chided for intruding themselves too much into the case.[56] Moreover, lords sometimes were, or believed themselves to be, more knowledgeable in French, German, or Italian, and challenged the translations given.[57]

It remains to say something about the counsel appearing for and against the bill. Together they constituted a formidable array of legal talent, including three future chancellors and two future chief justices.[58] This is not altogether surprising, given the nature of the case. What is surprising is the fact that the leading counsel on both sides were almost not permitted to appear. According to the standing orders of the House of Commons, MPs could not appear as counsel on legislation before the House of Lords. This was to prevent such MPs either from experiencing a conflict of interest, or from exerting improper influence in the promotion of private bills.[59] On 12 July, therefore, Brougham was obliged to move that the Commons' standing orders be so far waived as to allow him and Denman to appear for the Queen.[60] This waiver was extended to the Crown's law officers over Brougham's objection that, as the case was merely one of public interest, their presence was not required. The identity of opposing counsel was not the only problem that the defence had with the proceedings. Brougham complained about what he described as the 'mixed capacity' of peers, which enabled them to display their political or judicial demeanours as these suited them.[61] This tendency was particularly evident in their examination of witnesses. Brougham later recalled, 'When successful, they were like advocates; but when they failed, straightway they became judicial, and must only be considered to put the question as judges anxious to draw out the truth.'[62]

The lawyers were not alone, however, in having grievances. For their part, the lords found the lawyers' tone, particularly that of the defence counsel, rude and overbearing.[63] In part this was probably due to the fact that the lawyers represented opposite political as well as legal positions. This combination rendered the trial both tantalising and frustrating for able and ambitious advocates like Copley and Brougham. On the one hand, it provided an unparalleled opportunity to display one's professional skills and thereby advance one's career. Copley, in particular, would have been aware that an impressive performance would strengthen his claim to succeed Eldon on the Woolsack. On the other hand, however, the trial exposed the advocate to the dubious mercies of over 200 'judges', some of whom were one's political enemies and many of whom were capable of asking awkward questions through ignorance, boredom, or irritation. It is tempting, certainly, to assign some of Brougham's aggressive manner towards the House to his own situation as an opposition lawyer, and to his knowledge that the greatest professional prizes were beyond his reach.

Finally, the trial was both long and complicated. In terms of duration and intensity, it was unparalleled in contemporary English law. The average criminal trial in the early nineteenth century was extremely brief – certainly several per day during an average assize or Old Bailey session.[64] Even a complex and politically sensitive trial, such as Thomas Hardy's prosecution for 'constructive treason' in 1794 had only lasted seven days.[65] Judicial proceedings in Parliament tended either to be short or to occupy only a limited amount of the House's attention at any one time. The closest parallels to the Queen's trial were the impeachments of Lord Melville and Warren Hastings. Melville was acquitted after proceedings of fifteen days. Hastings's impeachment lasted 142 days, but these were spread over a period of eight years. During that time, interest in the case varied according to the press of other business and the dedication of the impeachment managers.[66] During the Queen's trial, by contrast, little, if any, other business was done in the House. The combination of long hours, enforced attendance, and frequently complex legal arguments took its toll. On 2 September, Lady Granville confided to her sister, 'The Lords are all tired and suffocated'.[67] In a letter to George Canning Liverpool confessed, 'in the whole course of my life I do not recollect to have undergone such continued fatigue'.[68] There were certainly opportunities for the attention of participants to wander. During one pause the Chancellor amused the judges by drawing a caricature of himself and circulating it among them.[69] Nor did the inquiry itself fail to provide scope for entertainment. Holland recalled that he spent much of his time 'writing nonsensical puns and epigrams on the various indecencies which occurred'.[70] The Queen, perhaps finding less enjoyment in such pursuits, typically kept to her apartment adjacent to the chamber, where she played backgammon with the former Lord Mayor of London.[71]

Despite the efforts made to provide for likely difficulties, the House of Lords was not sufficiently familiar with the pains and penalties process to deal effectively with the range of issues that arose as the trial progressed. Nor is this surprising, as the procedure had last been used against Bishop Atterbury almost a hundred years previously.[72] In fact, the pre-trial concentration on such matters as seating appears slightly naive when contrasted with the issues that were not considered beforehand, and that were muddled through once they did arise. For example, prior to the appearance of the first prosecution witness, Lord King queried the authority of the House in the event of perjury. Could they punish like a court of record, or only commit the malefactor for falsehood and prevarication during the term of their sitting?[73] The Chancellor did not know the answer to this question, nor did he know whether a prosecution for perjury, supposing one would lie, could commence without a special order of the House. Having made inquiries, Eldon reported that a prosecution could be maintained, and the House approved his motion to suspend their privileges in the event of such a prosecution.[74] The time of adjournment also caused awkwardness, as the House could not agree whether it preferred to adjourn at four o'clock or at five.[75] A third, more important, decision concerned voting rights. Were those who did not attend every day of the trial eligible to vote on the bill? Debate on this issue exposed differing views, but no explicit resolution, as peers questioned whether any absence, or only absence for a significant – but unspecified – period ought to disqualify.[76]

The issues of perjury, adjournment, and voting could be classed as procedural irritations – they never threatened to derail the proceedings. Other issues were much more dangerous in this respect. In attempting to vindicate the Queen, her lawyers issued a series of procedural challenges to the House, which had two obvious benefits for the defence. If successful, they could help strengthen the Queen's case. If unsuccessful, they could still help to discredit the case against her. A third benefit, which may or may not have been the ultimate aim of Brougham and company, was so to protract and complicate the trial by the discussion of these challenges that the entire process would be condemned as unworkable. Whether any of the benefits were actually achieved is uncertain. What is clear, however, is that the manner in which the House dealt with these challenges demonstrates how uncertain was their grip on their own procedure.

The first challenge came before the trial proper had begun, when Brougham requested that the defence be given a list of prosecution witnesses.[77] The statute of 7 Anne *c.* 21 (1708) provided that all persons indicted for treason should receive a list of witnesses ten days prior to trial. Brougham's request, however, caused peers to argue whether they should extend the privilege to the present case. Erskine favoured provision of a list, and to avoid the objection that this would place an unfair restriction upon the prosecution, he proposed that the list exclude rebuttal witnesses.[78] This prompted the Chancellor to complain that Erskine wanted not merely to apply a rule that was unique to treason, but to alter the very rule deemed so valuable. Rather than adopt such a dangerous innovation, Eldon advised the House 'to go on in the ordinary and established course'.[79] A committee was appointed to examine the records of bills of attainder, pains and penalties, and impeachments, to determine whether there was precedent for granting Brougham's request. Three days later it reported that there was not.[80] The absence of precedent did not, however, immediately determine the issue. Lord Lansdowne complained that it was not for the government, having put the unfamiliar process in train, either to invoke precedent or to decry its absence.[81] Lord Ellenborough, however, accused the defence of making the request to create a popular effect, while Lauderdale believed that Erskine's partial list would not really protect the accused.[82] The motion was defeated.[83] Ten days later, on 24 July, the House dealt with a variation of the witness list question. Erskine presented a petition from the Queen, seeking 'a specification of the place or places in which the Criminal Acts are charged to have been committed'.[84] Holland and the Chancellor debated whether the bill against the Queen was or ought to be as specifically framed as an indictment or as other bills of pains and penalties since the Revolution. In contrast with his earlier wish to conform as closely as possible to regular legal procedure, Eldon argued that there could be no necessary analogy between the common law and a proceeding before Parliament. Holland agreed that the House could lay aside questions of law in favour of 'substantial justice', but he felt that substantial justice in this case warranted compliance with the Queen's request. The petition was not granted.

The next challenge from the defence followed the examination, cross-examination, and re-examination of the first prosecution witness. Brougham requested that the witness be recalled and subjected to a further cross-examination. The Chancellor objected, but relented when Brougham promised to limit himself to three to five questions.[85] Almost immediately, however, the Chancellor had cause to regret his leniency. Brougham grossly exceeded his three to five questions, and two days later he announced his intention of repeating the process with another prosecution witness. This announcement, and the likelihood that the examination of every important prosecution witness would become protracted and complicated, provoked a lengthy debate on the best way forward. Brougham based his request on the lack of a witness list. Because the defence had no prior knowledge of a prosecution witness, they could only cross-examine immediately on points that arose from the direct examination, and then return to matters that subsequently came to light.[86] This argument, apart from compensating the defence for the lack of a privilege to which they were not entitled, presented several procedural problems. Should the defence have complete freedom to choose whether and when it would conduct a second cross? When would the prosecution conduct its re-examination – only after the defence had either conducted a second cross or determined that it would not do so? How would the divided cross affect questioning by peers? Would this occur after the possible second re-examination? And if their questions revealed new information, might this provide grounds for a third cross-examination and re-examination? Eldon feared that the consequence of these deviations from regular practice would result in proceedings 'moving on in an endless circle.'[87]

The decision to allow counsel to divide the cross-examination was reached by a tortuous route over the next few days. On 26 August the House decided that counsel should state any proposed alterations to the usual practice. On 28 August, however, that decision was rescinded, and counsel were informed that they could speak to Liverpool's motion, namely that cross-examination should proceed as usual, with the possibility of a further cross on a showing of sufficient grounds. Following statements by prosecution and defence counsel, Liverpool announced a wish to withdraw his motion. He was convinced, he said, that it would be unjust now to withdraw from the defence what had been granted, or seemed to have been granted to them previously. Lauderdale objected to this change of tack, claiming that 'such an instance of inconsistency and vacillation of opinion . . . never had before been exhibited'.[88] Eldon attempted to preserve something like regular procedure, but he was unwilling to dictate to the House.[89] An amended version of Liverpool's motion, in line with his changed sentiments, was approved by a vote of 121–106, with Eldon and Lord Sidmouth, the Home Secretary, declining to support their colleague.

The third and most important challenge occurred midway through the defence, when it was alleged that several persons had attempted to bribe potential witnesses to testify against the Queen. Acknowledging, as all sides did, the offensiveness of the alleged conduct, they nevertheless wrestled with the question whether to admit evidence on the subject at present. Debate focused primarily on whether the bribery had tainted the evidence that had formed the basis of the bill or that had been adduced at trial, which in turn provoked two further questions. First, who was the principal behind the bill and the resulting trial, and what was the link, if any, between that principal and the alleged malefactors? Secondly, were any of the alleged malefactors in a position to affect the content of the evidence actually produced against the Queen?

The identity of the principal was not resolved. Liverpool accepted responsibility for the bill, but objected to the notion that either the Crown or the government was prosecuting the Queen.[90] Other peers suggested that the state, or the House of Lords itself, was the principal, motivated by a desire to see justice done.[91] Attempts were made, not always successfully, to establish that the alleged malefactors were the agents of the Milan Commission. While not itself the principal, the Commission had produced the evidence which had gone to the Secret Committee and which had been relied upon by the counsel for the bill in producing their case. The practical effect of the alleged bribery, therefore, would have been to affect the evidence against the Queen, and render that evidence unreliable. This, according to the defence, justified a thorough, immediate inquiry into the issues of bribery, corruption, and a conspiracy against the Queen.[92] On the other side, it was argued that the evidence of corruption of persons who actually testified, and of actual links between the alleged malefactors and the Milan Commission, was slight, and certainly did not justify such a lengthy divergence from their present course.[93]

The above points, it is submitted, demand considerable powers of analysis when set out in a coherent form. This is not, however, the manner in which they were presented in the House of Lords. Over the course of seven days, from 13 to 20 October, the issues were circled, suggested, rephrased, and contrasted, in the context of arguments over the conduct of the particular individuals. For example, was evidence of the conduct of Guiseppe Sacchi admissible either because he might have been an agent of the Commission or because this evidence confuted his prior testimony, and did it matter that his alleged conduct involved the attempted bribery of persons who had not testified? Or, could the defence question a witness about the statements of one Ricanti, allegedly an agent of the Milan Commission, as a follow-on from similar questions having been permitted about the statements of one Restelli, when the grounds for admitting the statements of Restelli had been his inability to testify, and not because he was an agent of the Commission? Finally, the defence lawyers, in particular, argued very aggressively. Long before the judges were even asked whether evidence of a conspiracy was admissible, the defence spoke as if the fact of a conspiracy had been proven. Brougham spoke of 'a conspiracy of the foulest kind' and Wilde stated that 'a detestable conspiracy had been formed' against the Queen.[94]

To say that peers dealt ably with the bribery issue would overstate the case, as even the legally trained peers helped to confuse the discussion. Furthermore, arguments based on regular legal practice were repeatedly undercut by explicit demands that they conduct their proceedings according to a vague notion of 'fairness' and without reference to the rules of evidence or the opinions of the judges. Eldon, attempting to steer his colleagues along recognised legal channels without appearing to act against the will of the House, displayed a growing anxiety over offering an opinion. An objection to the request to view some confidential correspondence actually prompted the Chancellor to remark, that 'he did not mean to support the objection, as an objection; but . . . he desired not to be included in the number of those who thought that there was no objection to it'.[95] Undoubtedly the bribery issue severely complicated and slowed the trial. It is no wonder that the Earl of Darnley feared that they would never reach a satisfactory conclusion. He complained that 'when he came daily to that House, and saw the paraphernalia by which they were surrounded, he doubted whether he was not waking from some feverish dream'.[96] By late October, he was probably not the only person who was coming to regard the trial as a nightmare.

The arguments of counsel finally concluded on 30 October. Following the speeches of thirty peers, the vote on the second reading of the bill was taken on 6 November. It was approved by a vote of 119–94.[97] From the government's perspective this result was ominous. Eldon had predicted a majority of around 50, a conservative figure in the context of recent voting patterns.[98] The House then went into committee and debated, *inter alia*, whether to retain the divorce clause. They resolved this in the affirmative, by a vote of 129–62. The signals from this vote were mixed, as some peers supported the clause because they felt a divorce was justified, and some because they considered the clause as likely to sink the bill.[99] The vote suggested, however, that the government's usual supporters were divided and likely to prove unreliable. When the vote on the third reading was taken on 10 November the majority fell to 9.[100] Rightly deciding that the bill could not survive the Commons, Liverpool moved to delay consideration for six months. This was approved without a division. Effectively, the bill was thrown out.

The immediate result of the bill's failure was public adulation for the Queen. In the subsequent months, however, both her popularity and her value as a political weapon against the government or the King faded. Many people felt that the case against her had been proven, even if the House of Lords had not shown itself particularly keen to punish her. She became the object of sly humour, as with the popular riddle, 'Why is the Queen like the Bill of Pains and Penalties? Because they are both abandoned.'[101] In February 1821

Parliament settled an annual sum of £50,000 upon her without a division, but attempts to discredit in the Lower House the government's conduct in the Upper were soundly defeated. Both Houses continued to receive petitions in support of the Queen until mid-February, after which public sympathy for her situation seems to have faded. Despite the decision by the privy council on 4 July that she could not be crowned against the King's wishes, she attempted to disrupt, or at least to attend, the coronation on 19 July. While she was cheered on her way to Westminster Abbey, her tearful retreat occasioned boos from the assembled crowds.[102] This proved to be the nadir of her career. She did not live either to return to Italy or to endure further loss of status in England. Her health rapidly declined, and she died on 5 August 1821 following complications resulting from an intestinal obstruction

But what of the House of Lords itself? How did it bear the burdens imposed upon it during the summer and autumn of 1820? The verdict here must be largely positive, given the difficulty of the situation. Queen Caroline's 'case' was one that the government had tried hard to avoid. Legally obscure, politically dangerous, and generating considerable public disquiet, it had been forced upon ministers by the refusal of both the King and Queen to compromise. The bill of pains and penalties seemed to offer a means of transferring much of the burden and at least some of the opprobrium of the case onto the House of Lords. The judicial nature of the proceedings, the freedom with which the House could conduct the 'trial', and the obligation of maximum participation among peers were attractive features for ministers hoping to avoid full responsibility and also to shield the King. Each of these features, however, made the trial extremely awkward for the House. The pains and penalties process had a judicial component, but it was both cumbersome and unfamiliar to all those attempting to administer it. While the House enjoyed the power to regulate its conduct at every step, the majority of its members lacked the legal training necessary to use that power effectively. Indeed, many peers were not used to devoting substantial time and energy to public matters, and their enforced participation weakened the House as a deliberative body. For all its judicial trappings, moreover, the Queen's trial was not merely a judicial occasion, and the House of Lords was not merely a court. The House could not be expected wholly to abandon its political character, and the curious mixture of political signals received during the trial – the equivocal leadership from the government, the vocal public support for the Queen, and the suspicion that the conduct of neither royal party was particularly admirable – complicated any political element to the House's decision. Despite these formidable difficulties, the House avoided the pitfalls that could so easily have been its portion of this unfortunate proceeding. It was neither incompetent nor lacking in integrity. It did not give the government the easy victory that might have been anticipated.[103] On the contrary, having struggled through the complexities of the trial, the House convinced ministers that further hostilities against the Queen must cease. Ministers had chosen a bill of pains and penalties to placate the King while avoiding the most obvious legal and political costs of a prosecution against the Queen. The House of Lords demonstrated to the King and the government that every 'trial' has its price.

Notes

A version of this essay was published in *Parliamentary History*, 20: 3 (2001), 155–76, and appears by permission of The Parliamentary History Yearbook Trust.

1 Queen Caroline has been the subject of many biographies, which naturally include the trial. A modern account of the trial is provided in Roger Fulford, *The Trial of Queen Caroline* (London: B. T. Batsford Ltd, 1967); and E. A. Smith, *A Queen on Trial: the Affair of Queen Caroline* (Stroud: Sutton, 1993) contains excerpts from contemporary letters, diaries, and other relevant documents. Several contemporary accounts of the trail were published, among them J. H. Adolphus, *A Correct, Full and Impartial Report of the Trail of Her Majesty, Caroline* (London: Jones & Co., 1820); Anon., *Trial of Queen Caroline*, 2 vols (London: W. Wright, 1821). The latter has been used in the present chapter, as providing the most complete account.
2 Tresham Lever (ed.), *The Letters of Lady Palmerston* (London: John Murray, 1957), p. 44, letter from Emily Lamb to Frederick Lamb, 20 August 1820.
3 The observations are those of Richard Rush, the American Secretary of State, and George Canning. R. Rush, *The Court of London from 1819 to 1825*, ed. B. Rush (London: Richard Bentley & Son, 1873), p. 271.
4 Thomas Creevey quoted this statement by Lord Granville. Sir H. Maxwell (ed.), *The Creevey Papers* (London: John Murray, 1923), p. 322.
5 Membership of the commission consisted of Lords Grenville, Erskine, Spencer, and Ellenborough, and Sir Samuel Romilly, the Solicitor General.
6 See, e.g., Anon., *Royal Investigation* (London: J. F. Hughes, 1807).
7 See, e.g., R. Edwards (ed.), *The Book!* (London: privately published, 1813); Spencer Perceval (ed.), *The Genuine Book*, 3rd edn (London: W. Lindsell, 1813); Spencer Perceval, *The Royal or Delicate Investigation* (London: Hamblin & Seyfang, 1813).
8 54 Geo. III *c*. 160 (1814).
9 Public Record Office, London (hereafter PRO), HO126(3) Cabinet minute draft, 1 August 1816; see also *ibid.*, the opinions of the law officers to Lord Chancellor Eldon, 29 July and 1 August 1820. Ministers felt that, having been made aware of the activities of the Austrian government, the Princess would be on her guard, and further investigations would prove fruitless.
10 The so-called 'Milan Commission' consisted of John Powell, a solicitor; William Cooke, a Chancery barrister; and Major, subsequently Colonel, Thomas Browne.
11 It was felt that, while the Regent might have been willing to forgo a divorce so long as his daughter remained his heir, her death removed any wish to protect her, and might inspire him to contract a second marriage for dynastic reasons. See, e.g., the discussion in C. Hibbert, *George IV* (London: Penguin Books, 1976), p. 541.
12 C. D. Yonge, *Life and Administration of Robert Banks Jenkinson, Earl of Liverpool*, 3 vols (London: John Murray, 1868), vol. 3, p. 17, Cabinet minute, 17 July 1819.
13 J. W. Croker maintained that he told ministers that the liturgy effectively determined the larger issue of the Queen's status. 'If she is fit to be introduced to the

Almighty, she is fit to be received by men, and if we are to *pray* for her in Church we may surely bow to her at Court. The praying for her will throw a sanctity round her which the good and pious people of this country will never afterwards bear to be withdrawn.' Ministers had previously considered the legal aspects of the liturgy, but not the moral and religious aspects. L. J. Jennings (ed.), *The Croker Papers*, 2nd edn, 3 vols (London: John Murray, 1885), vol. 1, pp. 159–60.

14 British Library, London (hereafter BL), Liverpool papers, Additional MS 38565 f. 29, Cabinet minute, 10 February 1820.

15 *Ibid.*, f. 79, letter from George IV to the Cabinet, 17 February 1820. See also *ibid.*, fos 49, 63, for an exchange of letters on 12 and 14 February 1820.

16 Hansard, *Parl. Debs*, 2nd ser., vol. 1, cols 1152–60 (19 June 1820).

17 *Ibid.*, col. 1320 (24 June 1820).

18 *Journals of the House of Lords*, vol. 53, pp. 249–50 (4 July 1820).

19 J. H. Baker, *An Introduction to English Legal History*, 4th edn (London: Butterworths, 2002), pp. 491–3, 495. See W. S. Holdsworth, *A History of English Law* 17 vols (London: Methuen & Co. Ltd, 1903–72), vol. 11, p. 629 fn. 9; A. H. Manchester, *Modern Legal History* (London: Butterworths, 1980), p. 374.

20 See Baker, *English Legal History*, p. 493; PRO, HO126(3), letter from the law officers to the Lord Chancellor, 1 August 1816.

21 25 Edw. III st. 5 *c*. 2 (1351).

22 PRO, HO126(3), letter from the law officers [probably to the Chancellor], 17 January 1820.

23 *Ibid.*

24 *Ibid.*

25 BL, Liverpool papers, Add. MS 38565 f. 29, Cabinet minute, 10 February 1820.

26 *Ibid.*

27 *Ibid.*

28 Yonge, *Life of Liverpool*, vol. 3, pp. 104–6.

29 See Liverpool's statement on the public nature of the bill, in Hansard, *Parl. Debs*, 2nd ser., vol. 2, cols 1384–5 (7 September 1820).

30 Liverpool explained the decision to begin in the House of Lords when he introduced the bill on 5 July. See *ibid.*, cols 207–9. His reasoning found some favour with the opposition. See R. Grenville, 2nd Duke of Buckingham and Chandos, *Memoirs of the Court of George IV 1820–1830*, 2 vols (London: Hurst & Blackett, 1859), vol. 1, p. 49.

31 A. Aspinall (ed.), *The Letters of King George IV 1812–1830*, 3 vols (Cambridge: Cambridge University Press, 1938), vol. 2, pp. 354–5.

32 Advanced age was designated as over 70 years, and bereavement constituted a valid excuse where the death was of a wife, parent, or child. Foreign travel justified absence either when undertaken for royal service, or when commenced prior to 10 July, when the date for the second reading was announced. See Table 4.1.

33 *Lords Journal*, vol. 53, p. 355 (25 July 1820).

34 In addition to the twenty-one peers who were not members of the House of Lords, eighty-eight submitted excuses or had experienced some problem in receiving the summons. *Ibid.*, pp. 371–2 (17 August 1820).

35 The average figure of 231.92 is based on those peers answering the daily call of the House between 17 August–6 November. This forty-nine-day period includes not only the 'trial' proper, but also the summing-up by counsel and peers.

36 A more precise figure of 52.72 can be obtained by averaging daily attendance in 1815, 1820, and 1825. See Table 4.2. The number of English peers in the House of Lords remained stable during the first quarter of the nineteenth century. John Cannon states that the peerage stood at 267 in January 1800, while a call of the House in February 1825 reveals a figure of 278. See J. Cannon, *Aristocratic Century* (Cambridge: Cambridge University Press, 1987), p. 15.

37 Lords were restricted as to the orders of admission they could grant. A rota system was imposed, with archbishops, dukes, marquesses, and earls giving orders to admit one person each on the first day, and all other ranks giving orders on the second day. *Lords Journal*, vol. 53, p. 369 (16 August 1820).

38 See Rush, *Court of London*, pp. 300–7.

39 To reduce noise and the possibility of disruption, vehicular traffic in front of Parliament was restricted during the hours when the House was sitting, and Household troops were deployed to control the anticipated crowds. *Journal*, vol. 53, pp. 367–8 (15 August 1820).

40 Anon., *Trial*, vol. 1, p. 321. On the general attitude of both Houses towards newspaper reporters, see Holdsworth, *English Law*, vol. 10, pp. 547–8.

41 Hansard, *Parl. Debs*, 2nd ser., vol. 2, col. 870 (23 August 1820).

42 Anon., *Trial*, vol. 1, p. 233.

43 C. Greville, *The Greville Memoirs*, ed. H. Reeve, 3 vols (London: Longmans, 1874), vol. 1, pp. 35–6.

44 F. Hawes, *Henry Brougham* (London: Jonathan Cape, 1957), p. 158. See also, Greville, *Greville Memoirs*, vol. 1, p. 38.

45 E. Phipps, *Memoirs of the Political and Military Life of Robert Plumer Ward*, 2 vols (London: John Murray, 1850), vol. 2, p. 81.

46 The following peers questioned witnesses: Alvanley, Anson, Auckland, Balcarras, Bathurst, Belhaven, Belmore, Blessington, Brownlow, Buckingham, Calthorpe, Carnarvon, Cathcart, Clarence, Clifden, Colville, Combermere, Darlington, Darnley, De Clifford, De Dunstanville, De Lawarr, Derby, Donoughmore, Downshire, Duncan, Dynevor, Eldon, Ellenborough, Enniskillen, Erskine, Falmouth, Gosforth, Grantham, Grantley, Grey, Grosvenor, Hamilton, Harrowby, Holland, Hood, Huntley, Kenyon, King, Kingston, Lansdowne, Lauderdale, Limerick, Liverpool, Mansfield, Melville, Morley, Morton, Oxford, Prudhoe, Redesdale, Richmond, Rosebury, Rosslyn, Rous, Walsingham, and Winchelsea.

47 See, e.g., Hansard, *Parl. Debs*, 2nd ser., vol. 2, col. 925 (24 August 1820); Anon., *Trial*, vol. 1, p. 254, vol. 2, p. 323.

48 Anon., *Trial*, vol. 1, p. 78.

49 Hansard, *Parl. Debs*, 2nd ser., vol. 2, col. 912 (24 August 1820). See also Anon., *Trial*, vol. 1, p. 151, for an anecdote Eldon contributed on the subject of oaths.

50 Hansard, *Parl. Debs*, 2nd ser., vol. 3, col. 381 (7 October 1820). It is difficult to determine whether Holland meant to be taken seriously. The image conjured up by his suggestion – of judges kept in isolation from the trial – is certainly in keeping with his reputation for arch humour. In the Queen's trial, however, the high court judges were summoned to explain the relevant legal principles but not to evaluate the evidence, and Holland may have felt that they could best speak to general principles if they were not exposed to, and perhaps influenced by, specific facts and opinions.

51 *Ibid.*, col. 388 (7 October 1820).

52 Phipps, *Plumer Ward Memoirs*, vol. 2, p. 66.
53 H. Brougham, Lord Brougham and Vaux, *The Life and Times of Henry Lord Brougham*, 3 vols (London: William Blackwood & Sons, 1871), vol. 2, p. 384. See also, Sir J. Arnould, *Memoir of Thomas, First Lord Denman*, 2 vols (London: Longmans, 1873), vol. 1, p. 171; H. E. Fox, 4th Baron Holland, *The Journal of the Hon. Henry Edward Fox 1818–1830*, ed. the Earl of Ilchester (London: Thornton Butterworth Ltd, 1923), p. 45.
54 Phipps, *Plumer Ward Memoirs*, vol. 2, p. 80 and fn; Greville, *Greville Memoirs*, vol. 1, p. 38.
55 For an assessment of Eldon's conduct during the Queen's trial, see R. A. Melikan, *John Scott, Lord Eldon (1751–1838) the Duty of Loyalty* (Cambridge: Cambridge University Press, 1999), pp. 281–94.
56 See, e.g., Hansard, *Parl. Debs*, 2nd ser., vol. 2, col. 848 (22 August 1820); Anon., *Trial*, vol. 2, pp. 293–4.
57 See, e.g., Hansard, *Parl. Debs*, 2nd ser., vol. 2, col. 971 (26 August 1820).
58 Copley (Lord Lyndhurst), Brougham (Lord Brougham and Vaux), and Wilde (Lord Truro) all held the Great Seal. Denman became chief justice of King's bench, and Tindal became chief justice of Common Pleas. Gifford also held the latter post, prior to becoming Master of the Rolls. Lushington and Robinson each presided in the admiralty court, and Williams became a judge in the court of King's bench.
59 See the discussion in Hansard, *Parl. Debs*, 2nd ser., vol. 2, col. 363 (11 July 1820).
60 Brougham stated that if the bill reached the Commons, he and Denman would refrain from voting upon it. *Ibid.*, col. 364 (11 July 1820).
61 Brougham, *Life of Brougham*, vol. 2, p. 381.
62 *Ibid.*, p. 396.
63 See, e.g., Hansard, *Parl. Debs*, 2nd ser., vol. 2, col. 1333 (7 September 1820).
64 See, e.g., the discussion in V. A. C. Gatrell, *The Hanging Tree: Execution and the English People (1770–1868)* (Oxford: Oxford University Press, 1994), p. 536.
65 Hardy's trial is found at T. J. Howell (ed.), *A Complete Collection of State Trials and Proceedings for High Treason and other Crimes and Misdemeanours*, 33 vols (London: T. C. Hansard, 1816–26), vol. 24, pp. 199–1408.
66 A breakdown of the number of days per year dedicated to the impeachment is provided in K. Feiling, *Warren Hastings* (London: Macmillan & Co., 1954), p. 352. As early as May 1790, Edmund Burke was complaining that, at most, a mere three hours per day were being spent on the Hastings' case. Hansard, *Parl. Debs*, 1st ser., vol. 28, col. 786 (11 May 1790).
67 Hon. F. Leveson Gower (ed.), *The Letters of Harriet Countess Granville 1810–45*, 2 vols (London: Longmans, 1894), vol. 1, p. 173.
68 Yonge, *Life of Liverpool*, vol. 3, p. 106, letter from Liverpool to George Canning, 12 September 1820.
69 H. Arbuthnot, *The Journal of Mrs Arbuthnot (1820–1832)*, ed. F. Bamford and the Duke of Wellington, 2 vols (London: Macmillan & Co., 1950), vol. 1, pp. 36–7.
70 H. R. V. Fox, 3rd Baron Holland, *Further Memoirs of the Whig Party 1807–1821*, ed. Lord Stavordale (London: John Murray, 1905), p. 289.
71 See P. Quennell (ed.), *The Private Letters of Princess Lieven to Prince Metternich 1820–6*, (London: John Murray, 1937), p. 70; J. Farington, *The Farington Diary*, ed. J. Greig, 8 vols (London: Hutchinson & Co., 1924), vol. 8, p. 267.

72 9 Geo. I *c*.17 (1722).
73 *Parl. Debs*, 2nd ser., vol. 2, col. 803 (21 August 1820).
74 *Ibid.*, cols 906–7, 914 (23, 24 September 1820).
75 See, e.g., Anon., *Trial*, vol. 1, pp. 94, 121–2, 443, vol. 2, p. 46.
76 See *ibid.*, vol. 1, p. 173. The issue of voting by absentees remained open, and the Queen raised it in a protest on 7 November. See *Parl. Debs*, 2nd ser., vol. 3, col. 1702.
77 *Ibid.*, vol. 2, cols 252–3 (6 July 1820).
78 *Parl. Debs*, 2nd ser., vol. 2, col. 315 (10 July 1820). See also cols 431–2 (14 July 1820).
79 *Ibid.*, col. 317 (10 July 1820). See also cols 440–5 (14 July 1820).
80 Of the 116 cases perused, only two mentioned witness lists, and in neither instance was it clear that the list had actually been produced. The committee considered twenty-four bills of attainder (1539–1746), twenty-seven bills of pains and penalties (1610–1805), and sixty-five impeachments (1620–1805). *Lords Journal*, vol. 53, pp. 307–8 (14 July 1820).
81 *Parl. Debs*, 2nd ser., vol. 2, col. 446 (14 July 1820).
82 *Ibid.*, cols 464, 470 (14 July 1820).
83 The vote was 28–78. *Ibid.*, col. 472 (14 July 1820).
84 *Lords Journal*, vol. 53, p. 352 (24 July 1820).
85 Anon., *Trial*, vol. 1, p. 164.
86 *Ibid.*, p. 199.
87 *Parl. Debs*, 2nd ser., vol. 2, col. 1058 (29 August 1820).
88 *Ibid.*, col. 1052 (29 August 1820).
89 *Ibid.*, col. 1058 (29 August 1820).
90 See, e.g., Liverpool's comments, *ibid.*, vol. 3, cols 680–1, 684 (16 October 1820).
91 See, e.g., the statements of Holland, Ellenborough, and Lansdowne, *ibid.*, cols 630–2, 683 (14, 16 October 1820).
92 See Brougham's assertions, *ibid.*, cols 688–9 (16 October 1820).
93 See the assertions of the Attorney General and Solicitor General at *ibid.*, cols 704–5, 722 (16 October 1820).
94 *Ibid.*, cols 699, 719 (16 October 1820).
95 *Ibid.*, col. 899 (20 October 1820).
96 *Ibid.*, col. 917 (20 October 1820).
97 Peers whose voting records thus far in the Queen's case would have justified the government's reliance on their support, but who voted against the second reading, included Arden, Loftus, Fitzgibbon, Selsea, Fisherwick, Berwick, Bagot, Walsingham, Dynevor, Clinton, Caledon, Enniskillen, Farnham, Gosford, Carrick, Mansfield, Egremont, Dartmouth, Plymouth, and Pembroke. Craven and Bradford were ill on 6 November, and several other potential supporters attended the proceedings on that day but failed to vote.
98 Phipps, *Plumer Ward Memoirs*, vol. 2, p. 69. The failure of opposition motions on significant political occasions in the preceding eighteen months indicates very considerable support for the government in the House of Lords.
99 On 1 September Liverpool had sought the King's authority to abandon the divorce clause before the defence began if judged advisable by ministers, and on 6 September the King had acquiesced. See Aspinall, *George IV Letters*, vol. 2, pp. 362, 366.

100 The following peers defected from the government side when final approval of the bill was sought: Bayning, Falmouth, Portsmouth, the Bishop of Gloucester, and the Archbishop of Tuam. Prudhoe, Gambier, Brownlow, Stamford, Thomond, Harrowby, and the Bishop of Chester were present but failed to vote. Lonsdale and Huntington were ill. Aylesford and the Bishop of Bristol (who had been present but failed to vote on the second reading) were excused. Most galling was the failure of Harrowby, the Lord President, to support the third reading.

101 C. Bury, *Diary of a Lady-in-Waiting* ed. A. F. Steuart, 2 vols (London: John Lane, 1908), vol. 2, p. 451.

102 See, e.g., Lever, *Palmerston Letters*, pp. 86–7, letter from E. Lamb to F. Lamb, 20 July 1821.

103 In a letter to the King prior to the trial, the Queen had complained that she could not receive a fair hearing in the Lords. Not only were ministers among her judges, it was 'too notorious, that they have always a majority in the House'. BL, Liverpool papers, Add. MS 38565 f. 255, letter from Caroline to George IV, 7 August 1820.

5

The invention of trials *in camera* in security cases

A. W. Brian Simpson

Even in peacetime in Britain it is possible to be tried for very serious criminal offences *in camera*, in particular for offences against the Official Secrets Acts (hereafter OSA). The most remarkable trials *in camera* have been cases thought to involve national security. For example, in 1961 George Blake was convicted of five OSA offences and sentenced to forty-two years' imprisonment after proceedings largely conducted in secret, though the sentence itself was pronounced, as the law required, in open court. After Blake had been sentenced, and Prime Minister Harold Macmillan had made a brief statement, a question was asked by Arthur Holt MP. 'Is the Prime Minister aware that what is troubling many people is why, if the Russians know all about this person, security reasons prevent the House of Commons knowing more about him?' Macmillan replied, 'Anyone who has been engaged upon or has knowledge about these matters knows that is rather too simple a view. It was for that reason that the Lord Chief Justice decided to hold the trial in camera.'[1] Blake decamped to Russia, but to this day nothing is available in the Public Records.[2] In 1983 the so-called Cyprus Eight (or seven) were tried, largely *in camera*[3] and acquitted, and during the twentieth century there were many other examples.

Originally the common law criminal trial on indictment was open. Thus Sir William Blackstone in the *Commentaries* does not even trouble to mention the fact that there were no secret trials on indictment – one does not state the obvious. The public and theatrical nature of the criminal trial is well illustrated by the great state trials: even trials of very important people by their peers were held in public. The trial of Queen Ann Boleyn is said to have been attended by over two thousand people.[4] Indeed the people participated, albeit informally, in the trial. Thus when Thomas Howard, Duke of Norfolk, was convicted of high treason in 1571 the account published in the *State Trials* tells us that, 'Then the Lord Steward broke his rod *and the people cried God Save the Queen.*'[5] The people might also express approval of an acquittal, as they did at the trial of Lord Dacre of the North in 1535, when there gave forth, 'The greatest shoute and crye of joy the like no man livying may remember that ever he heard.'[6]

The public nature of the criminal trial persisted into the nineteenth century. When William Corder was convicted in 1828 for the murder in the Red Barn, not only were his trial and execution public, the dissection of his body took place in public in the shire hall and the mangled remains exhibited in the courtroom. Charles Cottu, a French judge, travelled the northern circuit in 1819. He was struck by the publicness of English trials.[7] David Cairns comments: 'Publicness comprised two characteristics. Firstly access, which enabled spectators to see the law in action. The public's right of access was enhanced by conducting the trial as a single and fast event. . . . The second feature of publicness is orality, by which the audience in court could follow every step of the trial.'[8] And by the 1830s those who could not attend could read extended newspaper accounts of trials, defendants' last moments, and executions.

In the nineteenth century all this began to change. Punishment became progressively more secret within the new penitentiaries. Press attendance at executions finally passed out of use in the 1920s. In the end the Home Office succeeded in suppressing the publication of any information concerning executions or final hours, with the executioners bonded to reveal no details. Secret execution always had its critics, including Lord Wensleydale. He argued,

> The fundamental principle which governs the administration of the criminal law in this country was that all proceedings involving life and liberty should be conducted in public, and it was only in accordance with it that the punishment should be carried out in public. By that means the public are certain that everything was done fair and right, and that justice had been done.[9]

But the critics lost.

The trial itself remained open. As late as 1905 the editors of *Archbold's Pleading*, simply do not mention that criminal courts do not sit behind closed doors. It had never occurred to anyone that they could. Secret trials were associated with evil institutions such as the Star Chamber, or the Spanish Inquisition. The 1910 edition of *Archbold*, however, strikes a different tone.

> At common law a trial on indictment or criminal information must be held in a public court with open doors. . . . In dealing with certain classes of criminal trial the presiding judge not infrequently *asks* women and young persons to leave the court, and there is undoubted power to exclude or eject persons who disturb the proceedings.[10]

Later editions vacillate on whether the judge could order the women and young persons out, or merely request them to leave.

Archbold mentions two statutes which gave express power to hold proceedings *in camera*, or exclude sections of the public: the Punishment of Incest Act 1908; and the Children Act 1908.[11] Section five of the Punishment of Incest

Act stated baldly that 'All proceedings under this Act are to be held *in camera.*' It was added as an amendment proposed by Lord Halsbury; he believed that press publicity would produce 'a crop of similar offences at other Assizes'.[12] The provision was repealed in 1922.[13] Thereafter the press in general apparently did not report cases of incest, or cloaked them in euphemism, and this too provoked judicial criticism. In 1925 Mr Justice Roche lamented that 'there was a stratum of society who did not realize that incest was a crime'. He favoured calling a spade a spade. '[T]he Press would be rendering the best service to the community if it put down perfectly plainly that a prisoner was convicted of incest.'[14] Mr Justice McCardie expressed the same view two years later at the Warwick Assizes.[15] Whether the proletariat amended their ways one can but wonder. The Children Act provided for the exclusion of everyone except parties, lawyers and *bona fide* members of the press when a person under 16 was giving evidence of an indecent nature, and introduced a general exclusion of persons under 14 in such cases.[16] The statutory powers were given 'in addition to, and without prejudice to any power which a court may possess to hear proceedings in camera'.

By 1900 it had become a little uncertain whether civil proceedings could be heard *in camera* with the consent of the parties. There were situations in which there was thought to be such a power, but it is not until 1913 that we get a leading case on the subject – *Scott* v. *Scott*.[17] In *Scott* the House of Lords firmly laid down the general principle that courts were open, and judges had no general discretion to exclude the public even with the consent of the litigants. There were, however, some exceptions – cases involving wards of court and lunatics, and actions concerning the protection of trade secrets. Also individuals might be excluded to preserve order. Lords Haldane and Loreburn went a little further: other cases might arise when it was proper to exclude the public, so long as this was necessary to achieve the paramount aim of doing justice.

The enunciation of this vague principle opened the way to an extension of the world of the secret trial. There are two reported divorce cases soon after *Scott* v. *Scott* in which women were permitted to testify in private because the nature of the evidence might have inhibited them from testifying in public. In *Cleland* v. *Cleland and McLeod* (1913)[18] Mr Justice Bargrave Deane, no doubt from his employment something of a connoisseur, described the case as 'about as horrible a case as I ever came across', and in *Moosbrugger* v. *Moosbrugger* (1913)[19] both counsel and Mrs Moosbrugger, agreed that 'The whole case is so horrible.'

So far there has been no explicit mention of the possibility of holding criminal trials *in camera*, nor of national security, nor the need to control espionage, as a ground for doing so. Victorians did not bother too much about spies.[20] Attitudes changed with the German spy scare of the early years of the twentieth century, and the establishment of the Secret Service Bureau in 1909; 'MI5', a name it has popularly retained.[21] The first OSA of 1889 said nothing whatever about secret trials, and was indeed very little used. The first achievement of the Secret Service Bureau was to secure the passage of the OSA of 1911,[22] directed against espionage. It made, however, no provision for holding trials *in camera*. A number of supposed spies or agents were tried for OSA offences shortly before the First World War: Lieutenant Siegfried Helm (1910), Dr Max Schultz (1911), Heinrich Grosse (1912), Armgaard Graves (1912), George Parrott with Karl Hentschel (1913), Wilhelm Klauer (1913), and Frederick Schroeder (1914).[23] All these trials were quite public.[24]

After some uncertainty the military persuaded the government to introduce what amounted to a form of martial law legitimised by emergency legislation under the Defence of the Realm Acts (hereafter DORA). The first DORA allowed regulations to be made 'for securing the public safety and the defence of the realm' and specifically:

> (a) to prevent persons communicating with the enemy or obtaining information for that purpose or any purpose calculated to jeopardise the success of the operations of any of H.M. forces or to assist the enemy; or
> (b) to secure the safety of means of communication or of railways, docks or harbours . . .[25]

The original maximum penalty for DORA offences was penal servitude for life, but the third DORA of 27 November permitted, but did not require, the death sentence for offences committed with the intention of assisting the enemy.[26] Under this and the consolidated regulations of 28 November 1914[27] DORA offences became triable either by court martial, or summarily. DORA offences tried summarily could attract only six months' imprisonment.

So spies were normally charged with DORA offences carrying the death penalty, and not with OSA offences.[28] During the war these regulations were continuously amended and made more stringent. The most extreme example, and one which is in such blatant conflict with the rule of law as to be barely credible, is Regulation 18A.[29] This required anyone who had been in communication with a spy, or had attempted to communicate, to prove his innocence. He must show that he did not know the person was a spy, and had no reason to believe he was. A spy was very widely defined – it included someone convicted under Regulation 18, or reasonably suspected of having infringed it, with intent to assist, or anyone outside Britain who was suspected of being a receiver of information. Anyone who had the address of such a spy, or other information about him in his possession, was deemed to be in communication unless he could exonerate himself. In effect the regulation, tailored to fit the meagre evidence which MI5 could offer a court, normally derived from postal censorship, was designed to ensure that anyone the authorities suspected of being a spy was more or less bound to be convicted if put on trial. MI5 was unable to produce proof that suspected spy addresses abroad *were* spy addresses, so convictions for attempting to send letters to such addresses had to depend on suspicion alone. Nevertheless there were supposed spies who were interned because it was thought impossible to secure convictions; one can only assume that the evidence against such persons was very weak indeed.[30] Some must have been wholly innocent. In some cases the problem was that the individual had done nothing which could, by any stretch of the imagination, rank as an offence.[31]

It might be thought that DORA or its regulations would have introduced trials *in camera*. But neither the original DORA of 8 August 1914 nor the second DORA of 28 August did so.[32] The first espionage trial from which the public was excluded from part of the proceedings, and this in a capital case, was that of Carl Hans Lody, alias Charles Inglis, which took place on 30 and 31 October and 2 November 1914. He was shot in the Tower on 11 November. Lody was a naval reserve officer, who certainly had been openly active as a spy, and he did not really deny this at his trial, much of which was devoted to demonstrating what a noble fellow he was, and how decently the British had treated him. His trial was, legally, very curious. He was not charged either with OSA or DORA offences. Instead, by a decision of the Cabinet on 8 October, he was charged with commission of a war crime, specifically war treason. The theory was that engaging in espionage rendered him liable under the international law of war, after a trial, to the penalty of death, or some more lenient sentence.[33]

Spies, unlike other combatants who had become prisoners, were traditionally liable to be executed. The 1894 edition of *The Manual of Military Law* states briefly that 'Spies, when taken, are punishable by death since, as Vattel observes, there is scarcely any other means of guarding against the mischief they do.'[34] From the citations it is clear that this refers only to persons operating in disguise, or under false pretences. The edition of February 1914 deals with the matter in a much more elaborate way. This rewriting was provoked by the Hague Rules of 1907,[35] whose definition of a spy reads: 'A person can only be considered a spy when, acting clandestinely or on false pretences, he obtains or endeavours to obtain information in the zone of operations of a belligerent, with the intention of communicating it to the hostile party.' As the *Manual* points out, people acting openly outside the zone of operations (like Lody) were not covered. The *Manual* therefore recommends that such persons should be charged with war treason. 'Indeed in every case where it is doubtful whether the act consists of espionage, once the fact is established that an individual has furnished or attempted to furnish information to the enemy, no time need be wasted in examining whether the case corresponds exactly to the definition of espionage.'[36]

The *Manual* then explains that espionage and war treason are types of the more general category of war crime, and gives a very wide definition of war treason, which includes 'obtaining, supplying and carrying of information to the enemy' or attempting to do so; war treason also covered such activities as sabotage, and aiding prisoners to escape.[37] Those accused were entitled, the *Manual* points out, to a trial, which would be by a military or civil court. They might be punished by death, or suffer a more lenient sentence, not including corporal punishment. The juridical basis was the law and usages of war.

The 1914 edition of the *Manual* was relied upon in Lody's case. The background to the Cabinet decision was very curious. In August 1914 an unnamed person, believed to be German, and equipped with a concealed radio transmitter was, so the War Office thought, captured by the police and lodged in Bodmin Prison.[38] Lord Kitchener, the Secretary of State for War, consulted the Lord Chancellor, Lord Haldane, and ruled that the individual should be tried by court martial and, if guilty, hanged. Haldane set out his theory of the matter thus:

> If an alien belligerent is caught in this country spying or otherwise waging war he can, in my opinion, be Court Martialled and executed. The mere fact that he is resident here and has what is popularly called a domicile is not enough. . . . When war breaks out an alien becomes *prima facie* an outlaw, . . . if he is a spy or takes up arms . . . and he becomes a person without legal rights. By international law he must have a trial before punishment but the trial may be by Court Martial. He cannot invoke the jurisdiction of the civil courts.[39]

The Adjutant General wondered whether Haldane really meant a military tribunal, not a court martial, and also wondered whether DORA had not limited the power of punishment to penal servitude for life.[40] Haldane's theory makes no reference either to the prerogative or to the usages of war.

In reality there was no such person in Bodmin Prison. But the thinking inspired by this phantom, and by the *Manual*, led to the form of proceeding used for the unfortunate Lody. After a discussion in Cabinet the Army Council on 9 October instructed that Lody be tried under international law, and not under DORA, so as not to limit the penalty to penal servitude for life. The military tribunal, though not legally a general court martial, behaved exactly as if it was one. It was presided over by a retired Major General, Lord Cheylesmore, sitting with eight other officers; he would preside over all courts martial for spies held in Britain during the war.

There was no concealment of the name of the accused, nor the fact that he was on trial, and only part of the trial was held *in camera*. The request came from the prosecution, handled by Archibald H. Bodkin.[41] The trial was very fully reported in *The Times* from 29 October to 11 November, when Lody was shot. Accounts of his execution read like stories from R. G. Henty's novels or the *Boy's Own Paper*. He wrote a letter of thanks to those arranging for his killing, shook hands with the Assistant Provost Marshal, Lord Athlumney, and he even arranged the romantic gesture of sending a ring to an unidentified lady in America.[42] His native village planted a tree as a permanent memorial, and a destroyer named after him escorted the doomed battleship *Bismarck* at one point during her final voyage.[43]

Two questions arise out of Lody's trial. The first is whether his spying did constitute a war crime, war treason. The 1958 *Manual of Military Law* argues that the view that a spy commits a war crime is incompatible with Article 31 of the Annex to the Hague Convention of 1907, which entitles a spy who rejoins his own side and is later captured to be protected as a prisoner of war. If spying was a war crime such a person could still be tried and punished. The *Manual* diffidently suggests that the idea that persons like Lody were guilty of war treason was doubtful, without mentioning his case.[44] At the time the Adjutant General, as we have seen, had expressed doubts. It seems fairly plain that Lody's execution was unlawful both under domestic and international law. The second question is whether Lord Cheylesmore's action in clearing the court was lawful. There was certainly no statutory basis for it, but then there was no statutory basis for the trial anyway, and the theory under which Lody was tried was one that required a trial under international law, but whose form was unregulated. So if we assume that the trial was lawful then it was surely lawful to hold it partially or wholly *in camera*.

No later spy trials in the First World War in Britain followed the precedent of Lody's case; from late November 1914 it became possible to impose a death sentence under DORA. Abroad matters were different. The register of trials before military tribunals (not courts martial) between October 1916 and October 1917 records a number of trials of civilians for war treason.[45]

Under the DORA of 27 November 1914[46] the military was given the power to try anyone, including civilian British subjects, by court martial for DORA offences, even offences involving a possible death penalty. Courts martial were regulated by the Army Act (1881) and procedural rules made under it.[47] These allowed the President to clear the court, but only for deliberation among its members. A note added that a person who interfered with the proceedings might nevertheless be excluded, 'a power incident to every court as necessary for the proper conduct of the proceedings'. *The Manual of Military Law* of 1914 said that except for deliberation: 'the court must be open to the public, military or otherwise, so far as the room or tent in which the court is held can receive them. It is not usual to place any restriction on the admission of reporters for the press.'[48] So, unless courts martial possessed some inherent power to exclude the public in the interests of security, they could not sit *in camera* in spy trials or any other trials.

So far as I am aware the issue had never arisen before the First World War. No doubt it was easy enough to keep the public away from courts martial, if this was desired. There was, furthermore, no appeal from a decision by court martial, though its decision had to be confirmed. So if a court martial did decide to sit *in camera* the legality of this could not be raised by way of appeal. In theory it would be possible to apply to the civil courts for *habeas corpus*. Indeed Lody could have done this, though if he was simply an outlaw the civil court would not have heard his application. But neither he nor anyone else, so far as I know, had ever done this; the pioneer was, as we shall see, one Doyle in 1917.

The first supposed spy tried by court martial after the DORA of 27 November 1914 was a Swede, Rolf Jonsson, who was tried at Falmouth on 26 February

1915, and acquitted.[49] I have discovered nothing about him. The next was that of Robert Rosenthal, but his trial took place after an important change in the law in 1915, which I shall first describe.[50] The fact that civilians could be tried for capital DORA offences by courts martial produced opposition, to which the government capitulated. So the DORA of 16 March 1915 allowed civilians to claim civil trial by judge and jury.[51] This right could be withdrawn in the event of an invasion, or, by proclamation, for any 'other special military emergency arising out of the present war'. This restoration of the right to jury trial in 1915 had been strongly opposed by the War Office. The Adjutant General argued that courts martial were better able to judge the gravity of offences from a military point of view, provided speedier trials, a more effective deterrent, and were not hampered by technicalities of procedure and rights of appeal. Sentences were, however, subject to executive review. In Ireland only trial by court martial provided any hope of securing a conviction. But the War Office view did not prevail. The War Office rejected a compromise, which would have been to either drop the death penalty for DORA offences, or introduce an appeal is such cases.[52]

It was this DORA which provided the first statutory warrant for holding a common law criminal trial which might lead to the death penalty *in camera*. Section 1 (3) provided:

> In addition to and without prejudice to any powers which a court may possess to order the exclusion of the public from any proceedings . . . if . . . application is made by the prosecution, in the interests of national safety, that all or any portion of the public should be excluded during any part of the hearing, the court may make an order to that effect, but the passing of the sentence shall in any case take place in public.

This was made part of the bill by a Lords amendment.

Somewhat surprisingly the Act made no provision for holding courts martial, as distinct from regular civil courts, *in camera*. I have found no material explaining this; it is unlikely to have been an oversight. Possibly the reason was that in practice Lord Cheylesmore could be relied upon to clear the court if deemed necessary, and any challenge would be technically difficult. Given wartime conditions, and the attitude of the judiciary, a challenge through *habeas corpus* would be unlikely to succeed. Had the provision allowing trials *in camera* been applied to courts martial there would also have been a difficulty over announcing the sentence in open court. For the military practice was to promulgate sentences of death in private, once confirmed. At the conclusion of a court martial on a capital charge the convicted person knew of the conviction, but was not then told whether he was to be killed or not.[53] Most capital sentences were not confirmed.[54]

After the change in the law a considerable number of espionage or similar cases arose, and arrangements had to be made to settle which would go to the civil courts, and which to courts martial. In June 1915 the Director of Public

Prosecutions, Sir Charles Mathews, obtained a ruling from the Attorney General, Sir John Simon, approved by the Secretary of State for War, Lord Kitchener, 'that trials of all persons accused of espionage (except British subjects) should be by Court Martial; cases of alleged spies for whom there is a reasonable ground for believing they are of American nationality to be reported to DPP for special consideration by the AG'.[55] In the whole course of the war there were twenty-six courts martial of supposed spies under DORA in Britain, and one trial, Lody's, under international law.[56] Fourteen death sentences were imposed, four being commuted to penal servitude for life.[57] Nine persons were shot in the Tower,[58] and one hanged in Wandsworth Prison.[59] There were two ten-year, three five-year, and one three-year sentences of penal servitude; one two-year, one eighteen-month and one twenty-eight-day sentences of imprisonment with hard labour; one twenty-eight-day and one seven-day term of imprisonment; and two acquittals.[60]

The first spy trial for a DORA offence to take place civilly after the Act of 1915 was never completed; it was that of Anton Kupferle, and it was partly heard *in camera*.[61] He had been arrested on 19 February, and caught through the postal censorship. He claimed to be a US citizen. The case predates the ruling by the Attorney General, but the Army Council, no doubt because of Kupferle's citizenship claim, instructed that he should not be tried by court martial. The trial opened at the Old Bailey on 19 May. To enhance the jollity of the proceedings the practice of carrying bouquets of flowers was revived. After some evidence had been given the Attorney General applied for the trial to continue *in camera*; the defence did not object. The accused gave evidence and was cross-examined, but the evidence presented *in camera* and the hearing were not reported. Kupferle committed suicide during the trial, on 20 May, *The Times* publishing his suicide note, written on a slate. This was the first civil trial for espionage conducted almost wholly *in camera*. But the fact that the trial was taking place, the name of the accused, and details about his death, were all made public, as was much of the evidence.

The first civil spy trial conducted entirely *in camera* was that of Karl Friedrich Muller, tried with Peter Hahn in June 1915.[62] They were tried jointly, and since Peter Hahn was a British subject, though of German extraction, they were not tried by court martial. The Grand Jury was charged *in camera* on 20 April. At the request of the prosecution the entire trial was held *in camera*, though the court was opened before sentence. Muller was sentenced to death and Hahn to seven years' penal servitude. Muller appealed, and the appeal was also held *in camera*, though a reporter from *The Times* was allowed to attend. The appeal was dismissed on 22 June.[63] Muller engaged in the normal courtesies, shaking hands with the firing squad which then shot him. This was on 23 June. Although the trial had been *in camera* the fact that Muller and Hahn were to be tried, the trial itself, the sentence, the appeal, and the execution were all reported in the press at the time.

The first spy trial by court martial after the legal change in 1915 was that of Robert Rosenthal, who was German.[64] On 6 July 1915 *The Times* announced in advance that the entire trial would be held *in camera*, so there had been an executive rather than a judicial decision on this matter. The general court martial opened on 11 July. The fact that Rosenthal's trial was to take place was not concealed; a large crowd gathered outside the Westminster Guildhall, but members of the public were excluded by armed soldiers. Rosenthal, who had made two suicide attempts, was hanged in Wandsworth on 15 July, and not shot. In 1932 MI5 tried to discover the reason for this.[65] The files did not provide any explanation, but the officer who looked into the matter had heard at the time 'that the Court considered a bullet too good for him on account of his extremely cowardly behaviour during the trial'. Being shot, rather than hanged, was considered to be an honourable way to die. An alternative explanation offered by S. T. Felstead was that some unspecified administrative problem in the Tower, where executions were carried out in the miniature rifle range, lay behind the decision.[66] Rosenthal's execution was reported in the press.

In the world of the secret state matters always seem to get worse, and the cases of Haicke Marinus Petrus Janssen, and Wilhelm Johannes Roos, in July 1915, introduced a more extreme form of secrecy.[67] They were among seven agents arrested in May and mid-June 1915.[68] They were tried by general court martial on 16 and 17 July 1915 for the DORA offence of espionage against Regulations 18 and 48. Both were convicted, sentenced to death, and, after confirmation, shot in the Tower on 30 July 1915. Roos earned some praise for having asked and received permission to finish his cigarette. The public was allowed to know little about this at the time. On 15 July *The Times* announced, without giving any names, 'The authorities announce the arrest of two alleged spies. Their trial will take place by general Court Martial to-morrow [16 July] at the Middlesex Guildhall. The whole proceedings will be *in camera*. They will be charged with collecting and attempting to collect for communication to the enemy information about his Majesty's Fleet.' Then, on 31 July, 'It is officially announced that the two persons who were charged with espionage and found guilty by General Court Martial at the Westminster Guildhall on July 16 and 17 were found guilty and sentenced to death. The sentence was duly confirmed and was carried out yesterday morning.' So it had come about that persons could both be tried in secret and then executed, with only the barest public revelation of what they were supposed to have done, or even who they were.

There were, after this, some cases where there was no secrecy.[69] But from July 1915 the authorities surrounded most espionage trials with enhanced secrecy. Thus on 11 September 1915 the following appeared in *The Times* after the event, that is to say, too late for any person outside the secret state to influence the outcome:

Unnamed Spy Executed.

Tried by Court Martial.

> It is officially announced that a person who was charged with espionage and tried by General Court Martial on August 20 and 21 was found guilty and sentenced to death. The sentence was duly confirmed and carried out yesterday morning.

This laconic announcement refers, as we now know, to one Ernst Waldemar Melin. A Swede, Melin had been tried by general court martial on 20 August, sentenced to death, and shot in the Tower on 10 September after, somewhat like Muller, shaking hands with his guard, a variant form of socially acceptable behaviour. He died, it was said, like the gentleman he had once been.[70]

A similar announcement was made on 18 September about 'Another Unnamed Spy', in fact Augusto Alfredo Roggen or Roggin, a Uruguayan, tried with Melin, and shot on 17 September.[71] And on 20 October the Secretary of the War Office announced that two prisoners, tried by general court martial on 28, 29, and 30 September had been convicted, and one sentenced to death, the other to five years' penal servitude. The execution had taken place on 19 October, so this announcement too came after the event. The executed man was Fernando Buschman, a Brazilian.[72] Thomson waxes eloquent over his noble bearing. He played his violin until a late hour the night before his execution, finally kissing the instrument and saying, 'Goodbye, I shall not want you any more.' As if this were not enough he refused to have his eyes bandaged, 'facing the rifles with a courageous smile'.[73] The individual sentenced to five years' penal servitude was Josef Marks, who was eventually repatriated to Germany after the war, probably in October 1920.[74]

Why did the authorities arrange to try spies *in camera*? Most spies were caught through postal censorship; trials *in camera* concealed the details. MI5 knew that certain addresses were used by spies, who employed either secret ink, or codes.[75] Thus Buschman was caught because he communicated with two addresses in Rotterdam which featured in other spy cases. MI5 may have sent false information to the Germans purporting to emanate from a spy who had in reality been caught and shot, an anticipation of the double agent system operated in the Second World War. Secret trials would be essential to this. According to Thomson this was done in Muller's case, and payment was indeed received for the information; Felstead has the same story.[76] This seems very implausible in Muller's case. Although his trial was held *in camera* his arrest, trial, and execution were openly announced in *The Times*.[77]

The enhanced level of secrecy soon spread to civil trials. Thus, when George Breeckhow (alias George Parker, alias Reginald Rowland) was tried with Lizzie Wertheim in September 1915 before Justices Bray, Sankey, and Low, the prosecution applied for the whole case to be heard *in camera*. Mr Justice Bray asked, 'Are there any objections? [there were none] Then let it be so.' The judges were told that secrecy was 'necessary in the interests of the national safety' and simply accepted this. Indeed I know of no case in which an application by the Crown for a trial *in camera* has ever been rejected, though there may have been such cases. On 26 September *The Times* reported the fact of the trial and the sentences – death for Breeckhow and ten years for Wertheim – but gave no names. There was an unsuccessful appeal on 18 October to the full Court of Criminal Appeal. This too was heard entirely *in camera*. Breeckhow was shot on 27 October; *The Times* announced next day that an unnamed spy had been executed. He had claimed US citizenship, probably falsely. Wertheim, who had acquired British citizenship through marriage to a naturalised German, died in Aylesbury prison in 1920.

So the position had now been reached when not only aliens, but even British citizens, could be tried and sentenced for offences involving the risk of a death penalty behind a veil of almost complete secrecy, for this was no isolated case. Courtenay (or Kurt) Henslop de Rysbach, a British subject by birth though of Austrian extraction, was tried civilly *in camera*, and, the jury having disagreed, was retried in October 1915.[78] He was sentenced to penal servitude for life, and Thomson records that 'His name was not made public at the time; only the fact that a British subject had been found guilty of espionage was disclosed, and the papers began to wonder why a British spy had been so leniently treated.' Felstead confirms this, and quotes a leader from the *Westminster Gazette* expressing mild surprise at the sentence.[79]

Those who did not have British citizenship could hardly expect to be treated better. A curious example is provided in Eva de Bournonville. She was described by Thomson as 'probably the most incompetent woman spy ever recruited by the Germans', and in her prison file as refined, of superior education, a brilliant linguist, and very neurotic.[80] She was a mercenary spy, caught through postal censorship, sending low-grade information on the result of a Zeppelin raid of Croydon. Although she was not a British citizen she was tried civilly in January 1916 before Justices Darling, Scrutton, and Rowlatt. A civil trial was favoured by the Attorney General and Home Secretary, though opposed by Bodkin. The context was the Edith Cavell affair, which produced enthusiasm for demonstrating that the British, unlike their opponents, knew how to treat women decently.[81] Bournonville was sentenced to death, and this was upheld by a full Court of Criminal Appeal, but following Cavell's execution her sentence was commuted to penal servitude for life. Had she been male she would certainly have been executed. *The Times* announced the charge, trial, failure of her appeal and outcome, but not her name.[82] This information came from some official, but one file[83] indicates that it was not until 20 July 1916 that the security service itself, through its chief of counter-espionage, Major R. J. Drake, issued a press notice which was cleared with Matthews, the Director of Public Prosecutions. This merely said: 'The letter "M" was attached to a woman of Danish origin, Swedish by naturalization, who was sentenced to death in January, 1916, by a Civil Court, the sentence being confirmed on appeal, but subsequently commuted to penal servitude for life.' In 1920 she was still in prison, and on 17 July 1920 Mr Justice Darling wrote to the Home Office urging clemency. MI5 recommended that she should serve ten years in prison, which would have led to her release in 1926 at the age of around 51.[84] But as a result of an initiative taken by Winston Churchill she was released on licence in 1922 and deported to Sweden.

The legality of trials *in camera* on security grounds in cases not covered by the DORA of 1915 came before the civil courts in two reported cases, an action of detinue in 1916, and a challenge to a court martial by *habeas corpus* proceedings in the following year. The story behind *Norman* v. *Matthew and Another* (1916)[85] was a curious one. A magistrate, in connection with a prosecution under DORA Regulation 27 (prohibition against alarming reports etc.), had made an order under Regulation 51A[86] which authorised the police to raid premises occupied by the Independent Labour Party. They seized documents aimed at discouraging recruiting. The magistrate heard the case *in camera* and made a destruction order. An unsuccessful attempt was made to quash the order by *certiorari* as being *ultra vires*. The Divisional Court upheld holding the proceedings, which were said not to constitute a trial at all, *in camera*, and this in a case which had nothing whatever to do with espionage.[87] Some of the documents belonged to C. H. Norman of the City of London branch of the ILP, who was the founder of the Stop the War Committee; they were thought to have been retained by the authorities, in particular by the Director of Public Prosecutions and the Metropolitan Police Commissioner. So he sued them in the Westminster County Court. The suit was dismissed as frivolous and vexatious, and here too the proceedings were *in camera*. The Divisional Court (Justices Lush and Sankey) affirmed that the County Court had an inherent power to proceed *in camera*, and was correct in doing so under the principles laid down in *Scott* v. *Scott*. According to Mr Justice Lush, 'if there are materials before the Court for concluding that it is necessary in order to secure that justice is done, the proceedings should be *in camera*'.[88] Mr Justice Sankey put it rather differently, thinking the case came within one of the exceptions mentioned in *Scott* v. *Scott* – here 'secrecy is of the essence of the cause'.[89] Both judges thought the power should be exercised with caution, but Sankey revealed that the practice of holding proceedings *in camera* was by this time becoming common. '[N]umerous other cases have been before the Courts recently where a similar course has been taken.'[90] The Court of Appeal refused leave to appeal. The disease was clearly spreading.

The legality of holding courts martial *in camera* first came before the civil courts in *R.* v. *Governor of Lewes Prison ex parte Doyle*,[91] arising out of the Irish Easter Rising. Gerald Doyle had been tried *in camera* by field general court martial on 5 May 1916, and had been transferred to England to serve his sentence of three years' penal servitude. He made an application for *habeas corpus*, one ground being 'The conviction was bad because the field general court martial heard the case *in camera*.' The Attorney General warned that 'If this contention prevailed the consequences would be very serious; at the trial of a spy, for instance, where the most secret matters were in question, it would be impossible to exclude the public.' He further argued that the requirement, under the applicable rules of procedure, that the proceedings should be held in open court only meant that the accused, his legal representative, and anyone officially entitled to be there, should be admitted. This rubbish was too much for the court, but it nevertheless ruled that the trial had not been invalid. General Maxwell had put in an affidavit that there was unrest and fighting in Dublin at the time, and the court accepted that there had been a need to exclude the public. There was no affidavit from the president of the court martial. The Lord Chief Justice justified the decision by *Scott* v. *Scott* – trial *in camera* was necessary in the interests of justice: 'In the existing local circumstances it was necessary to the public safety and the defence of the realm that neither the public nor the press should be admitted to the trial. It must be assumed that the members of the Court-martial took the same view.' This suggested that the judges would always allow a court martial to sit *in camera* if some sort of military necessity was asserted by the general officer commanding.

This is the only reported decision on the legality of secret trials by court martial; it was not an espionage case. The seventh edition of the *Manual of Military Law*, in reliance on it, states: 'A court-martial is an open court like other courts of justice, but it has inherent powers to sit *in camera* if such course is necessary for the administration of justice.[92] Spies could surely expect no more sympathy from the judiciary than the rebellious Irish.[93]

All this was in wartime. But once security services obtain powers in wartime, they are reluctant to give them up in peacetime. Thus MI5 argued the powers it had acquired, including the power to try espionage cases *in camera*, needed to be retained. The underlying rationale was the Red Menace. Before the armistice of 1918 the War Office Emergency Legislation Committee, in its first interim report of 4 April 1918, had pointed out that during the war the Directorate of Special Intelligence[94] had dealt with espionage cases under DORA regulations, to the practical exclusion of the OSA. There would be serious inconvenience if DORA came to an end and the only weapon was the OSA.[95] It proposed a peacetime National Security Act. The plan was to repeal the OSA of 1911 and incorporate its provisions in the new act, which would also widen the range of offences by incorporating a number of DORA and other offences. MI5 particularly wanted to be able to obtain convictions without having to prove their case in court, as they had been able to do during the war. In the name of national security the rule of law was to be abandoned.

This produced an appalling clause 2, based on Regulation 18A of DORA, which made it an offence to be found in the United Kingdom having communicated or attempted to communicate with a foreign agent or someone reasonably suspected of being a foreign agent, unless the accused could prove that he did not know and had no reasonable grounds for supposing the person to be an agent. The National Security Bill also included provisions allowing cases to be heard *in camera*, though it retained the requirement that the sentence to be pronounced in public.

At a meeting in March 1919 the Home Office, in the person of Sir Edward Troup, the Permanent Under Secretary, with Sir Frederick Liddell, the Chief Parliamentary draughtsman, strongly resisted the proposed clause 2. What shocked them was the reversal of the burden of proof. A letter by C. D. Carew Robinson, expressing Troup's view, said the clause 'goes far beyond anything for which there is a justification in peace time in making an innocent person guilty of an offence unless he can prove his innocence'. Liddell described MI5's view that the offence was committed by simply coming to the United Kingdom as 'too fantastic to hold in a court of law'. So Walter Moresby, MI5's legal officer, went gloomily away to water down the definition of the new offence. But the Home Office, a department deeply committed to secret government, did not object to the provision for trials *in camera*.

The interdepartmental committee finished its work in March 1919. Sir Vernon Kell, the Director of MI5, was anxious that in some form Regulation 18A should be kept in being after peace officially dawned, as it did on 31 August 1921. 'It is vital to the national interest that the Regulation should be continued until it becomes, as may be expected, part of our permanent legislation.'[96] For a while nothing was done. In late 1918 an interdepartmental committee had indeed been set up under Sir Reginald Brade, Secretary to the War Office, to consider which DORA regulations and orders might be revoked or cancelled without harm to the national interest; it made recommendations which were accepted by a committee of the War Cabinet under Lord Cave, which thought other regulations might need to be revoked if the armistice held.[97] However by 1920 little had been done to implement the policy of getting rid of unnecessary DORA regulations.

The imminence of the official ending of the war provoked action at last. On 20 October 1918 the Home Affairs Committee had rejected the idea of a National Security Act, fearing political opposition. It recommended simply amending the OSA, 'confining such amendments to the most important changes it was desired to make'.[98] An interdepartmental committee was set up to thrash out the details. The consequence was the OSA of 1920, which implemented so much of MI5's scheme as had survived Troup and Liddell.[99] Section 2 of the new OSA was the watered-down version of the old DORA Regulation 18A; whereas 18A had made the fact of communication with a reputed spy an offence unless the accused provided his innocence, the OSA version treated communication as merely *evidence* that an offence might have been committed. Section 8(4) made permanent the provision in the DORA of 1915 on trials *in camera*, now applied to OSA offences, 'on the ground that the publication of any evidence to be given or any statement to be made in the course of the proceedings would be prejudicial to the national safety . . . but the passing of sentence shall in any case take place in public.' So, in a form which could have been much worse but for the opposition of the Home Office, MI5 succeeded in carrying into peacetime, for the first time, statutory authorization for the holding trials *in camera* for offences involving security.[100]

By now, however, the courts had allowed the OSA to be used in cases which had nothing whatever to do with espionage or national security, thereby indirectly permitting trials *in camera* in cases which had no connection with espionage. The first example seems to be the case of Emile Jules Depuis in March 1915. He made use of information obtained as a postal censor for a form of blackmail.[101] In 1926 Major F. W. H. Blake was prosecuted under the OSA for revealing to the *Evening News* a confession by the convicted murderer Frederick Bywaters. Blake was a retired prison governor, and this was the first use of the OSA against a fairly senior official.[102] D. Hooper states that in 1919 a War Office clerk, Albert Crisp, and Arthur Homewood, company secretary of a tailoring firm, were prosecuted, Crisp having passed on information about clothing contracts.[103]

In the period between the wars there were a number of trials under the OSA which took place partially *in camera* – for example that of Dr Herman Goertz in March of 1936;[104] that of Walter John Butterfield in September of the same year;[105] and that of Percy Glading, Charles Munday, George Whomack, and Albert Williams in the Woolwich Arsenal case in 1938.[106] In at least one case the defence objected, but without success.[107] There seems to have been no public complaint. Two trials by court martial did, however, give rise to official anxiety, and led to proposals for general legislation on trials *in camera*.

One involved an aircraftman, John Donelly. He was convicted by a court martial held *in camera* for stealing confidential manuals and blueprints in 1928.[108] He was thought to be connected with the IRA, and MI5 was involved. An application was made to the Judge Advocate General, Sir Felix Cassels, for a transcript. The trial had taken place under the Air Force Act of 1917, whose section 124 was based on section 124 of the Army Act of 1881, which long predated the invention of trials *in camera*. Under this a person convicted by court martial was explicitly given a right to obtain, on payment, a copy of the proceedings, including the transcript of the hearing. Was Sir Felix legally entitled to refuse to supply a transcript, or to edit it, or to supply it on conditions, where the trial had been held *in camera*? Of course Donelly had been at the trial, and he or his lawyer might have made notes. But a transcript might include details otherwise forgotten, and there was no way of telling what use might be made of it. Sir Felix had edited out names in transcripts provided to Irish prisoners tried under the Restoration of Order in Ireland Act 1920. In the *Donelly* case he allowed counsel to inspect the transcript, but he did not supply a copy. The same solution had been adopted by the director of public prosecutions in the case of Wilfred R. F. McCartney, who had been tried civilly *in camera* for OSA offences in January 1928, where the problem arose under section 16(1) of the Criminal Appeal Act of 1907.[109] Sir Felix and the Treasury Solicitor considered seeking the law officers' opinion, but decided ignorance was bliss. '[I]t might be embarrassing to obtain too clear-cut a reply from the Law Officers, and that it was wise to leave the legal position a little vague, and, therefore, more open to the interpretation which the public interest demanded.' Sir Felix was prepared in any case in which defence interests might be affected to find ways and means of dealing with a demand for a transcript of secret evidence. Sir John Salmond, recently appointed to the Air Council as Air Member for Personnel, was also of opinion that a reference to the law officers was 'a gamble which it would be unwise to take'.[110] Thus did officialdom reconcile itself to blatant law breaking in the public interest.

In March 1933 the issue arose again. Norman Baillie-Stewart, a lieutenant in the Seaforth Highlanders, was tried by general court martial for a number of OSA offences.[111] The names of some witnesses were suppressed, and part of the hearing was *in camera*. Baillie-Stewart was convicted, cashiered, and sentenced to four years' imprisonment. The Judge Advocate General, Sir Henry F. MacGeagh, anticipated being asked for a copy of the proceedings, which, on release from prison, Baillie-Stewart would sell to the press. It was felt that the issue could no longer be ducked. The law officers, Sir Thomas W. Inskip, and Sir Donald B. Somervell, gave it as their opinion that such a request could not lawfully be refused.[112]

This opinion produced consternation in the War Office. It was feared that Baillie-Stewart might try to compel the release of a transcript by bringing *mandamus* proceedings. At a meeting on 11 March 1935, at which neither the Home Office nor Scottish Office were represented, the favoured solution was a new OSA, covering both military and civil trials, which would allow the Secretary of State, 'if satisfied that it is expedient in the interests of national safety' to withhold all or part of the transcript of proceedings heard *in camera*. A bill was drafted, and the Lord Chancellor said he was happy, so long as there was a right to inspect a transcript. But although discussions continued into 1936 the plan was, by 24 July, dead. The Home Office, in the person of Sir Alexander Maxwell, strongly opposed the idea as involving 'a grave departure from the accepted principles of justice'.[113] The Scottish Office called it 'an unwarranted interference with the Courts of Justice'.[114] The law officers emphatically agreed.[115] On 4 March 1937 the Army Council formally dropped the idea. The Judge Advocate General made it clear that he would in future observe the law, and provide copies of proceedings. With an air of menace he said that if the Secretary of State directed him not to do so, and legal proceedings were brought to compel him to provide copies, a rule *nisi* being granted, 'the Attorney General will have the situation clearly before his mind when he appears on the hearing of the rule'. But Baillie-Stewart never did demand a copy of the proceedings, nor, so far as I know, did anyone else. And so the matter rested until the passing of the Army Act of 1955, which made explicit provision for the problem.[116]

Legal preparations for the Second World War started back in the 1920s,[117] and when war eventually came an elaborate scheme of Defence Regulations (hereafter DRS), authorised by a parent Emergency Powers (Defence) Act, came into force. Under this new version of DORA the power to hold legal proceedings *in camera* was hugely extended.[118] Any legal proceedings whatsoever, whether commenced before or after the Act, could be heard *in camera*, and the court could prohibit or restrict the disclosure of information about the proceedings if 'satisfied that it is expedient in the interests of the public safety or the defence of the realm'.

During the First World War the normal practice had been, as we have seen, to try alien spies by court martial under DORA. The legal arrangements in the Second World War were rather different. The DRS did not provide for courts martial, which Maxwell of the Home Office strongly opposed.[119] Nor did the regulations permit the death penalty.[120] It was assumed that spies and serious saboteurs would be charged with treason. Hence when the war began there was no specific special provision for the trial and execution of spies and saboteurs.

Doubts soon arose as to whether a recently landed enemy agent would be amenable to the law of treason, which applies only to those who owe allegiance. Resident enemy agents would owe allegiance, but it was hard to see how an agent who arrived by parachute in order to blow up some installation, or whatever, could sensibly be treated as owing allegiance upon touching down. The whole question came before the Home Policy Committee of the War Cabinet in 1939.[121] At a meeting in the War Office on 1 December, MI5, represented by Sir Eric B. Holt Wilson and Brigadier O. A. Harker, favoured trial of all supposed spies by courts martial. The War Office accepted this, and did not want the army to be left merely with the disagreeable disposal task of shooting spies convicted by civil courts. Maxwell was informed, and on 6 December he objected, pointing out that trial of British subjects by courts martial would be unacceptable politically, and arguing that it would be impossible to treat aliens differently – for example an American who had lived in Britain for ten or twenty years. The War Office continued to press for trial of aliens by courts martial though it did not think that the *Lody* precedent for military trial for a war crime would be likely to be followed.[122]

It was decided to deal with the whole question by drafting a bill which would permit the death penalty for acts done with intent to assist the enemy. The mode of trial remained controversial until a compromise was reached at a conference on 22 February 1940 – enemy aliens were to be tried by courts martial, but only if the Attorney General gave his consent.[123] The bill became the Treachery Act of 1940. In the event only one spy was tried by the military during the war, Josef Jakobs, alias Joseph Rymer. He arrived by parachute on 29 January 1941 and was arrested near Ramsey in Huntingdonshire on 1 February, having broken his ankle on landing. He was tried *in camera* on 4 August 1941, and shot in the Tower on the fourteenth. His name does not feature in the Foreign Office list of 1945 nor in the reply, based upon it, of 'Spies Convicted under the Treachery Act by Civil Courts During the War'.[124]

However, the account given by Lt Col. R. W. G. Stephens states that he was tried under the Treachery Act and this is correct.[125] Quite why he was tried by court martial is unexplained; perhaps the reason was that he had been arrested by the military, and was thus in their custody.

A story, which has no satisfactory archival basis, has been told that two SS parachutists were dropped in Britain near Luton Hoo on 28 May 1941 to assassinate Rudolf Hess, who had arrived in Scotland on 10 May on his strange peace mission.[126] Quite how they were to achieve this feat is wholly obscure. They were, it is said, captured and summarily executed – conceivably after some form of trial.[127] It is possible that the two parachutists, if they ever existed, were killed in an attempted arrest by trigger-happy soldiers, or members of the Home Guard. The 1958 edition of *The Manual of Military Law* states that 'In the Second World War *most* spies were tried under the now spent Treachery Act 1940 on the direction of the Attorney General.'[128] The odd thing about this passage is the hint that there might have been more than one exception, but the reference could be to a trial abroad. It could also refer to the double cross system, under which some spies were never tried at all. Its meaning is obscure.

All documented trials for spying and similar offences in Britain during the war, apart from Jakobs's, were conducted before civil courts, and a considerable number of these trials took place entirely *in camera*. The most remarkable example is that of Captain John Herbert King.[129] King had served in the First World War in the Artists Rifles, and, according to his own account, suffered a severe mental illness in 1917 – presumably shell shock. From August 1920 he was employed by the Foreign Office as a cypher officer. This was not a pensionable job, and cypher officers, whose work was extremely boring and poorly paid, were treated no doubt as somewhat lowly creatures, about on a par with a footman, by the socially elevated diplomats. In 1933 or 1934, according to his confession, he met Henry Pieck, a Dutchman and, it is said, an artist, at the International Club in Geneva. The man who introduced them was Raymond C. Oake, another cypher officer. Oake was then courting the stepdaughter of Captain C. F. B. Harvey, who was Passport Control Officer at Geneva.[130] This was an intelligence job, and Harvey would have been connected with the Foreign Office intelligence service. Pieck was a friend of Harvey, and he knew others in the Foreign Office: J. P. Russell, R. Kinnaird, Captain H. B. W. Maling, and H. C. F. Tubb.[131] Pieck claimed that money could be made on the stock exchange by advance knowledge of political developments, and King gave as this as the reason why he handed over material. He gave, for example, reports of conversations between Hitler and Sir Neville Henderson, and claimed that none was of any importance. In 1933 King met one Helen Wilkie, said to have been American, and started an affair. In 1936 Pieck left London, and King's contact then became a Hungarian, Petersen, who pressed him to provide the cypher itself.[132] He strongly denied handing it over. King was paid substantial sums, £50 – £200 a time by Pieck and £100 – £150 a time by Petersen. In all he earned, so he claimed, £2,500.

King was discovered through information provided by Walter Krivitsky, who defected to the US. After having claimed that the money received from Pieck and Petersen constituted gambling winnings King confessed on 28 September, apparently in order to exonerate Helen Wilkie; charges against her were dropped. In his diary Alexander Cadogan refers to the use of the third degree, and another story, leaked from MI5, is that King was filled with drink at the Bunch of Grapes public house in Curzon Street until he mournfully broke down.[133] Although others were suspected, only Oake was actually dismissed, on 1 January 1940. Other cypher officers, who may well have been exonerated, were moved to other employment. After a committal for trial *in camera* on 10 October at Bow Street King was tried *in camera* at the Central Criminal Court on 17 October for OSA offences, to which he presumably pleaded guilty; he was sentenced to ten years imprisonment. The fact that a trial had taken place at all was kept entirely secret; Allason notes that no press announcement was made at the time. Information leaked out in 1956, when the Foreign Office issued a statement on the case.[134] Whether the judge simply broke the law by not pronouncing sentence in open court, or whether some sort of fictitious observance of the law took place, arrangements having been made to ensure that nobody knew what was going on, is not known. He could have passed sentence in public and still made an order that no reporting take place. No other wartime trial, so far as I know, was entirely concealed. Little short of incredible though it may seem, the position had now been reached that a British citizen could be sent to prison for ten years (or for that matter I suppose for some longer period) in conditions of complete secrecy, the public being unaware that any trial had taken place at all.

Numerous other trials were conducted *in camera*. One group involved prosecutions of spies, or associates of spies, on capital charges under the Treachery Act. With the exception of Jakobs all such persons were tried civilly, and a list in the Foreign Office papers, which does not include Jakobs, gives the names of thirteen persons so tried and sentenced to death. Three were British (George Armstrong, Jose Estella Key and Oswald John Job).[135] By the time the Parliamentary question for which the list had been prepared was answered three more names had been added, one being that of the British-born Duncan A. C. Scott-Ford.[136] So the total number sentenced to death, if we include Jakobs, comes to seventeen. One of these persons, Menezes, was reprieved, and the other sixteen executed. One person, tried on a capital charge under the Treachery Act, Sjoern Pons, was acquitted, and then interned under Regulation 18B. Christobel Nicholson was also interned after acquittal in a trial conducted *in camera*, but it is probable that she was charged with a non-capital offence under the OSA.[137] Though not viewed as a spy or agent but as a saboteur, Dorothy P. O'Grady was also tried *in camera* under the Treachery Act and sentenced to death, though her sentence was reduced to fourteen years' imprisonment on appeal.[138] Capital charges, presumably under the Treachery Act, were also preferred against Nora C. L. Briscoe and Gertrude

B. Hiscox, but withdrawn in a trial conducted *in camera* on 16 June 1941.[139] Most of those liable to the death penalty had done no harm whatever; the function of liability was to coerce agents into providing information or joining the double cross system.

None of these trials, however, was concealed. Whether the legal requirement that the sentence be pronounced in open court was actually observed in a realistic sense seems doubtful. Although the evidence is uncertain, what may have happened is that the court was ritually opened but, since members of the public and reporters had no idea that this was going to happen, none attended. The practice of the Ministry of Home Security and Home Office was, in collaboration with MI5, to issue a press statement immediately *after* spies had been executed, and the Home Office had been informed that they were dead.[140] Why this extraordinary practice was adopted, no announcement having been made either before trial or after conviction and before execution, it is impossible to say; no documentation exists. Thus in the case of Josef Waldberg and Karl Meier a press release was issued at 9.25 am on 10 December 1940 stating their names, dates of birth and citizenship, a brief account of their capture, their conviction under the Treachery Act on 22 November, and their execution at Pentonville. This was accompanied by a 'Notes to Editors' stating 'Editors are asked not to press for additional facts or to institute enquiries. Editorial comment might profitably take the form of drawing public attention to loose talk of all kinds, particularly in the presence of strangers.'

That same evening a talk was given by someone from military intelligence on the BBC; this gave further information and followed the same line. There were similar releases in the cases of Charles A. van den Kieboom[141] and George Johnson Armstrong. In the case of Karl Theo Drueke and Norman Heinrich Waelti, executed on 6 August 1941, MI5 seems to have tried to seize the initiative by presenting a draft to the Home Office; in any event it was MI5 which had the whole story. But in accordance with a procedure which had been settled on 31 July the Home Office press officer prepared a draft, which was then vetted by Frank Newsam for the Home Office, and by MI5. The press was given quite a good story to print, and a communication from the Chief Press Officer of the Ministry of Information told editors to treat the release as 'the sole source of information on the subject. Any further details would be liable to involve breaches of security and will not be passed by the censorship.'

Trouble with the press broke out over the case of Jakobs. The War Office issued a brief statement on 15 August 1941 which was ill received in Fleet Street. The censor intended that nothing further be published, but both the *Star* and the *Evening Standard*[142] investigated the matter and published fuller accounts of his capture; that in the *Star* was passed by a censorship accident. The outcome of this affair was a meeting of the Home Defence (Security) Executive on 28 August.

The problem, as the Chairman, Lord Swinton, saw it, was to release sufficient information to dissuade the press from pursuing further enquiries, whilst allowing the Security Service to decide what might not be told. The solution adopted was for MI5 to produce a full statement of the case from which the Home Office or War Office press officer and an MI5 officer would draft an appropriate statement. This would then be released and the press told that this was all the information they could use. Editors who stepped out of line would be prosecuted. MI5 strongly opposed allowing the press officer access to the transcript of the trial; however, the other members of the Home Defence Executive felt that MI5 had no grasp of what would generate a good story and keep the press happy.

The new procedure was first followed in the case of Karel Richard Richter, executed on 10 December 1941 after a violent struggle with the executioner.[143] There was a formal press release setting out his name, citizenship, place of birth, trial, and appeal, noting they had been held *in camera*. This was followed by unofficial notes giving an account of his capture and providing material for a story. Francis Williams for the Ministry of Information added a memorandum telling editors that they must make no further enquiries, and threatening a total information blackout that if any editor misbehaved. So far as the press were concerned the new system provoked virtually no further trouble; the authorities presented it as a sort of bargain with the press.

Unhappily, however, it enraged such judges as had been involved in trials *in camera*. Having acceded to prosecution requests to try spies *in camera*, and having warned witnesses and jurors that they must reveal nothing whatever in public, judges now saw chatty accounts of those same trials in the newspapers. Attempts by the Attorney General to soothe the Lord Chief Justice, Lord Caldecote, and explain the need both to hold the trials *in camera*, and to secure the co-operation of the press, were not initially successful. Lord Caldecote regarded the statements that had been issued as amounting to contempt of court. By 15 December 1941 peace was restored. It was settled that in future the procedure would include securing the permission of the trial judge and, if there had been an appeal, the Court of Criminal Appeal. This involvement of the judges was, however, to be a mere formality; they would not be shown the statement that was to be issued, which was not based upon what had gone on in the courts. There is no evidence that they pressed for any undertaking to release details of trials *in camera* after some decent interval, much less for public information that a trial was to take place or had taken place, to be issued before the individual was dead.

The available file[144] contains the statements released in the cases of Duncan A. C. Scott-Ford (3 November 1942), Johannes M. Dronkers (31 December 1942),[145] and the original draft of that for Oswald J. Job (executed 16 March 1944).[146] The form of these statements followed that in Richter's case. That for Scott-Ford says that he 'volunteered' a statement admitting his guilt; he was, at the request of Helenus ('Buster') Milmo, subjected to the rigorous methods of interrogation employed in Latchmere House.[147] In one case, however, there was no statement; this was the case of Rogerio de Magalhaes Peixto de Menezes, an employee at the Portuguese Embassy.[148] He was arrested and lodged in Latchmere House on 22 February 1943,[149] and sentenced to death in April 1943 under the Treachery Act. His appeal was dismissed on 13 May, all the proceedings taking place *in camera*. The judge had given the jury an assurance that a press statement would be made. A Cabinet decision, not recorded in the normal minutes, was made on 27 May approving his reprieve and commuting his sentence to life imprisonment in return for co-operation from the Portuguese government in clearing up a German spy ring in Lisbon.[150] The Home Secretary, Herbert Morison, thought that a statement would have to reveal why the sentence had been commuted, which was impossible without revealing 'matter which it was in the public interest should be kept secret'. Therefore, 'notwithstanding the obvious objection to not publishing the results of trials held in secret, he was against making any public statement'.

The Cabinet agreed, comforting itself that a mere life sentence was involved, and a public statement might be made at some later date. So far as I am aware this was not done officially until 1990, though information must have been leaked to Allason for his *MI5* (1981).[151] The reply to a Parliamentary question on 18 October 1945 revealed that Menezes had been tried and sentenced to death, but did not reveal that he had not been executed.[152] Presumably the trial judge and judges of the Court of Criminal Appeal were squared at the time, but the file, much of which has been destroyed, has nothing on this.[153] Presumably at some point he was deported to Portugal.

A number of less serious OSA and DRS violations were tried *in camera* during the war; even magistrates were able to exclude the public from hearings of summary offences. Thus George Wace Wall, a radio engineer engaged on secret experimental work, was publicly sentenced to six years after a trial *in camera* for improper recording of information under the OSA in September 1940.[154] In July of that year, an engineer who had been working on airfield construction chatted incautiously with a canon of the Church of England, who could have been a spy in disguise; the canon reported him and his case was heard by magistrates partly *in camera*. He went to prison for three months.[155] Fusilier Michael Hopper collected information with a view to writing a book after the war; his court martial was held partly *in camera*.[156] But many cases were tried in open court for offences of one kind or another against the OSA or DRS, as when a typist in the naval intelligence section of the admiralty took some documents home with no sinister purpose; she went to prison for a month.[157] The more ridiculous cases mainly occurred in 1940 and 1941.

With the end of the war the emergency legislation went, and the explicit power to hear cases *in camera* returned to substantially what it had been in the interwar years. One legacy of the war, however, was the extended doctrine of Crown privilege established in the case of *Duncan* v. *Cammell Laird*.[158] This was a suit for damages arising out of the loss of the submarine *Thetis*, which sank during trials with considerable civilian loss of life. The admiralty wanted the hearing to be *in camera* by judge alone to preserve the secrecy of some of the features of the submarine, but the plaintiff's lawyers were not prepared to consent to this. In the event the case was heard in open court, but the Crown refused to make available numerous documents which contained sensitive information. The House of Lords upheld the Crown's power to withhold documents in litigation, essentially at its discretion. Had the case been tried *in camera* the issue would never have arisen.

Although quite a number of documents connected with trials *in camera* are now available in the Public Record Office there is no policy of always releasing papers, including transcripts, under the thirty-years rule, much less a policy of early release. Nor, so far as I know, is there any policy of not destroying records of such trials. The tendency has been for departments, which operate either under rules which are not made public, or under no rules at all, to place relevant files under extended closure, or simply retain them. And under the banner of 'national security' numerous trials *in camera* have taken place since the Second World War; the ratification and recent incorporation of the European Convention on Human Rights has not affected the practice.[159] In general the judiciary appear to be perfectly comfortable with this aspect of the secret state, as with others. In participating in secret trials they have, perforce, joined it, in dereliction of their fundamental duty to respect and further the rule of law.

Notes

This is an expanded version of the Atkin Memorial Lecture originally delivered at the Reform Club on 19 May 1994, which happens to be the day of St Ivo of Kermartin, the patron saint of lawyers. Since writing this I have come across Leonard Sellers's *Shot in the Tower* (London: Leo Cooper, 1997), which deals with a number of the trials discussed by me. Sellers provides interesting further information about the individuals concerned, but does not address the issue of holding trials *in camera*.

1 Hansard, *Commons Debs*, 5th ser., vol. 639, col. 1618 (4 May 1961).
2 See M. Randle and P. Pottle, *The Blake Escape* (London: Harrap, 1989); and G. Blake, *No Other Choice* (London: Jonathan Cape, 1990), chs 9 and 10.
3 See R. M. Thomas, *Espionage and Secrecy: the Official Secrets Acts 1911–1989* (London: Routledge, 1991), pp. 193–6.
4 E. W. Ives, *Anne Boleyn* (Oxford: Basil Blackwell, 1986), p. 386.
5 *Cobbett's Complete Collection of State Trials*, 10 vols (London: R. Bagshaw), vol. 1, p. 1032.
6 *Ibid.*, p. 407.
7 See, for example, C. Cottu, 'On the administration of the criminal code in England and Wales and the spirit of English government', *Pamphleteer*, 16: 31 (1820), 21, 51.
8 I am indebted for the example and for the passage quoted to David J. A. Cairns, *Advocacy and the Making of the Adversarial Trial 1800–1865* (Oxford: Clarendon Press, 1998), p. 16.

9 R. McGower, 'Civilizing punishment: the end of public executions in England', *Journal of British Studies*, 33 (1994), 257.

10 W. F. Craies and H. D. Roome (eds), *Archibold's Pleading, Evidence & Practice in Criminal Cases*, 24th edn (London: Sweet & Maxwell, 1910), p. 217 (emphasis added).

11 8 Edw. VII *c*. 45 *c*. 67 (1908).

12 V. Bailey and S. Blackburn, 'The Punishment of Incest Act 1908: a case study of law creation', *Criminal Law Review* (1979), 708.

13 12 & 13 Geo. V *c*. 56 (1922), section 5.

14 *The Times*, (6 June 1925).

15 *Ibid.*, (6 July 1927).

16 8 Edw. VII *c*. 67 (1908), sections 114 and 115.

17 [1913] A.C. 417.

18 (1913) L.T.R. 744.

19 (1913) 29 T.L.R. 658.

20 See B. Porter, *Plots and Paranoia: a History of Political Espionage in Britain 1790–1988* (London: Routledge, 1992), esp. chs 5 and 6.

21 See C. Andrew, *Her Majesty's Secret Service. The Making of the British Intelligence Community* (London: Heinemann, 1985), ch. 2. The critical report is Public Record Office, Richmond (hereafter PRO), CAB 16/8.

22 1 & 2 Geo. V *c*. 28 (1911).

23 *The Times* (16 September1910), PRO, DPP 1/14 (Helm); *The Times* (29, 30 August. 1911), PRO, FO 371/1126 file 32404 (Schultz); *The Times* (10 February1912), PRO, DPP 1/16 (Grosse, alias Captain Grant); *The Times* (23, 24 July 1912) (Graves, or Arngaard Karl); *The Times* (17 January 1913), *R.* v. *Parrott* (1913) 8 CAR 186, PRO, DPP 4/48 and 1/20 (Parrott; the case against Hentschel was dropped); Hampshire Assizes 7, 14, 21 March 1913 (Klauer, alias William Clare); PRO, DPP 1/28, PRO, CRIM 1/45/2 (Schroeder, alias Gould, charged with his wife). See also Andrew, *Her Majesty's Secret Service*, pp. 61–2, 64–5, 67–9.

24 There are some books of importance on spy cases. Basil Thomson, who was head of the CID and Special Branch, gave accounts based on firsthand knowledge, notably *Queer People* (London: Hodder & Stoughton, 1922), and *The Scene Changes* (London: Collins, 1939). S. T. Felstead, a journalist, wrote an officially approved account, *German Spies at Bay* (London: Hutchinson, 1922) and edited *Steinhauer: the Kaiser's Master Spy* (London: Bodley Head, 1930). The corresponding work for later developments is Nigel West [Rupert Allason], *MI5: British Security Service Operations 1909–1945* (London: Bodley Head, 1981). J. Bulloch's *M.I.5.* (London: Arthur Barker Ltd., 1963), is also based on leaked information. On counter-espionage especially during the Second World War, see J. Curry, *The Security Service 1908–1945* (London: Public Record Office, 1999).

25 4 & 5 Geo. V *c*. 29 (1914), section 1(a).

26 4 & 5 Geo. V *c*. 8.(1914), section 4.

27 DORA, Consolidated Regulations (28 November 1914), section 56.

28 Karl Gustav Ernst was convicted on 11 November 1914 for OSA offences committed before the war. He could not have been tried by court martial for DORA offences, as DORA was not retrospective. His trial was not held *in camera*. PRO, DPP 1/27; Andrew, *Her Majesty's Secret Service*, pp. 70–1.

29 Regulation 18A was introduced by Order in Council No. 715 (28 July 1915).

30 This probably was the case with the spies arrested at the outbreak of the war, listed by Felstead, *German Spies*, pp. 8–9. Felstead explains the failure to take criminal proceedings by the need to conceal the fact of the arrests, which assumes that they could not have been tried *in camera*. A later example is Lionel Max Preiznitser (Thomson, *Queer People*, pp. 159–60, name a pseudonym). Felstead, p. 111, suggests that numerous agents had to be interned for lack of proof.

31 For example, Conrad Leyter was interned in 1915; see Thomson, *Queer People*, p. 133, Felstead, *German Spies*, pp. 85–7. The cases of Meta Brunner and Hilda Howsin may be similar; see Felstead, p. 197; Thomson, *The Scene Changes*, pp. 266–8, 270–2, 278.

32 4 & 5 Geo. V *c*. 29 and *c*. 63 (1914).

33 Andrew, *Her Majesty's Secret Service*, 182–4; Bulloch, *M.I.5.*, p. 95; Felstead, *German Spies*, pp. 23–33, Thomson, *Queer People*, pp. 122–5. See PRO, DPP 1/29 (transcript); PRO, WO 71/1236, 141/82. See also WO 32/4588, which includes Haldane's minute. G. Oram, *Death Sentences Passed by Military Courts of the British Army* 1914–24 (London: Francis Boutle, 1998), has Lody tried under DORA, but this is a mistake.

34 G. A. R. Fitzgerald (ed.), *Manual of Military Law*, 3rd edn (London: H.M.S.O., 1894), para. 41.

35 Under the International Convention Concerning the Laws and Customs of War on Land, signed 18 October 1907 and ratified by the UK 27 November 1909.

36 H. Godley (ed.), *Manual* (1914), para. 167.

37 *Ibid.*, para. 445.

38 PRO, WO 105/Gen. No./1829.

39 PRO, WO 32/4588, memorandum of 13 August 1914.

40 PRO, WO 32/4588 minute by the Advocate General.

41 At this time junior treasury counsel and senior counsel at the central criminal court, later director of public prosecutions.

42 See Thomson, *The Scene Changes*, pp. 249–51; *Queer People*, pp. 122–6; and Felstead (ed.), *Steinhauer*, p. 45.

43 Felstead (ed.), *Steinhauer*, p. 38; Burkard Baron von Müllenheim-Rechberg, *Battleship Bismarck: a Survivor's Story*, trans. Jack Sweetman (London: Arms & Armour Press, 1991), pp. 83, 101.

44 See H. Lauterpacht (ed.), *Manual* (1958), pp.106 and 108.

45 See PRO, WO 215/12. WO 32/4898 has a list of 'Spies tried by military courts' abroad. There are forty-nine names, the trials taking place at Alexandria (1), Douglas (1) H.Q. 10th Division (1), Ahmednagar (14), Kiraissi in Macedonia (12), in the field (1), Salonika (9), Port Sudan (6), Malta (4). Of these persons nine appear to have been executed. Oram, *Death Sentences*, has one Egyptian hanged under martial law in what may have been an espionage case. He also has, at p. 39, one M. S. Hussein acquitted of war treason; this is a mistake as Hussein was executed.

46 4 & 5 Geo. V *c*. 8 (1914).

47 44 & 45 Vict. *c*. 58 (1881).

48 Godley (ed.), *Manual* (1914), ch. 5, para. 71.

49 PRO, WO 32/4898 with reference to folio 17/1. This has a complete list.

50 In what follows I have used Oram's valuable *Death Sentences*, but my account differs in some respects, and is based on a more extensive archival basis. Oram does not, of course, deal with civil trials.

51 5 Geo. V *c.* 34 (1915).
52 See PRO, WO 32/5526.
53 PRO, WO 32/3989 and 3990; practice changed by Army Council Instruction 570 of 22 March 1918.
54 Oram, *Death Sentences*, p. 15.
55 PRO, DPP 1/41, case of Robert Rosenthal. He had falsely claimed American citizenship, and was tried by court martial.
56 PRO, WO 32/4588 and 4898.
57 The four were Rikard Leopold Vieyra (14 December 1916, Dutch); G. V. Bacon (26 February 1917, American); A. Hagn (27 August 1917, Norwegian); L. Goten (24 September 1917, Belgian). Dates give the start of each trial.
58 C. H. Lody (30 October 1914, German); H. M. P. Janssen (16 July 1915, Dutch); W. R. Roos (16 July 1915, Dutch); E. W. Melin (28 October 1915, Swede); A. A. Roggen (20 August 1915, Uruguayan); F. Buschmann (28 September 1915, Brazilian); I. G. Ries (4–5 November 1915, American); A. Meyer (5 November 1915, Danish, on whom see PRO, WO 141/83); L. H. J. Zender (20 March 1916, Peruvian).
59 R. Rosenthal (11 July 1915, German).
60 PRO, WO 32/4898 also lists ten spies tried by court martial and thirty-nine by military tribunals abroad of whom seven were executed. I have not investigated whether these trials took place *in camera*.
61 Alias Copperlee. For accounts, see Thomson, *Queer People*, pp. 126–9; Felstead, *German Spies*, pp. 33–40; PRO, WO 141/1/3, CRIM 1/153/3, HO 144/1429/288639. *The Times* (19, 20, 21 May 1915).
62 PRO, DPP 1/38, CRIM 1/683, 684, 685, WO 141/2/2; *The Times* (28 May, 21 April, 5 June, 22 June, 24 June 1915); Felstead, *German Spies*, pp. 44–52; Thomson, *Queer People*, pp. 130–3.
63 Reported as *R.* v. *M.*, 32 T.L.R. 1 (1915).
64 PRO, DPP 1/41, WO 32/4898, 141/1/5, HO 144/288639; Felstead, *German Spies*, pp. 54–7; Thomson, *Queer People*, p. 148.
65 See PRO, WO 32/4588.
66 Felstead, *German Spies*, p. 56.
67 PRO, DPP 1/33, WO 71/1312, 92/3, 32/4898; Thomson, *Queer People*, pp. 135–7; Felstead, *German Spies*, pp. 102–9; *The Times* (15 July 1915).
68 Thomson, *Queer People*, p. 137; Felstead, *German Spies*, p. 109; J. Bulloch, *M.I.5.*, pp. 116–21. Bulloch indicates they were Janssen, Roos, Wertheim, Breeckow, Buschmann, and Guerrero. However Felstead, p. 110, indicates that Buschman was not one, and Oram, *Death Sentences*, has Buschman executed on 19 October 1915, relying on PRO, WO 92/3 and 71/1313. His text suggests that Auguste Alfredo Roggen, a Uruguayan, executed 18 September 1915 was, and that another suspect was deported. This may be Raymonde Amondarin, Guerrero's girl friend, against whom charges were dropped.
69 For example, the case of Ernst Gustav Waldemann Olson. *The Times* (13 July 1915); PRO, DPP 1/37, 4/49.
70 PRO, DPP 1/35, WO 71/1237, 141/2/3, 92/3; Felstead, *German Spies*, p. 134; Thomson, *Queer People*, p. 146.
71 PRO, DPP 1/40, WO 141/61, 92/3; Thomson, *Queer People*, pp. 144–6; Felstead, *German Spies*, p. 125.

72 PRO, DPP 1/31. Thomson, *Queer People*, p. 141, has him tried at the Westminster Guildhall on 20 September but this is incorrect. See also PRO, WO 92/3, 71/1313.

73 Thomson, *Queer People*, pp. 141–3.

74 PRO, DPP 1/34, WO 32/4898; Thomson, *Queer People*, pp. 171–3; Felstead, *German Spies*, pp. 181–2.

75 One file in the Public Record Office, CRIM 1/683, contains a wizened lemon whose juice was, presumably, employed as ink.

76 Thomson, *The Scene Changes*, p. 357; Felstead, *German Spies*, p. 52.

77 *The Times* (21, 28 May, 1, 5, 19, 22, 24 June 1915). Curry, *Security Service*, p. 76, states that in one case a German agent was impersonated after his execution, but does not provide a name.

78 PRO, DPP 1/42, WO 32/4898; Thomson, *Queer People*, pp. 157–9, *The Times* (26 October 1915); Felstead, *German Spies*, pp. 152–6.

79 Felstead, *German Spies*, p. 155.

80 Thomson, *Queer People*, pp. 187–90; Felstead, *German Spies*, pp. 187–96; PRO, DPP 1/32 (case papers), 4/51 and 52 (transcripts), PCOM 8/245 (with photo), WO 32/4898 (release and list of spies still in prison after the armistice).

81 Lauterpacht (ed.), *Manual* (1958), part 3, p. 183, states that Edith Cavell was convicted of what might be called war treason – aiding prisoners to escape.

82 *The Times* (13 January, 18 February 1916).

83 PRO, DPP 1/32.

84 See PRO, WO 32/4898.

85 (1916) 85 L.J.K.B. 857, 32 T.L.R. 303 (Divisional Court) and 369 (Court of Appeal). Andrew, *Her Majesty's Secret Service*, pp. 192–3; and F. L. Carsten, *War Against War* (London: Batsford, 1982), pp. 55–6, are referring to a different incident.

86 DORA, Regulation 51A (28 July 1915).

87 See *ex parte Norman* (1916) 114 L.T.R. 232, and K. D. Ewing and C. A. Gearty, *The Struggle for Civil Liberties. Political Freedom and the Rule of Law in Britain, 1914–1945* (Oxford: Clarendon Press, 2000), pp. 65–8.

88 (1916) 85 L.J.K.B. 857, 859.

89 *Ibid.*, pp. 860–1.

90 *Ibid.*, p. 861.

91 [1917] 2 K.B. 254, more fully reported at (1917) 33 T.L.R. 222. See Ewing and Gearty, *Civil Liberties*, pp. 343–5.

92 Godley (ed.), *Manual* (1939), ch. 3, para. 37. ch. 8, para. 41, n. 5 mentions a case in Calcutta (*Ricketts* v. *Walker*, 1841) where a reporter whose notes were seized after he had been ordered not to take notes was awarded nominal damages. The case is reported in W. Hough, *Precedents in Military Law* (London: W. H. Allen & Co., 1855), p. 718.

93 All courts martial held in connection with the Easter Rising were *in camera*, and since this chapter was written some material dealing with their legality has been released in the PRO, which I have not had an opportunity to consult. See in particular WO 141/21 (shooting of civilians by troops in 1916) and WO 141/27 (supply of copies of courts martial proceedings).

94 The institution which handled counter espionage work in Britain during the First World War was called MO5g until January 1916, when it was renamed MI5.

This formed part of MO5, the institution being referred to, rather than the Directorate of Intelligence within the Home Office established in 1919 and run by Thomson. There was also within GHQ a unit concerned with obtaining intelligence related to revolutionary movements and industrial unrest in Britain, set up in 1919. Thereafter the army wanted wished to have no connection with domestic secret intelligence, and this unit went early in 1920, but in response to pressure from Lloyd George and Winston Churchill a small liaison unit continued, called MO4x, but this was disbanded in 1922. See PRO, WO 32/5553, 106/45/525; Andrew, *Her Majesty's Secret Service*, pp. 343–4.

95 See PRO, WO 32/13733.

96 PRO, WO 32/4896.

97 See PRO, CAB 24/109 (CP No. 1604 of 1920. Review of the Defence Regulations, paper circulated by Churchill 12 July 1920). The report of the Cave Committee is PRO, GT 6350 and should be in CAB/70.

98 PRO, PRO 32/13733.

99 10 & 11 Geo. 5 *c*. 75 (1920).

100 The history of OSA 1911 and 1920 is discussed in D. Williams, *Not in the Public Interest* (London: Hutchinson, 1965), ch. 1; Thomas, *Espionage and Secrecy*, ch. 1; and D. Hooper, *Official Secrets: the Uses and Abuses of the Act* (Sevenoaks: Coronet, 1988), ch. 2.

101 See Williams, *Public Interest*, p. 33; PRO, DPP 1/25.

102 *The Times*, (16 November, 8 and 16 December 1926); PRO, HO 144/1982; Williams, *Public Interest*, p. 63; PRO, CRIM 1/380; Hooper, *Official Secrets*, pp. 38–40. Another case two years later involved Archibald Taylor, a junior civil servant engaged in corruption. See Hooper, *Official Secrets*, p. 40.

103 Hooper, *Official Secrets*, p. 32.

104 Goertz was convicted on 9 March and sentenced to four years' imprisonment. See *The Times* (5, 6, 7, 10 March 1936). See also PRO, CRIM 1/813.

105 *The Times* (25 September 1936).

106 See West, *MI5*, p. 81; A. Masters, *The Man Who Was M: the Life of Maxwell Knight* (Oxford: Basil Blackwell, 1984), ch. 4; *The Times* (4, 8, 12 February 1938). Williams, *Public Interest*, p. 104, notes that in the five years up to May 1938 the Attorney General had consented to OSA prosecutions in twenty-eight cases, and refused consent in ten. Hooper, *Official Secrets* Appendix I, lists three of these cases. For the period between 1920 and 1939 he lists seven cases: Michael Simington (June 1920, PRO, DPP 4/54); Lionel Ballard Frederick Budgen (June 1932); William Burger (January 1935); Albert Fulton (March 1935); James Goodrich and Sidney Norris (September 1937); Wilfred Vernon (October 1937); Edward Edwards (May 1939); Walter Moore (May 1939). He notes that Moore's trial was largely *in camera*. Probably so was that of Burger, who was connected with the Woolwich Arsenal case.

107 Case of Eric J. C. Camp, see *The Times* (27 October 1936).

108 See PRO, AIR 2/17425. Donelly's Air Ministry file was number 893013/28, but it is not available. I have also relied on AIR 2/718 and WO 141/60 (formerly PRO, WO 32/60). The case does not seem to have attracted the attention of the press.

109 The trial resulted from a raid on the Russian trade delegation in London on 12–14 May 1927. The only file listed in the PRO, CRIM 1/418, was not available

when I last ordered it. Accounts of the case are given in West, *MI5*, pp. 62–75; and Andrew, *Her Majesty's Secret Service*, pp. 467–73.

110 The reference is to his minute on 893013/28. See note 107 above.

111 PRO, KV 2/174–192, WO 71/1033, 209/114; West, *MI5*, pp. 100–10; *The Times* (21–5, 28–9 March 1933) (coverage of the trial itself). Under section 41 of the Army Act, if the accused was a serving officer, he could be tried by court martial.

112 PRO, WO 141/60 (formerly WO 32/60), law officers' opinion, 1 March 1933.

113 *Ibid.*, letter by Sir Alexander Maxwell, 23 June 1936.

114 *Ibid.* (Scottish Office memorandum).

115 *Ibid.* (law officers' opinion).

116 3 & 4 Eliz. II *c.* 18 (1955), section 94 (2).

117 See A. W. B. Simpson, *In the Highest Degree Odious* (Oxford: Oxford University Press, 1994), ch. 3.

118 2 & 3 Geo. VI *c.* 62 (1939), section 6. The provision of OSA was suspended.

119 PRO, WO 32/4588. The Home Office took the same line over the arrangements for an invasion in 1940–1. See Simpson, *Highest Degree*, pp. 190–2.

120 PRO, WO 32/4588, including a letter from Maxwell to Sir James Grigg, 31 October 1939.

121 PRO, HPC (39) 86.

122 PRO, WO 32/4588, memorandum by H. D. F. MacGeagh, Judge Advocate General, 24 November 1940.

123 See PRO, HPC (40) 66, memorandum by the home secretary, 15 March 1940; HPC (40) 105, 4 May 1940.

124 PRO, FO 371/5084, prepared for a parliamentary question of 18 October 1945 in Hansard, *Commons Debs*, 5th ser., vol. 414, col. 1513. F. H. Hinsley and C. A. G. Simkins, *British Intelligence in the Second World War*, 5 vols, (London: H.M.S.O., 1990), vol. 4, pp. 92, 97 n. (discussing press releases). PRO, HO 45/25595 has a note on the aftermath. See also West, *MI5*, pp. 324–8.

125 O. Hoare (ed.), *Camp 020: MI5 and the Nazi Spies* (Richmond: Public Record Office, 2000), p. 156. See PRO, WO 32/18144.

126 The story originated with one John McGowan, who was at the time a staff officer with fighter command; see *Luton Herald* (10 June 1979). The supposed executions do not feature in a list of death sentences carried out in PRO, WO 93/40.

127 See J. Douglas-Hamilton, *Motive for a Mission* (London: Macmillan, 1971), p. 197; J. Leasor, *Rudolf Hess, The Uninvited Envoy* (London: Allen & Unwin, 1962), pp. 149–50; L. Picknett, O. Prince, and S. Prior, *Double Standards: the Rudolf Hess Cover-up* (London: Little Brown, 2001), p. 309; P. Padfield, *Hess: Flight for the Fuehrer* (London: Weidenfeld & Nicolson, 1991), pp. 251–2.

128 Lauterpacht (ed.), *Manual*, (1958), pt 3, p. 108 (emphasis added).

129 West, *MI5*, p. 90; Cadogan Diary (Archives of Churchill College Cambridge as ACAD) September 1939; PRO, CRIM 1/1129, TS 27/1217; W. Cameron Watt, 'Francis Herbert King: a Soviet source in the Foreign Office', *Intelligence and National Security*, 3 (1988), 62–82; G. Brook-Shepherd, *The Storm Petrels: the First Soviet Defectors, 1928–1938* (London: Collins, 1977), pp. 172–80; Curry, *Security Service*, pp. 189–90.

130 Harvey had been appointed a cypher officer in 1919; he was still employed by the Foreign Office in 1940, and must have been exonerated.

131 Russell, Kinnaird, Maling, and Tubb were all apparently exonerated. Russell received an MBE in 1939.

132 G. Brook-Shepherd, *Storm Petrels*, p. 176, has it that King's controller was Theodore Maly, who was also known as Paul Hardt.

133 West's account, *MI5*, pp. 73–4, does not tally with the case papers, which indicate that in his first statement King did not confess. See PRO, CRIM 1/1129 and TS 27/1217.

134 *The Times* (8 June 1956).

135 PRO, FO 371/5084 (prepared for a Parliamentary question on 18 October 1945).

136 Hansard, *Commons Debs*, 5th ser., vol. 414, col. 1513 (18 October 1945). See PRO, CRIM 1/1449, HO 45/25763, KV 2/57–59. The others were Karl Theo Drueke (Drüke) and Francis Johannes Winter.

137 See Simpson, *Highest Degree*, pp. 154, 156, 241, 392.

138 See *The Times* (18 December 1940) and (11 February 1941).

139 PRO, HO 45/25741.

140 All material on press releases is taken from PRO, HO 45/25595. PRO, PCOM 9/2121 contains an example of the grim form returned to the Home Office after an execution had been carried out, which, for example, reported on the conduct of the executioners.

141 PRO, HO 144/21471–2.

142 *Star* (16 August 1941); *Evening Standard* (16 August 1941).

143 PRO, CRIM 1/1350, KV 2/30–33.

144 PRO, HO 45/25595.

145 See also PRO, CRIM 1/1454, HO 45/25603, KV 2/43–46.

146 See also PRO, HO 144/22028.

147 See PRO, HO 45/25763. There is an account by R. W. G. Stephens in Hoare (ed.), *Camp 020*, pp. 195–8, which maintains, however, that Scott-Ford willingly co-operated.

148 See Hoare (ed.), *Camp 020*, pp. 47–8, 237–9.

149 See PRO, HO 45/25111, which has lists of those in MI5's private prisons, Latchmere House (Camp 020) and Huntercombe Place (Camp 020R).

150 PRO, WM (43) 78th.

151 Accounts are in Hinsley and Simkins, *British Intelligence*, vol. 4, pp. 110–12, 186, 204; and in West, *MI5*, pp. 345–6.

152 Hansard, *Commons Debs*, 5th ser., vol. 414, col. 1513 (18 October 1945).

153 Judges known to have presided over the trial of spies during the war were Hilbery (King); Tucker (Kent, Wolkoff, Richter); Wrottesley (Waldberg, Kieboom, Meier, Pons, Dronkers); Lewis (Armstrong); Asquith (Waelti and Druecke); Humphreys (Key, Timmerman, Winter); Birkett (Scott-Ford); Stable (Job); Hallett (Vanhove).

154 *The Times* (19 September 1940); PRO, CRIM 1/1223.

155 Case of Harvey Blessington Young, *The Times* (17 July 1940).

156 *The Times* (2 September 1940).

157 Case of Ethel E. Mann, *The Times* (5 July 1940).

158 [1942] A.C. 642. See PRO, TS 32/101–17.

159 See A. W. B. Simpson, *Human Rights and the End of Empire: Britain and the Genesis of the European Convention* (Oxford: Oxford University Press, 2001), pp. 399, 465–6, 694, 732, 1061.

6

War crimes trials before international tribunals: legality and legitimacy

Dominic McGoldrick

I Introduction

An assessment of the historical place of any trials requires both a micro and a macro analysis. The microanalysis focuses on the internal processes and procedures of the trials. The macroanalysis focuses on the broader political and historical context. Both levels of analysis can review issues of legality and legitimacy.[1] This essay presents a comparative critique of war crimes trials before the International Military Tribunals at Nuremberg and Tokyo and the International Tribunals for the former Yugoslavia and for Rwanda. It also looks to future trials that could take place before the Permanent International Criminal Court.

Any trial can be viewed as a drama.[2] However, it is never an abstract drama. A trial or series of trials has to be localised in a system of criminal law and justice. International trials have to be localised in 'systems' of 'international criminal law' and 'international criminal justice'. However, the very existence of such 'systems' has been contested. This goes to the heart of issues of legality and legitimacy for international trials. For much of its history 'international criminal law', if it has existed at all, has been rudimentary, indeterminate, and ineffectual.[3] It existed in the nether regions of international humanitarian law, which existed in the nether regions of public international law. A system of 'international criminal justice' might be thought to require some consensus on the existence and values of the 'international community'. The existence of such a community in this sense and its values also remain contested.[4] What has not been contested is that the standards of legality and legitimacy by which international trials should be assessed have evolved. There has been a clear recognition of the need to comply with the human rights of defendants and to take greater account of the interests of victims.

The second section of this chapter briefly records the history of national and international trials for 'war crimes' (used in a broad sense to include war crimes in the strict sense, crimes against humanity, genocide), and considers the various purposes of war crimes trials. The third section is a comparative examination of the establishment and functioning of the Nuremberg, Tokyo, Yugoslavian and Rwandan tribunals respectively. The fourth section highlights the principal features of the permanent international criminal court. The fifth section concludes with an assertion that that war crimes trials before international tribunals have moved closer and closer towards satisfying purer norms of legality and legitimacy.

II National and international trials: an overview

National war crimes trials have a long and (un)distinguished history.[5] National courts may appear more legitimate than international ones or vice versa. The obligation on states to prosecute certain war crimes, 'grave breaches', is a central element of international humanitarian law.[6] National jurisdiction has also been exercised over crimes against humanity and genocide. The exercise of national jurisdiction over these three kinds of crimes would usually be based on the nationality of the offenders (nationality jurisdiction) or on the territorial location of the crimes (territorial jurisdiction). In addition, however, the three kinds of crimes are among the few areas of international law where there is general acceptance that states can, in principle, exercise jurisdiction over offences committed by any person anywhere in the world ('universal jurisdiction'). Perhaps the most famous national war crimes trial asserting universal jurisdiction remains the Israeli trial of Adolf Eichmann, who had been head of the Jewish Office of the German Gestapo.[7] That case raised legal controversy because the Israeli court asserted jurisdiction over a German national in respect of offences which had not taken place within the territory of Israel, and indeed, in respect of offences which had taken place when Israel did not even exist as a state.[8]

After the First World War, the Versailles Treaty (1919) required Germany to try its own war criminals. The resulting Leipzig trials were widely discredited; 888 out of 901 defendants were acquitted or had their cases dismissed. After the Second World War, international trials attracted the greatest publicity. However, the largest volume of war crimes trials were held in Germany in the four Allied occupation zones under Control Council Law No. 10, which allowed each occupying authority to carry out trials of persons held in its custody. Individual states that held war crimes trials in Europe and in Asia included the US,[9] the UK,[10] Australia, Nationalist China, France, Greece, the Netherlands, Poland, and the USSR.[11] Since the 1940s, war crimes trials have been spasmodic at the national level but in the 1980s and 1990s there was a resurgence of prosecutions in Australia,[12] Canada,[13] and a number of European states.[14] The passage of more than half a century since the Second World War means that the possibilities of Second World War related prosecutions are fast diminishing. In 1999 Anthony Sawoniuk was the subject of the first prosecution in the UK under the War Crimes Act 1991, which provided jurisdiction in relation to war crimes committed by non-British nationals in German-controlled territory during the Second World War.[15]

Like all 'trials', international war crimes trials serve a variety of purposes.[16] These include deterrence, punishment, reconciliation, establishing the historical facts, making societies come face to face with the past,[17] reinforcing the concept of accountability,[18] re-establishing legal and moral order and an ordered system of justice, education,[19] rebuilding civil society, establishing or reinforcing the supremacy of international law over national law, building an international society governed by an international rule of law,[20] and re-establishing international peace and security. Some of these purposes may conflict or appear to conflict at particular times.[21]

The earliest international prosecution is often suggested to have been that of Conradin von Hofenstafen in 1268 for waging aggressive war. In 1474 Governor Peter of Hagenbach was tried and condemned before a court of twenty-eight representatives of the Hanseatic cities at Breisach for various atrocities including murder, rape, pillage, and wanton confiscation.[22] Some five centuries later, Article 227 of the Treaty of Versailles (1919) made provision for the trial before an international tribunal of William II of Hohenzollern, formerly the German Kaiser, for 'a supreme offence against international morality and the sanctity of treaties'. However, the Netherlands refused to hand him over for trial.[23] In substance, therefore, 'The real history of international criminal law begins after WW II, and is often a history of institutions'.[24] Until the 1990s, the only successful historical precedents at the international level were the International Military Tribunals (IMTs) at Nuremberg and Tokyo.

III Nuremberg, Tokyo, Yugoslavia, Rwanda: a comparative analysis

Nuremberg

The Nuremberg IMT was undertaken only after other options, such as summary executions, were considered by the major Allied powers.[25] It was preceded by the establishment of the UN War Crimes Commission, but the Commission was not directly involved in the establishment of the Tribunal.[26] The agreement of the Allies on the trial of war criminals was expressed in a number of international statements but most notably in their Moscow Declaration of 1943. Under that declaration, minor criminals were to be judged and punished in the countries where they committed their crimes. 'Major war criminals whose offences have no particular geographical location' were to be tried and punished 'by the joint decision of the Governments of the Allies'.[27] Major or minor status depended on rank rather than the seriousness of the crime charged. To that extent, it was intended as a show trial (in the proper sense)[28] of the 'big fish'. With Adolf Hitler, Heinrich Himmler, and Josef

Goebbels dead, Reich Marshal Hermann Goering and former Foreign Minister Joachim von Ribbentrop were the major political figures. Alongside them were tried a mixture of other political figures, military and naval officers, economic and financial figures, and propagandists. In this way, the Nazi system was put on trial.

Nuremberg has been described as 'the most majestic forensic drama ever enacted on the stage of history'.[29] Its legality and legitimacy have been subjected to sustained critiques.[30] A significant number of participants have published accounts of the trial.[31] The judgement of the Tribunal remains of seminal importance.[32] The international legal authority of the Allies to set up the Tribunal can be argued to have derived from: (i) their authority as the *de facto* territorial rulers of a defeated state; (ii) from a pooling of jurisdiction that they could each have exercised over offences for which there was universal jurisdiction, or (iii) from a broader exercise of authority on behalf of the international community on the basis of universal jurisdiction. The Tribunal was established under the London Charter of 11 December 1946. This charter had been drafted by the US, the UK, France, and the USSR.[33] The later adherence of nineteen other Allied states to the charter increased its international legitimacy.[34] The judges and the prosecutors were appointed by the original four powers. It was intended that there would be other trials but, in the event, none was held. Article 1 of the charter provided that the defendants were to receive a 'just and prompt trial'. They were defended by German lawyers and received extensive legal assistance. The defence could cross-examine prosecution witnesses, submit evidence, witnesses, and documents. The defendants could and did testify on their own behalf. There were consistent complaints from the defence concerning access to and use of documents. The Control Council had some important responsibilities under the charter, including the right to reduce or alter sentences, but not to increase them.

The charter stated that the Tribunal and judges could not be challenged by the prosecution or by the defendants or by their counsel. The Tribunal stressed that the Allied powers had done jointly what they might have done singly. The making of the charter was the exercise of the sovereign legislative power by the countries to which the German Reich had unconditionally surrendered. It is often curiously overlooked that the IMT was designated as a 'military tribunal' (there was no civil authority in Germany). The London Charter was clearly selective. There was no possibility of prosecutions in relation to Allied actions such as the carpet bombings of cities, crimes against peace and against humanity by the USSR, or war crimes by various Allied states.

It is generally accepted that the Nuremberg Tribunal sought to apply rules of international law, rather than rules of national law. Article 6 of the charter provided for jurisdiction over three categories of offence for which there was individual responsibility: crimes against peace, war crimes, and crimes against humanity. The categories overlapped to some extent and were not carefully distinguished by the Tribunal. The second and third categories have formed the conceptual basis for the development of international criminal law since 1945.[35] War crimes was an accepted category in 1945 both in terms of treaty law and customary international law. Crimes against peace and crimes against humanity were much more controversial in terms of whether they violated the principle of *nullem crimen sine lege* and thus constituted retroactive criminalisation. Crimes against peace,[36] and in particular the waging of an aggressive war, was the most controversial in terms of whether they existed at all at the relevant time and, if they did, whether they gave rise to individual criminal responsibility as distinct from the responsibility of the state.[37] The Tribunal considered that the crimes did exist and in particular that international agreements had made aggressive war illegal in the 1930s. As for individual responsibility, the Tribunal stated that the maxim *nullem crimen sine lege* was not a limitation on sovereignty but merely a general rule of justice to which there could be exceptions, and the circumstances before them constituted such an exception. In its view, waging aggressive war did give rise to individual criminal responsibility. The Tribunal argued that, 'Crimes against international law are committed by men, not by abstract entities, and only by punishing individuals who commit such crimes can the provisions of international law be enforced.'[38]

Similarly controversial was the position in relation to crimes against humanity because this crime was concerned with a state's treatment of its own population, a matter which had classically been considered as within its domestic jurisdiction.[39] In the event, crimes against humanity were narrowly interpreted by reference to the terms of the charter on other offences and thus events before 1937 were excluded. On the evidence no defendant was convicted of crimes against humanity for an act committed before 1 September 1939.

The fourth charge was of conspiracy to commit offences within the three substantive categories. This was controversial for some of the Allies and for some of the judges. In the event, conspiracy was limited to crimes against peace, was strictly construed, confined to commanders and leaders, and limited to the period from 1938 onwards.

The personal jurisdiction of the Tribunal extended to organizations. If an organisation was found to be criminal, its members could be found guilty in subsequent proceedings before the lesser (national) court of the victorious power.[40] Much debate in the Tribunal was occasioned by this offence. There were no precedents for such international liability, and the Tribunal read in safeguards of voluntariness and knowledge. The SS, the Leadership Corps of the Nazi Party, and the Gestapo/SD were declared criminal but the SA, the Reich Cabinet, and the High Command were not.

In terms of evidence, there were no exclusionary rules.[41] The cases mainly rested on undisputed German documents. 'The trial had involved scrutiny of a hundred thousand documents, a hundred thousand feet of film and twenty five thousand still photographs.'[42] Those defendants who were convicted and hanged were effectively hoisted on the petard of Germanic efficiency in record keeping.[43]

Twenty-four defendants were charged. One committed suicide, and one was determined to be unfit to stand trial. Twenty-two were tried, one *in absentia* (Martin Bormann). The trial lasted ten months. Three defendants were acquitted. Sentencing was at the discretion of the Tribunal.[44] Of the nineteen convicted, twelve were sentenced to death (including Bormann), three received life sentences, and four received terms of imprisonment ranging from ten to twenty years. The Control Council affirmed all of the sentences of the IMT.

Goering committed suicide. Ten were executed by hanging, a method considered dishonourable by military personnel. Pleas by a number of them to be shot by firing squad were rejected. The convictions of Julius Streicher and Admiral Karl Donitz were the most controversial.

Nuremberg is the point in the constellation from which all legal discussion of war crimes trials proceeds or reverts. That crimes against peace and crimes against humanity were retrospectively criminalised remains at best technically arguable. The purpose of the rule against retrospective criminalisation is that individuals should not be punished for actions which they could not have reasonably considered to have been subject to criminal prohibition. International law was clearly evolving in the first half of the twentieth century, and the Nuremberg charges do not offend the purpose of the prohibition.[45] The law that the IMT applied was subsequently affirmed by the international community.[46] The concept of 'crimes against humanity' is now a central part of humanitarian law, and there is no requirement for the relevant conduct to be linked to an armed conflict.[47] The Tribunal interpreted the charges cautiously. As noted, three defendants were acquitted. The concept of 'crimes against peace' has fared less well. No crime of 'aggression' was included in the International Criminal Tribunal for Yugoslavia statute. The crime of 'aggression' has been included in the jurisdiction of the International Criminal Court, but this remains dependent upon agreement on its definition. Such an agreement has not been reached.[48]

Nuremberg is 'the' precedent.[49] Without Nuremberg there would almost certainly have be no Tokyo. Half a century later the light (or shadow) of Nuremberg lay on the paths to the two *ad hoc* tribunals for Yugoslavia and Rwanda, and to the International Criminal Court.[50] Nuremberg also played a crucial role in the development of international human rights law. Holding individuals responsible for violations of international law 'duties' necessarily involved regarding those individuals as subjects of international law. The atrocities committed by the Nazis were partly responsible for the notion of international human 'rights' as expressed in the UN Charter (1945), the Universal Declaration of Human Rights (1948), and subsequent myriad regional and international instruments. Lord Kilmuir, one of the British prosecutors, identified the European Convention on Human Rights of 1950 as one of the results of Nuremberg,[51] along with Nuremberg's demonstration of the dynamic of international law.[52] The piercing of the veil of sovereignty by the notions of human rights and duties, along with extensive international procedures to implement them, has moved international law away from its classical inter-state sovereignty focus.[53] None of this is to gainsay that human rights violations remain extensive in practice. However, they are at least assessed against normative standards and monitored under international procedures. They are no longer regarded as matters within the domestic jurisdiction of sovereign states.

However, it is in a broader ethical and legitimation context that Nuremberg shines most brightly. Even accepting, *arguendo*, the range of legal and legitimacy criticisms directed against it, it remains historically remarkable that after the most destructive and uncivilised conflict in human history, there should have been resort to the civilised institutional drama of a trial at law. The opening words of the US prosecutor Justice Robert H. Jackson are among the most cited and remain valid;

> That four great nations, flushed with victory and stung with injury stay the hand of vengeance and voluntarily submit their captive enemies to the judgement of law is one of the most significant tributes that power ever paid to reason.[54]

Nuremberg was also part of the broader political drama. 'A moment's reflection suggests that many of the significant forces that shaped the European and American transition from war to peace appeared in microcosm during the trial'.[55]

Tokyo

The Tokyo Tribunal was also a military tribunal. As Japan was solely under US control, the US effectively determined the court's establishment and functioning. The Charter for the Far East was set out in a Proclamation issued on 19 January 1946 by the Supreme Commander of the Allied Powers, General Douglas MacArthur.[56] Jurisdiction covered crimes against peace, war crimes, and crimes against humanity. The eleven judges from Allied states and territories were nominated by states but were appointed by MacArthur. There is evidence that MacArthur exercised substantial influence on the trials to ensure that they would not threaten the success of the occupation. The Tribunal applied rules of international law. The defendants were represented by Japanese counsel assisted by US attorneys.

The trial lasted two and a half years. Judgement was much more divided than at Nuremberg. There were disagreements between the judges as to whether the legal basis of the trial was (i) belligerent jurisdiction or (ii) the consent of Japan. There was no argument that it was done on the authority of the international community. The Tribunal indicted twenty-eight representative Japanese political and military leaders, and tried and convicted twenty-five of them.[57] Of the twenty-five, seven were sentenced to hang, sixteen to life in prison, one to twenty years in prison, and one to seven and a half years in prison. Conspiracy was charged. This was controversial but was brushed aside by the Tribunal. However, there was no provision for organisations to be charged. Allied Tribunals tried over 5,000 other Japanese for war crimes. As with Nuremberg, the Tokyo trial was selective.[58] There was no possibility of Allied prosecutions, for example, in relation to the nuclear bombings of Hiroshima and Nagasaki.

Tokyo has not left the same legacy as Nuremberg, and it became the poor relation.[59] Partly this is simply because Tokyo came afterwards and therefore was following the path of Nuremberg. However, there is also a sense in which Tokyo is seen as less legitimate than Nuremberg. There was less of a break in Japanese governmental authority as the Emperor was allowed to continue. As the Cold War descended in Europe, political pressures rendered the trial an embarrassment. The judgement itself was more divided than that of Nuremberg and contained bitter dissent on some issues.[60] In historical memory, the nuclear bombings have remained more prominent than the offences for which the Japanese were tried.

The International Criminal Tribunal for Yugoslavia (ICTY)[61]

In 1993, the Security Council (SC) established the International Tribunal for the Prosecution of Persons Responsible for Serious Violations of International Humanitarian Law Committed in the Territory in the Former Yugoslavia since 1991.[62] Its establishment was part of a wide range of international legal responses to the conflict and dissolution of Yugoslavia.[63] A Commission of Experts had been established by the SC in 1992 to collect information and examine the evidence relating to grave breaches of the Geneva Conventions and other violations of international humanitarian law committed in the territory of the former Yugoslavia.[64] A massive computer database had been established in the US. In its report to the UN Secretary-General, the Commission had recommended the establishment of an *ad hoc* tribunal.

The foundational document of the ICTY was a thirty-five-page report submitted to the SC by the Secretary-General.[65] That report was prepared at the request of SC and was unanimously adopted by it.[66] The Secretary-General presented the report on a pretty much take it or leave it basis. No options were presented. Although a number of members of the SC would have liked to propose changes, they did not do so for fear that this would engage a process of negotiation and unravelling of the report. The report asserted that the SC would not be legislating. The ICTY would only apply existing law. The legal basis for the ICTY was Chapter VII of the UN Charter, which deals with threats to the peace, breaches of the peace, and acts of aggression. Decisions under Chapter VII are legally binding on members of the UN. According to SC Resolution 827, the aims were to put an end to the crimes being committed, to bring to justice those responsible for them, and to contribute to the restoration and maintenance of peace.

The eleven judges of the ICTY, drawn from legal systems across the world, were elected by the General Assembly in September 1993 and took office on 17 November 1993.[67] The ICTY has been composed of experts in criminal law, human rights, and civil liberties protection, and has included senior judicial officers. Initially the ICTY faced financial and practical constraints. It took eighteen months to appoint the first Prosecutor. Additional courtrooms have had to be built. Additional judges have been appointed. A pool of twenty-seven *ad litem* judges was being established in 2001 to assist the ICTY to reduce the backlog.[68] The ICTY adopted a very pro-active and dynamic approach to its work. It was given the very important power to adopt its own rules of procedure and evidence[69] and took a substantial number of other practical steps. The first indictments were made public on 8 November 1994.

In Nuremberg and Tokyo the principal leaders and organisers were put on trial.[70] This has not yet occurred with the ICTY. There have been fourteen official convictions, two documented confessions, and two acquittals issued by the Tribunal. Of those detained at any time (forty-five in total), twenty-seven suspects have been of Serbian or Bosnian Serb background, fourteen of Croatian or Bosnian Croat background, three of Muslim or Bosnian backgrounds, and one of Macedonian background who also held Croatian citizenship. As of October 2002 forty-four of the suspects are in custody in the Tribunal's jail facility near The Hague, sixteen have been transferred or released. Eleven have been provisionally released. Major political and military leaders have been indicted but remain at large. However, the level of those tried has risen. In January 2001 Biljana Plavsic, former deputy to Radovan Karadzic and former President of the Bosnian Serb Republic, surrendered herself to the ICTY. She is the first woman to be indicted by the ICTY. The Milosevic trial began in 2001.

The establishment of the ICTY was a unique venture for the international community. There were partial precedents from the Nuremberg and Tokyo Tribunals. However, these 'were created in very different circumstances and were based on moral and juridical principles of a fundamentally different nature'.[71] The ICTY was not an organ of the victorious state, but an organ of the international community. The ICTY and the comparable Tribunal for Rwanda are technically subsidiary organisations of the Security Council,[72] but they are operationally independent.[73] Much was therefore done to avoid the impression of a partial judgement by the victors of a conflict. This was particularly evident when the ICTY Prosecutor considered whether to bring prosecutions in response to the NATO bombings of Kosovo in 1999.[74] It may be stating the obvious but it was, of course, of fundamental importance that Nuremberg and Tokyo had actually taken place. Any arguments that new law was being created were of much lesser weight after these tribunals.[75]

The most general critique aimed at the ICTY (and the International Criminal Tribunal for Rwanda) is an indirect one. This is that the international community only established it to salve its conscience for its failure to act to stop the 'ethnic cleansing' which had taken place.[76] There is no international criminal offence of ethnic cleansing, nor indeed any national law with a specific offence of this title. The concept of 'ethnic' groups is more familiar to the law relating to international minority rights and international group rights.[77] The concept of genocide was also well known.[78] The primary response to the term 'ethnic cleansing' was not so much one of legal reflection but rather that it harked back to the atrocities committed by Nazi Germany in the Second World War. The systematic destruction of the Jewish population in Germany and in territories occupied by Germany was literally explained as an attempt to cleanse those territories of that ethnic group. It was the spectre that similar practices were occurring in the former Yugoslavia that so shocked the conscience of Europe and the world and was encapsulated in the expression 'ethnic cleansing'.[79]

Principal legal features The place of the ICTY in international law and its general operation have been the subject of extensive investigation and analysis by international law scholars.[80] The most notable legal features of the process include the limitations on jurisdiction, the provisions for fair trials, and the punishments available.

There is concurrent jurisdiction between the ICTY and the domestic courts of the former Yugoslavia (that is, they can both exercise jurisdiction).[81] However, Article 9(2) of the ICTY Statute provides that the ICTY has primacy over national courts. Primacy can include retrial by the ICTY if the trial in the national court was for an ordinary crime, or if the national proceedings were not impartial or independent because they were designed to shield the accused from the ICTY, or if the case was not diligently prosecuted.[82] At any stage, the ICTY may formally request national courts to defer to its competence, and it has done so on a number of occasions.

The jurisdiction of the ICTY is, however, limited in several ways. The ICTY only has competence over natural persons.[83] Following the suggestion of the Secretary-General, the SC did not give it competence over legal persons or on the basis of membership of organizations. The focus is on individual responsibility, including command responsibility,[84] rather than vicarious or imputed liability. Therefore, organisations, legal persons, and states cannot be brought to trial. Jurisdiction is also limited to conduct since 1 January 1991. This was chosen as a neutral date in terms of whether the conflict(s) were international or not. There is no end date. Termination of the ICTY is not provided for in Resolution 827. According to the report of the Secretary-General, termination is linked to the restoration and maintenance of international peace and security in the territory of the former Yugoslavia, and SC decisions related thereto.[85] This could prove to be problematic if the SC were to intervene to terminate politically inopportune prosecutions. As of October 2002, the Prosecutor was continuing to seek indictments.[86] Jurisdiction is also limited to the territory of the former Yugoslavia. It thus clearly covered the conflict in Kosovo in 1999.[87]

In terms of substantive jurisdiction,[88] the ICTY is concerned with grave breaches of the Geneva Conventions, violations of the law and customs of war, genocide, and crimes against humanity.[89] The article on crimes against humanity is derived from Article 6 of the London Charter but adds express reference to rape[90] and torture. The Secretary-General stressed that the need to apply the principle of *nullem crimen sine lege* meant that the Statute had to be cautious and require the ICTY to apply rules that were beyond any doubt part of customary international law. However, a particular problem is that while the offences themselves may be undoubted, their constituent elements for criminal law purposes are not necessarily specified. The Statute does not expressly refer to common Article 3 of the Geneva Conventions of 1949, which would apply in a non-international armed conflict. However, the reference to 'violations of the laws or customs of war' in Article 3 of the Statute covers common Article 3.[91] Genocide and crimes against humanity are difficult to prosecute. The mental element (*mens rea*) for genocide requires a specific intent, which can be hard to prove.[92] It has been prosecuted at the ICTY but as of October 2002 there had been only one conviction (*Prosecutor* v. *Krstic*).[93]

Under Article 20 of its Statute, the ICTY's trial chambers are to ensure that a trial is fair and expeditious and that proceedings are conducted in accordance with the rules of procedure and evidence, with full respect for the rights of the accused and due regard for the protection of victims and witnesses.[94] The fair trial safeguards are very extensive and draw very heavily on Article 14 of the International Covenant on Civil and Political Rights (1966).[95] The accused must be present and may be questioned only as a witness in his own defence. The accused is entitled to the presumption of innocence, and guilt must be proved beyond reasonable doubt. In practice, the proceedings before the ICTY have been more adversarial than inquisitorial.[96]

Trial *in absentia* is not possible. Accused persons are held in a specially created detention unit that is housed within a Dutch prison. This is subject to the exclusive control and supervision of the UN. They are entitled to seek bail, which can be granted in exceptional circumstances. The individual facilities are provided so as not to force different ethnic groupings together. Prison sentences are served outside Yugoslavia.

There is no possibility of imposing the death penalty.[97] This reflects the principled objection of many states around the world to that form of punishment. In determining the terms of imprisonment, recourse is to be had to the general practice regarding prison sentences in the courts of the former Yugoslavia.[98] The longest sentence imposed has been forty-five years, in *Prosecutor* v. *Tihomir Blaskic* (2000).

Problems of implementation While many important legal powers and limitations were set out in the Statute, implementing those provisions, or interpreting the Tribunal's power in situations where the Statute was silent, proved a challenge for the ICTY. A particular difficulty in terms of dealing with the systematic practice of ethnic cleansing was whether the ICTY could punish those who organised and instigated the policy in addition to the particular individuals who carried it out. The argument was that, 'the Tribunal will never be able to bring to justice those in command: plainly, reference is made here to those responsible for planning or ordering large-scale breaches of international humanitarian law occurring in the Former Yugoslavia, or for omitting to prevent or punish the perpetrators of such breaches.'[99] The ICTY rejected this argument.

> This objection assumes that the Tribunal will be unable to bring to trial all those who, under its statute, may be charged with war crimes or crimes against humanity. That is an entirely wrong assumption: the Tribunal will proceed against any person, regardless of status and rank, against whom the Prosecutor has issued an indictment confirmed by a Judge of the Tribunal.[100]

Nevertheless, bringing these persons to trial is difficult. Although the ICTY may issue proceeding against the leaders or organisers of those who committed large-scale breaches, if the ICTY's orders or any action taken by the SC does not secure their presence, then the individuals cannot be tried because the Statute does not permit trial *in absentia*. This has happened in relation to a number of major political and military figures including Karadzic and Ratko Mladic.

The only possibility is for the ICTY to hold 'Rule 61' hearings. Rule 61 applies when a suspect remains at large a reasonable time after an arrest warrant is issued, and the judge who issued the indictment is satisfied that the Prosecutor and the Registrar have taken all reasonable steps to bring about the arrest. In these cases a panel of three judges, including the indictment judge, can hold a hearing in which the Prosecutor's office can present all of its evidence, including witnesses. After the hearing, the panel states whether there are reasonable grounds for believing that the accused committed all or part of the crimes charged in the indictment. If there are reasonable grounds, the panel will issue an international arrest warrant. At the prosecutor's request or of its own initiative, the panel can also order a state or states to adopt provisional measures to freeze the assets of the accused. The panel may also make a determination that a state has failed to co-operate with the Tribunal with regard to the accused in certain ways required by Article 29 of the Tribunal's Statute. The President of the ICTY can bring that matter to the SC.

Rule 61 hearings allow for further pre-trial enforcement efforts and serve a documentary function. They afford a means of redress for the victims of the alleged crimes committed by the absent accused, and give them an opportunity to testify in public and to have their testimony recorded for posterity. If an international arrest warrant is issued, the suspect becomes an international fugitive. The ICTY President has stressed that what was of particular importance to the victims or relatives of victims of rape, ethnic cleansing, torture, genocide, or wanton destruction of property was the punishment of the authors of those acts by an impartial tribunal. That, it was asserted, was at least in part a means of alleviating their suffering and anguish.[101] There have been five Rule 61 hearings involving eight indictees: Dragan Nikolic, Milan Martic, Milan Mrksic, Miroslav Radic, Ivica Rajic, Karadzic, Mladic and Veselin Sljivancanin.

One of the remarkable features of the conflict in the former Yugoslavia is the amount of official and non-official documentation available. It is probably the best-recorded crisis in the course of human history. Notwithstanding this, the trials before the ICTY have primarily been based on oral testimony. The uniqueness of the ICTY's task and the limited scope of the express provisions of its Statute left the ICTY with a substantial amount of discretion in approaching a variety of issues ranging from matters of evidence, procedure, administration, and organisation. The ICTY approached these with a commendable degree of sensitivity and intelligence particularly in dealing with the phenomenon of 'ethnic cleansing'. The ICTY has 'attempted to strike a balance between the strictly constructionist and the teleological approaches in the interpretation of the Statute'.[102] This balance is principally reflected in its rules of procedure and evidence. This is how the ICTY described its 'purpose-made set of rules'.

> As an ad-hoc institution, the Tribunal has been able to mould its uses and procedures to fit the task in hand. The Tribunal is charged with sole responsibility for judging the alleged perpetrators of some of the most reprehensible crimes known to man, committed not on some foreign battlefield but on their own home ground, acts of terror and barbarism committed against their own neighbours. The tribunal therefore decided, when preparing its rules, to take into account the most conspicuous aspects of the armed conflict in the former Yugoslavia. First among these is the fact that, in the former Yugoslavia, it is not simply a matter of wars between the armies of two belligerent States or even between a single disciplined force with clear command structure and a civilian population. Instead, there are a number of parties involved in the conflict, ranging from the regular armies of States to military and paramilitary groups, with conspicuous uncertainty about who is in control of the latter. Secondly, an internecine strife is under way, aggravated by ethnic and religious conflict, genocide, mass rape and other manifestations of large scale and widespread breaches of human rights. Ethnic hatred springs afresh to turn friend into foe and places the claims of ancient blood above those of common humanity and decency. Thirdly, the unbearable abuses perpetuated in the region have spread terror and deep anguish among the civilian population. It follows that witnesses of massacres and atrocities may be deterred from testifying about those crimes or else be profoundly worried about the possible negative consequences that their testimony could have for themselves or for their relatives. In drafting the rules of procedure and evidence, the judges of the Tribunal have endeavoured to incorporate rules that address issues of particular concern arising from those

aspects of the conflict, namely patterns of conduct, the protection of witnesses and sexual assault.

The rules of evidence thus adopted made provision for the admissibility of evidence relating to 'patterns of conduct'. Such evidence was considered to be particularly relevant in establishing coercion sufficient to vitiate any alleged consent in matters of sexual assault, and in establishing one of the basic requirements of genocide, namely 'the intent to destroy, in whole of in part, a group'. When the intent had not been expressly and specifically manifested, one of the means of ascertaining its existence could lie in investigating the consistent behaviour of groups or units, so as to determine whether that intent could be inferred from their 'pattern of conduct'.

A number of rules were concerned with the protection of witnesses, given an expected reluctance to appear before the Tribunal to testify. The principal witness against the perpetrator of a crime would often be the victim, who could feel threatened, either directly or indirectly, and who might still have family within an area held by forces sympathetic to an accused. To enable witnesses to testify freely provision was made for the submission of evidence by deposition. These could be made locally and taken by means of video-conference, if appropriate. In order to protect the 'equality of arms' (and, in particular, the rights of the accused), the procedure for taking depositions allowed for cross-examination of the witness. Arrangements have been made for the identity of witnesses who may be at risk not to be disclosed to the accused until such time as the witness can be brought under the protection of the ICTY. Witnesses may also be protected from public identification, if appropriate.

An important and innovative provision for the protection of witnesses was the establishment of a Victims and Witnesses Section within the Registry.[103] This was created to provide counselling, not only on legal rights but also to give psychological help and support, and to recommend protective measures, where required. The section has mainly dealt with female victims of rape and sexual assault. Its programmes cover over 300 witnesses or related persons from over twenty different countries.

As part of the special emphasis on crimes against women in the rules of procedure there are special provisions as to the standard of evidence, and matters of credibility of the witness, which may be raised by the defence. In particular, no corroboration of the victim's testimony is required in matters of sexual assault. The victim's previous sexual conduct is irrelevant and inadmissible. If a defence of consent is raised, the Tribunal may take note of factors that vitiate consent, including physical violence, and moral or psychological constraints. The rules are clearly gender-friendly.[104] Where trial before the ICTY is not possible because there are real practical or psychological difficulties in getting women to testify, an alternative recourse is to some form of Truth and Reconciliation Commission which would at least seek to achieve some record and atonement of the wrongs done.[105] The idea is being considered but has not proved politically acceptable to date.[106]

The ICTY has followed the pattern of the Nuremberg and Tokyo trials in that there are no technical rules for the admissibility of evidence. It did not wish to shackle itself to restrictive rules. The judges are thus responsible for weighing the probative value of the evidence before them. This is a common approach in international law. On this basis all relevant evidence maybe admitted to the ICTY unless its probative value is substantially outweighed by the need to ensure a fair trial, or where the evidence was obtained by a serious violation of human rights. Evidence could thus be excluded where it was obtained, for example, by torture, or inhumane or degrading treatment or punishment. An interesting addition is that the ICTY may order the production of additional or new evidence of its own motion. This is not normally the case in adversarial proceedings. The ICTY explained this by stating that 'it was felt that, in the international sphere, the interest of justice is best served by such a provision and that the diminution, if any, of the parties' rights is minimal by comparison'.[107] Finally, there are no rules on the granting of immunity or on plea-bargaining. Substantial co-operation by an accused, however, can be taken into account by the Chambers as a mitigating factor in sentencing as well as by the President for the purpose of granting pardon or commutation of sentence.

The ICTY has adopted a largely adversarial approach, but there are elements more familiar to inquisitorial systems. There is no investigating judge to collect the evidence. As in a common law regime, this task falls to the Prosecutor. After confirmation of the indictment by a judge, the defence is entitled to collect and to have access to all relevant evidence. Both the prosecution and the defence are reciprocally bound to disclose all documents and witnesses. In *Prosecutor* v. *Furundzia* (1998) the Prosecutor had failed to disclose that witness A had had psychological counselling. The trial chamber subsequently found that A's memory had not been affected by any psychological disorder she may have had. Individuals, organisations, or governments may, by leave, present written or oral submissions as *amici curiae*, and a number of such briefs have been submitted. This is unusual in a common law adversarial context of a prosecutor against the defence without any third party intervention. It is more common in continental systems of law. The third parties must be seen as representing the wider interests of victims or the values of elements of the international community.

Co-operation with the ICTY In accordance with SC Resolution 827 (1993) 'all states shall cooperate fully' with the ICTY and its organs, and shall take any measures necessary under their domestic law to implement the provisions 'and to comply with requests for assistance or orders issued by a trial chamber'.[108] States are thus under a binding legal obligation to co-operate with the ICTY in terms, for example, of arrest, search, surrender, or transfer of persons to the ICTY. Some states needed to enact implementing legislation to meet these requirements, while others claimed that they did not need to do so. Co-operation has generally been good, but there have been particular problems with the Federal Republic of Yugoslavia, Croatia, and Republika Srpska (the Serb part of Bosnia).[109]

Obligations on states stemming from the Statute 'shall prevail over any legal impediment to the surrender or transfer of the accused to the Tribunal' that may exist under national legal systems. A common national obstacle is that some constitutions or national laws prevent the extradition of nationals. This principle is in conformity with international law given the large number of states who follow the practice. In the *Lockerbie Case*, the International Court of Justice ruled that the obligation under Article 103 of the UN Charter that 'In the event of a conflict between the obligations of the Members of the United Nations under, the present Charter and their obligations under any other international agreement, the obligations under the present Charter shall prevail' overrode any rights of Libya under the Montreal Convention on aircraft highjacking.[110] Presumably, given that SC Resolution 827 (1993) was a binding decision adopted under Chapter VII, then the same argument would apply. The ICTY president explained that

> a few countries have laid down an *ad hoc* procedure, while others planned to apply *mutatis mutandis* their national provisions relating to extradition, though only as regards questions of procedure and without making the transfer of the accused to the ICTY subject to the same restrictions that apply to extradition (e.g. non-extradition of nationals or of persons accused of political crimes). In certain countries, provision has been made for appeals against or review of decisions of national courts on the ICTY's request for transfer.[111]

As suggested, though, this could raise some difficult issues of national law. In terms of methods of transfer to the ICTY, seven persons have been arrested by national police, fourteen have voluntarily surrendered, and twenty have been detained by international forces.

The other main area of domestic co-operation has been financial. In addition to UN funding, the ICTY has been supported by substantial financial contributions from individual states ($17.5 million). The largest voluntary contributor has been the UK (over $3 million). It contributed very substantial financing for the building of a second courtroom.

Legality and legitimacy Three of the principal issues of legality and legitimacy of the ICTY were raised in the *Tadic Case*.[112] First, Tadic argued that the Tribunal had not been lawfully established. The drafters of the UN Charter had not envisaged such a tribunal, the General Assembly had not been involved in its creation, the Council had not consistently created tribunals in other instances, the Council could not act in relation to individuals, there was no real threat to the peace, the Tribunal would not promote peace, and a political body could not create a judicial organ.[113] Secondly, the primacy over national courts which the SC resolution gave to the Tribunal was unlawful and violated the national sovereignty of the states affected. Thirdly, the Tribunal lacked subject matter jurisdiction in respect of the charges against the defendant.[114] The trial chamber and the appellate chamber rejected these arguments but differed in their legal arguments for doing so.[115] The most interesting part of the legal analysis was that the appellate chamber accepted that it had jurisdiction to determine whether it had been lawfully established (*la competence de la competence*). In principle, at least, this raised the possibility that the tribunal could have decided that it had been unlawfully established. It is difficult to determine the legal consequences in such a situation for the Tribunal, the judges, the Prosecutor and, not least, the defendants and indictees.[116] The political consequences for the SC's strategy would presumably have been devastating. Fortunately, the appellate chamber decided that the establishment of the ICTY was within the SC's powers under Article 41 of the Charter, and that the ICTY had been lawfully established. It took a broad, but not unlimited, view of the powers of the SC. It considered that the Tribunal had been 'established by law'.[117] All of Tadic's other arguments were also rejected.[118]

The ICTY has faced challenges to its credibility and effectiveness. Its progress has been painfully slow. Trials have been long and complicated involving substantial numbers of witnesses (over a hundred in a number of cases) and huge amounts of documentation. The longest trial to date was 223 days (*Blaskic*). The 2002–3 budget totals $223 million. As of May 2002, there were 1,248 staff members from eighty-two countries. The cost per person tried has been astronomical. Over one hundred individuals have been indicted. Fifty-five accused are in proceedings before the Tribunal; eleven have been provisionally released. Twenty-one indictees remain at large, including the two major figures.

The former President of the ICTY has examined the ICTY's development on three levels.[119] First, from an operational point of view, trial and appellate proceedings are regularly held, and decisions on 'both procedural and substantive matters are on the cutting edge of the development of international humanitarian law'.[120] For example, the decision in the *Tadic* appeal has had a worldwide impact on practice and doctrine. The ICTY has also developed an extensive jurisprudence on the narrower technical 'lawyers law'.[121] This includes the power and effect of ICTY decisions on individuals and on states,[122] command responsibility,[123] whether violations of the law of internal armed conflict can lead to criminal responsibility,[124] whether crimes against humanity require a connection with an international armed conflict,[125] abduction, whether rape could constitute torture,[126] and whether there is a distinction between the seriousness of a crime against humanity and that of a war crime.[127] Secondly, its experience has laid down the foundations for the establishment of a practical and permanent system of international justice. Without the ICTY there would probably have been no international tribunal in Rwanda. Without the two *ad hoc* tribunals there would almost certainly be no international criminal court. Thirdly, it is slowly beginning to have an impact on the former Yugoslavia. The ICTY's legitimacy has not been accepted by the Federal Republic of Yugoslavia, but co-operation is improving. March 2001 saw the first official handover by Yugoslavia of a suspect to the ICTY. The ICTY has an extensive outreach programme to inform the population in the region about its work and its significance.

Finally, in terms of a wider international law, it is of significance that the SC characterised violations of international humanitarian law as threats to international peace and security and therefore opened the door to collective action.

The International Criminal Tribunal for Rwanda (ICTR)[128]

The ICTR was established by the SC in 1994,[129] again after a report by a Commission of Experts.[130] Its establishment was in response to the massive number of killings and atrocities committed in Rwanda in 1994.[131] The perpetrators were mainly from the Hutu ethnic group, and the victims were mainly from the Tutsi ethnic group but also included pro-Tutsi Hutus. Interestingly, although the ICTR Statute was modelled on that of the ICTY, it was not drafted by the SC. Rather it was drafted by the US and New Zealand governments with some input from the government of Rwanda. As with the ICTY the argument is made that the establishment of the ICTR was partly due to embarrassment at the failure of the international community to intervene to stop the atrocities.[132]

The ICTR has fourteen judges, five of whom are assigned to the appeal chamber but are based at the seat of the Tribunal in Arusha, Tanzania. It shares the appellate judges and the Prosecutor with the ICTY. The argument for this sharing of personnel was that it was useful to try to develop a body of specialised expertise. In practical terms the effect of the arrangement was to render administration and the role of Deputy Prosecutors crucial, one based at each Tribunal. The investigatory and prosecutorial units of the ICTR are in Kigali, the capital of Rwanda, and the trial chambers sit in Arusha. For 2002–3, the ICTR's budget is $177 million and there are 810 staff representing over eighty nationalities.

With regard to jurisdiction, trial provisions, and punishment, the ICTR is similar, but not identical, to the ICTY. For example, as with the ICTY, the ICTR has concurrent but primary jurisdiction.[133] The jurisdiction of the ICTR is also restricted to natural persons. In terms of location, the Tribunal's authority is limited to crimes committed in the territory of the Rwanda or in the territory of neighbouring states in respect of serious violations of international humanitarian law committed by Rwandan citizens.[134] The Tribunal can only try crimes committed between 1 January 1994 and 31 December 1994. The principal effect of the limitation could be that offences of planning, preparation, or of aiding or abetting offences under Articles 2 to 4 of the Statute could be excluded.[135] If substantive offences occurred during 1994 then the prior planning would be within the ICTR's temporal jurisdiction. Presumably, the ICTR will terminate its operations when there are no outstanding investigations related to its temporal jurisdiction.

The subject-matter jurisdiction of the ICTR is different from that of the ICTY because the conflict was essentially a non-international one. The offences covered are genocide, crimes against humanity, and violations of common Article 3 of the 1949 Geneva Conventions and of Additional Protocol II (1977) to those Conventions.[136] Incitement to genocide appears as a freestanding offence which is not linked to the actual occurrence of subsequent acts of genocide.[137] The SC rejected Rwanda's view that jurisdiction should be confined to genocide. This avoided the appearance that the Tribunal would only be used against opponents of the government. In practice, no cases at the ICTR have involved members of the ruling government (Rwandan Patriotic Front).

The testimony of witnesses has been the principal form of evidence before the ICTR. More than 230 prosecution and defence witnesses from various African, European, and American countries have testified before the Tribunal. Like the ICTY, the ICTR has a Witnesses and Victims Support Section. It receives considerable assistance from non-governmental organisations.

The Statutes of both the ICTY and the ICTR prohibit the imposition of the death penalty.[138] ICTR sentences can be served in Rwanda if human rights standards for imprisonment are met. The tribunal maintains supervision over the sentence while it is being served.

The ICTR has indicted political, military, and media leaders, as well as senior governmental administrators. The ICTR rendered the first convictions by an international tribunal for genocide (*Prosecutor* v. *Akayesu*). In *Prosecutor* v. *Bayagwiza* the trial chamber in 1998 denied a motion to nullify Bayagwiza's arrest and detention. The appeal chamber in 1999 directed his release and dismissed the indictment against him with prejudice to the Prosecutor. That decision was heavily criticised. In 2000 the appeal chamber reviewed its decision ordering release and ordered a continuation of the proceedings. It reasoned that it had misunderstood the factual basis of the case. Bayagwiza has appealed. Over forty individuals accused of involvement in the 1994 genocide in Rwanda have been arrested. At present over fifty detainees are held at the ICTR's detention facility. June 2001 saw the first acquittal by the ICTR (Iganace Bagilishema).

Co-operation between the ICTR and states has generally been very good. The Tribunal's relationship with the government of Rwanda, however, has been somewhat problematic. Interestingly, the request for the ICTR's establishment came from the new Tutsi government of Rwanda, though the government then proceeded to disagree with a number of aspects, including the temporal limitation on jurisdiction. Eventually it was the only member of the SC to vote against its establishment.[139] Despite its vote, the government expressed the intention to support the ICTR and to co-operate with it.

Rwanda introduced a specific law to deal with national prosecutions for genocide. It came into force on 1 September 1996. This was in a context where the effective functioning of the Rwandese national judicial system had ceased. The law grouped the offences into four categories of seriousness and fixed penalties for each category with the possibility of substantial reductions for guilty pleas at various stages. The pleas had to be accompanied by an accurate and complete confession, disclosure of accomplices, and an apology. This serves a number of purposes in terms of establishing an accurate historical record.[140] An apology serves as part of the process of national reconciliation. In Rwanda only an offender charged with the most serious offences (Category One) of being one of the leaders and organisers of genocide and the perpetrators of particularly heinous murders or sexual torture could be subject to the death penalty. The national proceedings in Rwanda have raised major human rights concerns in terms of conditions of imprisonment and the possibility of fair trials. In 1995, the main prison in Kigali, designed for 750 persons, was holding 6,400. As of July 2001, 120,000 persons were in detention. Detention is based solely on denunciation. Western states have provided substantial financial assistance to Rwanda to fund national prosecutions. The Rwandan government objected to the absence of the death penalty under the ICTR because under the Rwandan Penal Code there was provision for the death penalty.[141] Their argument that those tried by the ICTR would face lesser penalties than those tried under Rwandan law has been borne out. In 1998, Rwanda held a public execution of twenty individuals found guilty of genocide.[142]

The legality of the establishment of the ICTR was challenged in *Prosecutor* v. *Kanyabashi (Jurisdiction)*.[143] The challenge was rejected with the ICTR ruling that the determination of a threat to peace was within the discretion of the SC, and that the creation of the ICTR was within the SC's powers under Article 41 of the Charter.

The work of the ICTR could have been allocated to the ICTY, but there were some fears that the situation in Rwanda would then be getting a second-class treatment. Nonetheless, the perception of the ICTR has always been that of the poor relation to the ICTY. It faced severe financial limitations and was blighted by maladministration and inefficiency. More specifically, the number of translators has been inadequate, and Rwanda has criticised the absence of the death penalty and the lack of a separate Prosecutor or Appeal Chamber. That judgements have not been translated into local languages has made it difficult for the work of the ICTR to appear relevant to the situation in Rwanda.

IV The Permanent International Criminal Court (ICC)

The idea of a permanent international criminal court has been discussed since at least the 1920s.[144] It had been on the UN's agenda almost since its inception but little progress was made. However, events in Yugoslavia and Rwanda transformed political thinking and, with the end of the Cold War, progress was astonishingly quick.[145] Agreement on a permanent international criminal court was reached in the Rome Statute in 1998.[146] The Statute has been signed by 139 states. It required ratification by sixty states before it came into force in July 2002. Although Germany had suggested Nuremburg as the location for an ICC, it is located in The Hague.

It is helpful in comparative terms to outline the principal features of the ICC which are central to its legality and legitimacy:[147] First of all, it is a permanent court. It has a relationship agreement with the UN but it is not a UN body. Under the Statute, the SC has power to refer situations to the ICC, and it also has the power to suspend investigations or proceedings at the ICC.[148] The jurisdiction of the court is based on a treaty, and reservations to the treaty are not permitted. There is, however, a limited possibility for a state to opt out of the court's jurisdiction in respect of war crimes for a period of seven years.[149] The conditions for the exercise of jurisdiction are based on the exercise of nationality jurisdiction or territorial jurisdiction. The ICC is based on the principle of 'complementarity'. It is only supposed to exercise jurisdiction when national courts are unable or unwilling to do so.

The ICC only has jurisdiction over natural persons. The crimes within its jurisdiction are genocide, crimes against humanity, war crimes, and aggression. Exercise of jurisdiction over aggression is dependent on agreement on a definition of the offence. No agreement has been reached as of October 2002. Agreement has, however, been reached by states on the 'Elements of Crimes'.[150] These are to be submitted to the judges of the ICC. Agreement has also been reached by states on Rules of Procedure and Evidence.[151] Extensive consideration of gender issues and the interests of victims are reflected in the Statute, the Elements of Crimes, and the Rules of Procedure and Evidence.

V Conclusions

Nuremberg has ensured that the Holocaust remains 'the' defining event of the twentieth century.[152] In a small number of countries it is a criminal offence to deny the Holocaust or the Nuremberg judgement.[153] With hindsight, Nuremberg and Tokyo have become precedents in the increasing criminalisation of international law.[154] This has taken place alongside the growth of the human rights movement and a decline of concepts of absolute sovereignty. There has been a move away from immunity and from amnesties for gross human rights violations. This is also reflected in transnational criminal prosecutions, such as in the *Pinochet* case,[155] and in civil claims. The ICC will not operate retrospectively, and there may still be *ad hoc* international or mixed national/international tribunals in the interim, such as for Cambodia and for Sierra Leone.[156] In principle, the ICC should spur national prosecutions so as to avoid ICC jurisdiction. The statute of the ICC, the Elements of Crimes, and its detailed rules of Procedure and Evidence go a long way towards satisfying standards of certainty and accessibility in the law. Its normative standards are already being cited by national and international tribunals. It is submitted in conclusion that war crimes trials before international tribunals have moved closer and closer towards satisfying purer norms of legality and legitimacy.

Notes

I am grateful to Catherine Le Mageuresse, David Turns, and Christine Byron for their comments on a draft of this chapter. Responsibility for the views expressed is mine alone.

1 See T. Franck, *The Power of Legitimacy Among Nations* (New York: Oxford University Press, 1990).

2 Some post-modern legal analysis has focused on the function of trials as 'storytelling'.

3 See J. J. Paust *et al.* (eds), *International Criminal Law – Cases and Materials* (Durham: Carolina Academic Press, 1996); C. Greenwood, 'Historical development and legal basis', in D. Fleck (ed.), *The Handbook of Humanitarian Law in Armed Conflicts* (Oxford: Oxford University Press, 1999), pp. 1–38; J. Barboza, 'International criminal law', *Receuil Des Cours – Collected Courses of the Hague Academy of International Law*, 278 (1999), 9–200.

4 See B. Simma, 'From bilateralism to community interest in international law', 250 *Receuil Des Cours – Collected Courses of the Hague Academy of International Law*, 250 (1994-IV), 217–384.

5 See T. L. H. McCormack and G. J. Simpson (eds), *The Law of War Crimes - National and International Approaches* (The Hague: Kluwer, 1997); Paust *et al.* (eds), *International Criminal Law*, pp. 707–857; H. McCoubrey, 'War crimes jurisdiction and a permanent international criminal court: advantages and difficulties', *Journal of Armed Conflict Law*, 3 (1998), 19–26.

6 Each of the Geneva Conventions of 1949 specifies what are grave breaches, as does Protocol I of 1977. See R. Wolfrum, 'Enforcement of humanitarian law', in Fleck (ed.), *The Handbook of Humanitarian Law*, pp. 517–50 at pp. 530–40; L. C. Green, *The Contemporary Law of Armed Conflict*, 2nd edn (Manchester: Manchester University Press, 2000), pp. 286–316. There is no acceptance yet of a general duty to prosecute for any war crime.

7 *Attorney-General of the Government of Israel* v *Eichmann* (1961) 36 I.L.R. 5. See P. Papadatos, *The Eichmann Trial* (London: Stevens, 1964); G. Bach, 'The trial of Adolf Eichmann', *Judicial Studies Board Journal* (1997), 15–17; J. N. Wenig, 'Enforcing the lessons of history: Israel judges the Holocaust', in McCormack and Simpson (eds), *The Law of War Crimes*, pp. 103–22 (this essay also discusses the *Damjanjuk Case* (1985) 79 I.L.R. 535.

8 The Jerusalem District Court found that the jurisdiction to try crimes under international law was universal.

9 See F. M. Buscher, *The U.S. War Crimes Trial Programme in Germany 1945–55* (New York: Greenwood, 1989).

10 See A. P. V. Rogers, 'War crimes trials under the royal warrant: British practice 1945–1949', *International and Comparative Law Quarterly*, 39 (1990), 780–800.

11 See J. Appleman, *Military Tribunals and International Crimes* (Indianapolis: Bobbs-Merrill, 1954).

12 See G. Triggs, 'Australia's war crimes trials: all pity choked', in McCormack and Simpson (eds), *The Law of War Crimes*, pp. 123–49.

13 See S. A. Williams, 'Laudable principles lacking application: the prosecution of war criminals in Canada', in McCormack and Simpson (eds), *The Law of War Crimes*, pp. 151–70.

14 See A. Marschik, 'The politics of persecution: European national approaches to war crimes', in McCormack and Simpson (eds), *The Law of War Crimes*, pp. 65–101; L. S. Wexler, 'The interpretation of the Nuremberg principles by the French court of cassation: from Touvier to Barbie and back again', *Columbia Journal of Transnational Law*, 32 (1994), 289–380.

15 See *R* v. *Sawoniuk (Anthony)*, [2000] *Criminal Law Review* 506. The investigations unit under the act has been wound up. The passage of the act was itself controversial.

16 National war crimes trials will have similar though usually more limited purposes.

17 Debate has continued on the role of the German people in Nazism. See D. Goldhagen, *Hitler's Willing Executioners – Ordinary Germans and the Holocaust* (London: Little, Brown, 1996); M. Minow, *Between Vengeance and Forgiveness: Facing History After Genocide and Mass Atrocity* (Boston: Beacon Press, 1999).

18 See S. R. Ratner and J. S. Abrams, *Accountability for Human Rights Atrocities in International Law* (Oxford: Oxford University Press, 1997).

19 'When education and understanding have spread through the family of nations there may be no need for international law'. G. Lawrence, Lord Oaksey, 'The Nuremberg trials and the progress of international law' (Birmingham: Holdsworth Club, 1947) p. 16.

20 See C. Bassiouni and C. Blakesley, 'The need for an international criminal court in the new world order', *Vandenberg Journal of Transnational Law*, 25 (1992), 151–82.

21 See A. D'Amato 'Peace vs accountability in Bosnia', *American Journal of International Law*, 88 (1994), 500–6; A. J. Colson, 'The logic of peace and the logic of justice', *International Relations*, 15: 1 (2000), 51–62; Symposium: 'State reconstruction after civil conflict', *American Journal of International Law*, 95 (2001), 1–119.

22 See G. Schwarzenberger, *International Law as Applied by International Courts and Tribunals, vol. 2: Armed Conflict* (London: Stevens, 1968), pp. 462–6. Hagenbach was convicted and beheaded.

23 The Netherlands was not a party to the Versailles Treaty. It further stated that the extradition would have violated Dutch law and its tradition of asylum.

24 R. Cryer, 'Towards an integrated regime for the prosecution of international crimes', (Ph.D. thesis, University of Nottingham, 2000), 315.

25 See B. F. Smith, *The American Road to Nuremberg – The Documentary Record 1944–45* (Stanford: Hoover Press, 1982); Smith, *The Road to Nuremberg* (New York: Basic, 1981); M. R. Marrus (compiler), *The Nuremberg War Crimes Trials, 1945–46: a Documentary History* (Boston: Bedford Books, 1997).

26 See E. Schwelb, 'The UN war crimes commission', *British Yearbook of International Law*, 23 (1946), 363–76.

27 Anglo-Soviet-American Communiqué from the Tripartite Conference in Moscow, 1 November 1943, *American Journal of International Law*, 38 (supplement, 1944), 3.
28 There were not show trials in the Stalinesque sense, see G. H. Hodos, *Show Trials: Stalinist Purges in Eastern Europe, 1948–1954* (New York: Praeger, 1987).
29 J. H. Morgan, *The Great Assize – an Examination of the Law of the Nuremberg Trials* (London: John Murray, 1948), 1. On the forensic aspects of the trial, see A. D. Gibb, *Perjury Unlimited* (Edinburgh: Green, 1954).
30 R. Ginsberg, *The Nuremberg Trial and International Law* (Dordrecht: Nijhoff, 1990); R. E. Conot, *Justice at Nuremberg* (London: Weidenfeld, 1983); A. Tusa and J. Tusa, *The Nuremberg Trial* (London: Macmillan, 1983); R. K. Woetzel, *The Nuremberg Trials in International Law* (London: Stevens, 1962); R. S. Clark, 'Nuremberg and Tokyo in contemporary perspective', in McCormack and Simpson (eds), *The Law of War Crimes*, pp. 171–87.
31 These include T. Taylor, *The Anatomy of the Nuremberg Trials* (New York: A. Knopf, 1992); B. F. Smith, *Reaching Judgment at Nuremberg* (London: Deutsch, 1977); D. A. Sprecher, *Inside the Nuremberg Trial: a Prosecutor's Comprehensive Account*, 2 vols, (Lanham, Md: Univ. Press of America, 1999).
32 See *Judgement of the International Military Tribunal for the Trial of German Major War Criminals*, 1946, (H.M.S.O., Cmd 6964); Proceedings, vols 1–23 (1946–51); H. Stimson, 'The Nuremberg trial: landmark in law', *Foreign Affairs*, 25 (1947), 179–89. The soviet judge dissented from parts of the Tribunal's legal analysis, the three acquittals, and the imposition of a life sentence rather than the death penalty for Rudolf Hess.
33 For the international agreement on establishing the Tribunal and the London Charter, see 82 United Nations Treaty Series, 279, 284.
34 In accordance with Article 5 of the charter.
35 See Paust *et al.* (eds), *International Criminal Law*, pp. 967–1080.
36 *Ibid.*, pp. 861–966.
37 For some broadly contemporary accounts see Oaksey, 'The Nuremberg trials' (supportive); Viscount Kilmuir, 'Nuremberg in retrospect' (Birmingham: Holdsworth Club, 1956, supportive); Morgan, *The Great Assize* (critical of references to international law rather than acts of *de facto* sovereigns and of the counts of conspiracy, aggressive war and crimes against humanity, and generally intemperate).
38 Judgement of the IMT, p. 223. A reverse argument is before the International Court of Justice (hereafter ICJ) in the case between Bosnia and Yugoslavia (Serbia and Montenegro). The latter has argued that genocide only bears individual criminal responsibility and not state responsibility. See *Case Concerning Application of the Convention on the Prevention*, I.C.J. Reports (1993), 3 and 325 (interim measures), I.C.J. Reports (1996), 595 (jurisdiction), I.C.J. Reports (1997) (counterclaim), I.C.J. Reports (2000) (request for revision).
39 See E. Schwelb, 'Crimes against humanity', *British Yearbook of International Law*, 23 (1946), 178–226.
40 See *Case of Ulrich Greifelt*, *Law Reports of Trials of War Criminals*, vol. 13, (London: H.M.S.O.), pp. 1–69.
41 Article 19 of London Charter.
42 See Tusa and Tusa, *The Nuremberg Trials*, pp. 487–8.
43 See J. Mendelson, 'Trial by document: the problem of due process for war criminals at Nuremberg', *Prologue*, 7 (1975), 227–34.

44 Article 27 of London Charter.
45 'The ambiguous legacies of Nuremberg linger at the margins of our unreliable moral memories; they inspire but also burden the conscience of our politics', D. Luban, 'The legacies of Nuremberg', *Social Research*, 54 (1987), 779–829 at 829. See also *S.W.* v. *UK*, (1995) 335-B ECHR, where it was held that judicial abolition of the common law marital rape exemption did not violate Article 7 of European Convention on Human Rights.
46 See General Assembly Resolution 95(I) (1946) and the International Law Commission's formulation of the Nuremberg Principles (1950).
47 See G. Robertson, *Crimes Against Humanity* (London: Penguin, 2000).
48 See D. Turns and C. Byron, 'The preparatory commission for the international criminal court', *International and Comparative Law Quarterly*, 50 (2001), 420–34.
49 H. Kelsen, 'Will the judgment at Nuremberg constitute a precedent?', *International and Comparative Law Quarterly*, 1 (1947), 153–71; G. Lawrence (President of the IMT), 'The Nuremberg trial', *International Affairs*, 23 (1947), 151–64; Q. Wright, 'The law of the Nuremberg trial', *American Journal of International Law*, 41 (1947), 38–72; G. Best, *Nuremberg and After: the Continuing History of War Crimes and Crimes Against Humanity* (Reading: University of Reading, 1984).
50 See C. Tomuschat, 'International criminal prosecution: the precedent of Nuremberg confirmed', in *Criminal Law Forum*, 5 (1994), 237–47. For an early call for permanent judicial machinery for enforcement of the Nuremberg law, see W. E. Jackson, 'Putting the Nuremberg law to work', *Foreign Affairs*, 25 (1947), 550–65.
51 See A. W. B. Simpson, *Human Rights and the End of Empire – Britain and the Genesis of the European Convention* (Oxford: Oxford University Press, 2001).
52 See Kilmuir, 'Nuremberg in retrospect'.
53 See S. L. Paulson, 'Classical legal positivism at Nuremberg', *Philosophy and Public Affairs*, 4 (Winter 1975), 132–58.
54 *Nuremberg Trial, Proceedings*, vol. 1, p. 49. See also *Report of Robert H. Jackson, U.S. Representative to the International Conference on Military Trials, London, 1945* (Washington, 1949).
55 B. F. Smith, *American Road*, p. xvi.
56 U.S. State Department, Publication No. 2675. See P. Lowe in this volume and the literature cited there; Lord Russell of Liverpool, *The Knights of Bushido: a Short History of Japanese War Crimes* (London, Cassell, 1958).
57 Two died and one became ill. Neither the Emperor nor any industrialists were indicted.
58 On rape and the use of comfort women by the Japanese, see D. Boling, 'Mass rape, enforced prostitution and the Japanese imperial army: Japan eschews international legal responsibility?' *Columbia Journal of Transnational Law*, 32 (1995), 533–90.
59 See S. Horwitz, 'The Tokyo trial', *International Conciliation* (November, 1950), 473–584.
60 See E. Kopelman, 'Ideology and international law: the dissent of the Indian justice at the Tokyo war crimes tribunal', *New York University Journal of International Law and Politics*, 23 (1991), 373–444.
61 C. Blakesley, 'Atrocity and its prosecution: the ad hoc tribunals for the former Yugoslavia and Rwanda', in McCormack and Simpson (eds), *The Law of War Crimes*, pp. 189–228; K. Lescure, *International Justice for Former Yugoslavia: the*

Workings of the International Criminal Tribunal of the Hague (The Hague: Kluwer, 1996); V. Morris and M. P. Scharf, *An Insider's Guide to the International Criminal Tribunal for the Former Yugoslavia* (Irvington NY: Transnational Publishers, 1995); J. C. O'Brien, 'The international tribunal for violations of international humanitarian law in the former Yugoslavia', *American Journal of International Law*, 87 (1993), 643–59; [Symposium], 'A critical study of the International Tribunal for the former Yugoslavia', *Criminal Law Forum* 5 (1994). For the internet sites see www.un.org/icty/ and www.un.org/ictr. These contain the annual reports of the tribunals to the General Assembly (hereafter GA) and the Security Council (hereafter SC).

62 SC Resolutions 808 (1993), 827 (1993). The Statute was amended by SC Resolutions 1166 (13 May 1998) and 1329 (30 November 2000).

63 See D. McGoldrick, 'The tale of Yugoslavia: lessons for accommodating national identity in national and international law', in S. Tierney (ed.), *Accommodating National Identity: New Approaches in International and Domestic Law* (The Hague: Kluwer, 2000), pp. 13–64; C. Greenwood, 'The prosecution of war crimes in the former Yugoslavia', *Bracton Law Journal*, 26 (1994), 13–22; T. Meron, 'The case for war crimes trials in Yugoslavia', *Foreign Affairs*, 72: 3 (Summer 1993), 122–35.

64 SC Resolution 780 (1992). See C. Bassiouni, 'The commission of experts established pursuant to SC Resolution 780: investigating violations of international humanitarian law in the former Yugoslavia', *Criminal Law Forum*, 5 (1994), 279–340.

65 United Nations Document S/25704 (1993); 32 I.L.M. (1993), 1159.

66 The secretary-general received reports from the Conference on Security Co-operation in Europe (S/25307) (1993), France (S/25266) (1993), and Italy (S/25300) (1993) and a number of states and non-governmental organisations made comments during the drafting of the report.

67 The list is submitted to the GA by the SC. The number was later increased to fourteen. The ICTY has had three female judges.

68 See SC Resolution 1329 (2000).

69 See ICTY, *Rules of Procedure and Evidence*, IT/32/REV.19; J. Katz Cogan, 'The problem of obtaining evidence for international criminal courts', *Human Rights Quarterly*, 22 (2000), 404–27.

70 See Smith, *Reaching Judgment*, 171–298.

71 First Annual Report of the Tribunal, submitted to the GA and SC, UN Doc. A/49/342, 29 August 1994.

72 See D. Sarooshi, *The United Nations and the Development of Collective Security* (Oxford: Oxford University Press, 1999), pp. 92–109; 'The legal framework governing United Nations subsidiary organisations', *British Yearbook of International Law*, 67 (1996), 413 at 428–31, 453–8.

73 There is necessarily some indirect UN control in terms of financing, appointment of judges and staff.

74 See 'Final report to the Prosecutor by the committee established to review the NATO bombing campaign against the Federal Republic of Yugoslavia' (ICTY, The Hague, June 2000). The bombings were in response to Serb human rights violation in Kosovo. See S. Tierney, 'The road back to hell: the international response to the crisis in Kosovo', in Tierney (ed.), *Accommodating National Identity*, pp. 89–130.

75 This did not preclude debate as to the applicable humanitarian law in respect of particular situations in the former Yugoslavia.
76 For a helpful collection of historical statements, see A. Cassese (ed.) *Path to The Hague* (The Hague: ICTY, 1996).
77 See P. Thornberry, *International Law and the Rights of Minorities* (Oxford: Oxford University Press, 1991), pp. 158–63; N. Lerner, *Group Rights and Discrimination in International Law* (Dordrecht: Nijhoff, 1991).
78 W. Schabas, *Genocide in International Law: the Crime of Crimes* (Cambridge: Cambridge University Press, 2000).
79 See D. Petrovic, 'Ethnic cleansing – an attempt at methodology', *European Journal of International Law*, 5 (1994), 342–59.
80 See A. Cassese, 'On the current trend towards criminal prosecution and punishment of breaches of international humanitarian law', *European Journal of International Law*, 9 (1998), 2–17.
81 Article 9(1) ICTY Statute.
82 Article 10 ICTY Statute. The ICTR Statute contains the same provision.
83 Article 7 ICTY Statute. Article 6 ICTR Statute is the same.
84 See I. Bantekas, *Principles of Direct and Superior Responsibility in International Humanitarian Law* (Manchester: Manchester University Press, 2002).
85 UN Doc. S/25704, para. 28.
86 See the annual reports of the ICTY for 1999 and 2000. For the trial of Slobodan Milosevic, see McGoldrick, in this collection.
87 On 10 March, 1998 the chief prosecutor, in a public statement, stated that the tribunal's jurisdiction covered the violence in Kosovo. Subsequently, the ICTY prosecutor requested the SC to amend Article 5 of ICTY Statute so as to cover events after the armed conflict in Kosovo.
88 See J. Paust, 'Applicability of international criminal laws to events in the former Yugoslavia', *American Journal of International Law and Policy*, 9 (1994), 499–521.
89 See Articles 2–5 of the Statute. Article 5 retains the link with an armed conflict. See C. Bassiouni, *Crimes Against Humanity in International Criminal Law*, 2nd edn (Dordrecht: Nijhoff, 1999).
90 On the controversy over rape, see C. Chinkin, 'The rape and sexual abuse of women in international law', *European Journal of International Law*, 5 (1994), 326–41; C. P. M. Clieren and M. E. M. Tijssen, 'Rape and other forms of sexual assault in the armed conflict in the former Yugoslavia: legal, procedural and evidential issues', *Criminal Law Forum* 5 (1994), 471–506.
91 See *Tadic Case*, Case IT-94-1, Appeals Chamber, para. 137 (2 October 1995); T. Meron, 'War crimes in Yugoslavia and the development of international law', *American Journal of International Law*, 88 (1994), 78–87; T. Meron, 'The international criminalization of internal atrocities', *American Journal of International* Law, 89 (1995), 554–77; D. Turns, 'War crimes without war? The applicability of international humanitarian law to atrocities in non-international armed conflicts', *African Journal of International and Comparative Law*, 7 (1995), 804–30.
92 See ICJ's decisions on interim measures and jurisdiction concerning eight member states of NATO and relating to NATO's intervention in Kosovo in 1999, I.C.J. Reports (2000).

93 See *Tadic*, and *Prosecutor* v. *Jelisic*, Case IT-95-10 (14 December 1999); G. Verdirame 'The genocide definition in the jurisprudence of the ad hoc tribunals', *International and Comparative Law Quarterly*, 49 (2000), 578–98.
94 See C. Warbrick, 'International criminal courts and fair trial', *Journal of Armed Conflict Law*, 3 (1998), 45–64.
95 For the extensive jurisprudence of the Human Rights Committee on Article 14, see D. McGoldrick, *The Human Rights Committee* (Oxford: Oxford University Press: 1991), pp. 395–458.
96 See M. Findlay, 'Synthesis in trial procedures? The experience of the international criminal tribunals', *International and Comparative Law Quarterly*, 50 (2001), 26–53.
97 Article 24 ICTY Statute.
98 *Ibid.* See D. Turns, 'The international criminal tribunal for the former Yugoslavia: the Erdemovic case', *International and Comparative Law Quarterly*, 47 (1997), 461–74; W. A. Schabas, 'Perverse effects of the *nulla poena* principle: national practice and the ad hoc tribunals', *European Journal of International Law*, 11 (2000), 521–39.
99 UN Doc. A/49/342, para. 48.
100 *Ibid.*, para. 49.
101 *Ibid.*, para. 51.
102 *Ibid.*, para. 53. A more purposive approach to interpretation is often taken by international human rights bodies.
103 There are also a Defense Counsel Unit and a Judicial Support Services Unit.
104 See K. D. Askin, 'Sexual violence in decisions and indictments of the Yugoslav and Rwandan tribunals: current status', *American Journal of International Law*, 93 (1999), 97–100; H. Charlesworth and C. Chinkin, *The Boundaries of International Law – a Feminist Analysis* (Manchester, Manchester University Press, 2000), pp. 324–37.
105 See P. B. Hayner, 'Fifteen truth commissions – 1974–1994: a comparative assessment', *Human Rights Quarterly*, 16 (1994), 597–655.
106 See ICTY Annual Report (1998), para. 225. A conference on the proposal was held in Bosnia in May 2001.
107 UN Doc. A/49/342, para. 73.
108 See Article 29 of the statute and rule 58 of the rules of procedure and evidence.
109 An Article in the Dayton Peace Agreement on the former Yugoslavia prohibits persons indicted before the Tribunal from holding political office. Radovan Karadic eventually stood down because of this. As of June 2001 co-operation with the Federal Republic of Yugoslavia was improving; a new law on co-operation was passed and former President Milosevic was surrendered to the ICTY. See McGoldrick in this volume
110 I.C.J. Reports (1992), 3 and 114.
111 UN Doc. A/49/342, para. 180.
112 *Prosecutor* v. *Tadic (Jurisdiction)* 35 I.LM. (1996), 35.
113 See R. Kerr, 'International judicial intervention: the international criminal tribunal for the former Yugoslavia', *International Relation*, 15: 2 (2000), 17–26.
114 See C. Greenwood, 'International humanitarian law and the *Tadic* case', *European Journal of International Law*, 7 (1996), 265–83.

115 See G. H. Aldrich, 'Jurisdiction of the international criminal tribunal for the Former Yugoslavia', *American Journal of International Law*, 90 (1996), 64–9; J. E. Alvarez, 'Nuremberg revisited: the *Tadic* case', *European Journal of International* Law, 7 (1996), 245–64.

116 See E. Lauterpacht, 'The legal effects of illegal acts of international organizations', in *Cambridge Essays in International Law: Essays in Honour of Lord McNair* (London: Stevens, 1965), pp. 88–112.

117 'For a tribunal such as this one to be established according to the rule of law, it must be established in accordance with the proper international standards; it must provide all the guarantees of fairness, justice and even-handedness, in full conformity with internationally recognised human rights instruments', *Tadic*, 35 I.L.M. 35 (1996) para. 45.

118 Judge Li dissented on the first issue arguing that ICTY had no competence to decide the issue. Judge Sidhwa dissented on the third issue. Tadic was later convicted and sentenced to twenty years, after an appeal on sentencing.

119 ICTY Annual Report, (1999); UN Doc. A/54/187.

120 *Ibid.*, para. 201.

121 See A. Klip and G. Sluiter (eds), *The International Criminal Tribunal for the Former Yugoslavia, 1993–1998 – Annotated Leading Cases of International Criminal Tribunals* (Antwerp: Intersentia, 1999).

122 See *Blaskic Case*, IT-95-14 (15 July 1994); S. Furuya, 'Legal effect of rules of the international criminal tribunals and court upon individuals: emerging international law of direct effect', *Netherlands International Law Review*, 47 (2000), 111–45.

123 See D. Sarooshi, 'Command responsibility and the Blaskic case', *International and Comparative Law Quarterly*, 50 (2001), 452–65; Bantekas, *Principles*.

124 The answer was yes, see *Tadic* Case.

125 The answer was no, see *ibid.*

126 The answer was yes, in certain circumstances, *Prosecutor* v. *Delalic and others*, IT-96-21 (16 November 1998), *Prosecutor* v. *Kunaric, Kovac, and Vokovic (Foca)*, IT-96-23 and IT-96-23/1 (22 February 2001).

127 The answer was no (by majority), *Prosecutor* v. *Tadic* (appeal on sentencing) (26 January 2000).

128 See Blakesley, *Atrocity and its prosecution*; J. Karhilo, 'The establishment of the international tribunal for Rwanda', *Nordic Journal of International Law*, 64 (1995), 683–713; 'Judging genocide', *The Economist* (14 June 2001).

129 SC Resolution 955 (1994).

130 SC Resolution 935 (1994).

131 See G. Prunier, *The Rwanda Crisis* (1995); *African Rights, Death, Despair and Defiance*, rev. end (London: Hurst, 1995); *The Administration of Justice in Post-Genocide Rwanda* (United Nations High Commissioner for Human Rights, Field Operation in Rwanda, UN Doc. HRFOR/JUSTICE/June 1996/E; A. J. Kuperman, 'Rwanda in retrospect', *Foreign Affairs*, 79: 1 (2000), 94–118.

132 See J. Alvarez, 'Crime of hate/ crimes of state: lessons from Rwanda', *Yale Journal of International Law*, 24 (1999), 365–483.

133 Article 8 ICTR Statute. See M. H. Morris, 'The trials of concurrent jurisdiction: the case of Rwanda', *Duke Journal of Comparative Law*, 7: 2 (1997), 349–74.

134 Article 7 ICTR Statute.

135 Unless the tribunal took the view that the substantive commission of the offence in 1994 brought all elements of it within its jurisdiction.
136 Article 4 ICTR Statute.
137 See Article 2(3)(c) ICTR Statute.
138 Article 24 ICTY Statute; Article 37 ICTR Statute.
139 It was purely coincidental that Rwanda was one of the non-permanent members of the SC at the time of the establishment of the ICTR. China abstained because it felt that there had not been enough consultation with Rwanda.
140 The same purpose can and has been served by post-conflict truth commissions in jurisdictions such as Chile, Argentina, and South Africa. See Minow, *Between Vengeance.*
141 Republic of Rwanda, Decret-Loi 21/77, Code Penal, Article 26.
142 There were international pleas to Rwanda not to carry out the executions but these were ignored.
143 ICTR-96-15-T (18 June 1997). See V. Morris, 'International decisions: *Prosecutor* v. *Kanyabashi*', *American Journal of International Law*, 92 (1998), 66–70.
144 See J. Brierly, 'Do we need an international criminal court?', *British Yearbook of International Law*, 8 (1927), 81–8.
145 See J. Dugard, 'Obstacles in the way of an international criminal court', *Cambridge Law Journal*, 56 (1997), 329–42.
146 See A. Cassese (ed.), *The Rome Statute for an International Criminal Court* (forthcoming, Oxford: Oxford University Press, 2001); D. McGoldrick, 'The permanent International Criminal Court: an end to the culture of impunity?', *Criminal Law Review*, (1999), 627–55.
147 See G. Boas, 'Comparing the ICTY and the ICC: some procedural and substantive points', *Netherlands International Law Review*, 47 (2000), 267–92.
148 This requires a decision under Chapter VII of the charter and is thus subject to the veto.
149 As on June 2001 only France has exercised this opt-out.
150 UN Doc. PCNICC/2000/1/Add.2.
151 UN Doc. PCNICC/2000/1/Add.1.
152 See P. Baldwin (ed.), *Reworking the Past: Hitler, the Holocaust and the Historians' Debate* (Boston, Mass.: Beacon, 1990); L. L. Langer, *Admitting the Holocaust: Collected Essays* (New York: Oxford University Press, 1995).
153 See D. McGoldrick and T. O'Donnell, 'Hate-speech laws: consistency with national and international human rights laws', *Legal Studies*, 18 (1998), 453–85.
154 See T. Meron, 'Is international law moving towards criminalization?', *European Journal of International Law*, 9 (1998), 18–31; T. Meron, *War Crimes Law Comes of Age* (Oxford: Oxford University Press, 2000).
155 *R.* v. *Metropolitan Stipendiary Magistrate, ex parte Pinochet Ugarte [No.3]* [1999] 2 All E.R. 97: no immunity for ex-head of state charge with torture. See D. Turns, 'Pinochet's fallout: jurisdiction and immunity for criminal violations of international law', *Legal Studies*, 20 (2000), 566–91.
156 See M. Frulli, 'The special court for Sierra Leone: some preliminary comments', *European Journal of International Law*, 11 (2000), 833–56; website of the Coalition for International Justice: www.cij.org

7

An embarrassing necessity: the Tokyo trial of Japanese leaders, 1946–48

Peter Lowe

In the middle of August 1945 Emperor Hirohito of Japan made an unprecedented radio broadcast to the Japanese people in which he informed his subjects that they must accept that Japan had experienced final defeat in the huge wars that had ravaged Eastern Asia and the Pacific. The dropping of the two atomic bombs on the cities of Hiroshima and Nagasaki, together with the decision of the Soviet Union to join the war against Japan, acted as the catalyst compelling surrender.[1] The role of Emperor Hirohito in the events preceding and following the outbreak of the Pacific war was to be the source of much argument and speculation, fuelled by the decision of the victorious Allies that the Emperor would not be prosecuted or permitted to give evidence in the Tokyo trial of political, military, and naval leaders between 1946 and 1948.[2] The end of the war ushered in the establishment of the Allied occupation, which continued until sovereignty was restored to Japan in April 1952, following ratification of the peace treaty concluded in San Francisco in September 1951.[3] However, in essence, the occupation was administered and controlled by the United States. President Harry S. Truman ultimately possessed more power to determine the fate of Japan than the other Allied leaders.[4] Truman was not deeply interested in Japan, however, and delegated decision-making to others. The most prominent of these was the man appointed by Truman to head the Allied occupation, General Douglas MacArthur.[5]

John Dower has produced an important, challenging reassessment of the occupation in which he has emphasised the impact of interaction on both occupiers and occupied. Each was affected deeply by the course of events, sometimes in a crude manner but often in very subtle ways. Dower sees the occupation as committed originally to fundamental reform yet increasingly focused on gaining the co-operation of the Japanese people.[6] MacArthur was 65 years of age when the occupation began. He was highly experienced and had served as a key commander in the Pacific theatre. In American politics MacArthur supported the Republican Party: he was critical of Roosevelt and

Truman. In Japan he acquired a strong sense of mission. He was determined to reform Japanese institutions fundamentally with the purpose of eradicating extreme nationalism and militarism and of ensuring that when Japan regained sovereignty, it would function as a democracy willing to accept American leadership.[7] MacArthur was responsible for setting up the International Military Tribunal for the Far East (IMTFE) and for considering appeals against the judgement of the tribunal.

The magnitude and scale of the atrocities committed in the Second World War rendered it urgent to decide, in 1945, how German and Japanese leaders should be punished. Some of the principal members of the Churchill coalition government preferred summary execution. This was the preferred solution of Winston Churchill and Anthony Eden, the Prime Minister and Foreign Secretary, and, interestingly, of the chief law officers of the Crown, the Lord Chancellor, Viscount Simon, and the Attorney General, Sir Donald Somervell.[8] The Truman administration believed that it was necessary to establish formal tribunals comprising judges, appointed from the victorious states, with the broad character of courts functioning in a domestic context. The British government was wary of creating an over-complex structure which could become cumbersome and time-consuming. Patrick Dean of the Foreign Office commented in November 1945 that caution should be shown in response to the American proposal to establish the IMTFE.[9] In the next few weeks, however, British opinion moved towards acceptance of the American proposal for creating international courts on which Britain and other relevant countries would be represented. Time was the chief cause for concern.[10] It was feared in London that the Truman administration might embark on an excessively ambitious series of trials which could entail the expenditure of much time and energy.[11]

The Truman administration decided to establish a large tribunal representing those states mainly responsible for fighting Japan between 1941 and 1945. At the beginning of 1946, it was unclear whether the jurisdiction of the tribunal would be restricted to charges of 'planning, preparation, initiation or waging of a war of aggressions, etc.' or whether crimes against the laws and customs of war and against humanity would also be pursued. It was decided to combine general and specific charges, the most important being Count 1, responsibility for advancing a broad conspiracy to secure Japanese domination of Asia and the Pacific by force. Evidence relating to the charge of crimes against peace was to be collected by the deputy British prosecutor who would assist in the preparation of the prosecution in Tokyo.[12] The chief prosecutor was an American, Joseph Keenan, who had liaised with the American Congress regarding New Deal legislation implemented by the Roosevelt administration and had then held office as assistant Attorney General in the criminal division in the Justice Department. This turned out to be a most unsatisfactory appointment. Keenan lacked the knowledge of international law and did not possess the ability or industry required in preparing a highly complex prosecution.

Instead, the bulk of the detailed preparation of the prosecution case was fulfilled by other lawyers, notably by Arthur Comyns Carr, Keenan's British deputy. The British Attorney General persuaded Comyns Carr to accept the appointment on the basis that the trial would be short and might be completed by May 1946 (the end came eventually in November 1948). An official in the Foreign Office commented that Sir Hartley Shawcross had given the assurance on timing in 'an over-sanguine moment'.[13] Comyns Carr was a prominent KC who had served briefly as a Liberal MP in 1923–4: he remained active in the Liberal Party, standing again for Parliament on several occasions and serving as the national president of the party in 1958–9. After returning from Tokyo Comyns Carr would serve as vice-treasurer and treasurer of Gray's Inn. In 1946, however, he was faced with the daunting task of assimilating large quantities of material rapidly and of undertaking much of the responsibility that should have been shouldered by Keenan. According to Roy Douglas, in a brief biographical assessment, Comyns Carr did not recover fully from the descriptions of the shocking atrocities he investigated.[14] It is not surprising that he complained not infrequently of the burdens he carried and protested at delays in sending him documentation. It was to the credit of Comyns Carr that the prosecution was as solidly prepared as it was, and that he performed ably in court. The disasters in the prosecution were usually associated with Keenan's under-prepared contributions. On the whole, the prosecution team worked hard and included several able American lawyers who were markedly better than their chief.

In total eleven countries were represented among the judges – Australia, Canada, China, France, India, the Netherlands, New Zealand, the Philippines, the Soviet Union, the United Kingdom, and the United States. The Truman administration was originally unwilling to include India but eventually agreed that an Indian judge should be nominated (India was part of the British empire in 1946 and became an independent state in 1947).[15] One of the obvious problems, and subsequently a cause of fundamental criticism, was the composition of the IMTFE: all of the judges came from countries hostile to Japan (admittedly, it was more complicated in the case of India where some Indians had fought against Britain in association with Japan but far more Indians fought against Japan). This gave rise to the accusation of 'Victors' Justice', a charge consolidated in Richard Minear's influential short study, published in 1971.[16] It is interesting to observe that Keenan, despite his numerous faults, did suggest, in January–February 1946, that Japan should be involved in the trial. He indicated that this could be accomplished either by including the Japanese government in the indictment among the countries submitting the charges, or by appointing a Japanese judge and a Japanese prosecutor. The British liaison mission in Tokyo reported in February 1946 that some Japanese were keen to assist in the prosecution, and that crimes committed against the Japanese people, such as the numerous assassinations of political figures in the 1930s, could be included in the charges. As Oscar Morland pointed out in a telegram from Tokyo, participation of Japanese citizens would modify the criticism of 'Victors' Justice'; however, Allied public opinion might not take kindly to such a development.[17]

L. H. Foulds of the Foreign Office observed that it was not desirable that Japanese should serve as judges or assistant prosecutors.[18] A telegram was sent to the British mission stating that Japan should not participate as Keenan had suggested: it would raise the issue as to why such a step had not been taken in the case of Germany, and public opinion in Allied states would resent such a course of action because of the atrocities committed by the Japanese armed forces.[19] B. V. A. Röling, the distinguished Dutch judge whose dissenting views and constructive retrospective criticisms will be considered later in this chapter, believed that Japanese should have taken part, as Keenan had proposed, and that a neutral judge (or judges) should have been appointed from countries not involved as belligerents in the Pacific war.[20] Röling envisaged that Japanese and neutral judges would have constituted a minority of the judges.

The judges appointed to serve in Tokyo were, in the main, safe and rather staid figures: the chief exceptions were Röling and the Indian judge, R. B. Pal. The American judge appointed originally, John P. Higgins, resigned shortly after the commencement of the trial and was replaced by Myron Cramer, who specialised in American military law. The British judge, Lord Patrick, came from the Court of Session in Edinburgh. Like Comyns Carr, Patrick had accepted the appointment on the understanding that the trial would not be protracted. He chafed at its length, and his Scottish colleagues complained of the pressure of business facing them during his absence in Tokyo. Patrick suffered from ill health and this contributed to his decision to decline MacArthur's offer of appointment as acting president (chairman) of the IMTFE when the president, Sir William Webb, was away temporarily in Australia. The head of the British mission in Tokyo, Alvary Gascoigne, and the Foreign Office were annoyed that Patrick refused MacArthur's offer without prior consultation.[21] MacArthur's appointment of the Australian, Webb, softened the image of American dominance of the deliberations. However, Webb's appointment was regrettable in several ways. The principal legal objection was that Webb had already been involved in investigating alleged Japanese war crimes, including cannibalism, in New Guinea on behalf of the Australian government. Surely this alone should have disqualified Webb from serving. As regards the daily functioning of the court, Webb lacked the diplomatic skill and urbanity required in a chairman, those qualities demonstrated so successfully by Webb's equivalent at Nuremberg, the British judge, Sir Geoffrey Lawrence.[22] Webb was a somewhat remote figure and did not enjoy good relations with his fellow judges.[23]

The Canadian judge, E. Stuart McDougall, was sound, and Harvey Northcroft, the New Zealand judge, was capable. The latter would indeed have been a more suitable appointment than Webb, but MacArthur held that New Zealand was too insignificant a country and could not provide the president of the Tribunal, when the question arose of replacing Webb during the latter's absence in Australia.[24] The French judge, Henri Bernard, did not contribute particularly but did dissent in part at the end of the trial. The Dutch judge, Röling, was the youngest and probably the ablest of the judges. He was 39 years of age when appointed and had specialised in the laws of the Netherlands East Indies (Indonesia). Röling was strongly committed to the trial of war criminals and to holding leaders responsible for the crimes carried out by their subordinates. At the same time, he was very critical of various aspects of the conduct of the trial.[25] The Soviet judge, I. M. Zaryanov, was a specialist in Soviet military law and spoke neither English nor Japanese, the two official languages of the trial. The Chinese judge, Mei Ju-no, was relatively young, possessed a law degree but had never practised. The judge from the Philippines, Delfin Jaranilla, had been a prisoner-of-war of the Japanese and was a survivor of the notorious Bataan death march in 1942. To an even greater extent than Webb, Jaranilla could not be seen as possessing the detachment required to sit as a judge. Pal was appointed by the British authorities in New Delhi when the Truman administration reluctantly permitted the appointment of an Indian judge. He was conversant with international law and was a former judge of the Calcutta High Court. He was also sympathetic to the accused because he regarded Japan as in part responsible for liberating Asia from occidental imperialism.[26]

Preparations for the Tokyo trial were influenced significantly by preceding arrangements for the analogous trial of Nazi leaders in Nuremberg. The charter for the IMTFE was very similar to the charter compiled at the London conference in the summer of 1945, which paved the way for the Nuremberg trial. However, as Röling later observed, major differences existed in the character of the trials of German and Japanese leaders. The most basic was that those prosecuted at Nuremberg had committed or ordered others to commit the acts of which they were accused. In the Tokyo trial it was much more difficult to identify orders to commit particular crimes.[27] The IMTFE was established in a proclamation issued by MacArthur on 19 January 1946.[28] The charter, defining the authority and powers of the Tribunal, was issued on 26 April 1946. Features worthy of particular note are that six out of the eleven judges constituted a quorum (Article 4(a)); decisions and judgements were arrived at by the majority vote of those present (Article 4(b)); if a judge had been absent, he could resume attendance without difficulty unless he stated in court that he could not continue because of inadequate knowledge (Article 4(c)). Article 5 defined jurisdiction over persona and offences. Acts defined as crimes falling within the terms of reference of the Tribunal comprised crimes against peace, conventional war crimes, and crimes against humanity. The Tribunal could impose the death penalty: the Supreme Commander for the Allied Powers (MacArthur) was responsible for determining appeals.[29]

The trial lasted far longer than anticipated, but this should have occasioned little surprise. The issues addressed at Tokyo were more sweeping and, to some extent, more vague than at Nuremberg. The geographical areas concerned were immense, ranging from the borders of India to New Guinea and from Manchuria to obscure Pacific islands. The difficulties of securing accurate, agreed translations from Japanese into English were considerable. The daily conduct of the trial was often delayed by challenges to translations or by corrections supplied by translators. Much evidence had been destroyed by the Japanese in the closing stages of the war or immediately after surrender. Some material was of an ambiguous nature. In retrospect, it is amazing that the British Attorney General and officials responsible for dealing with war crimes in the Foreign Office could ever have believed that the trial could be completed rapidly. MacArthur was frustrated at the protracted proceedings. According to Röling: 'the general told me explicitly that he had not wanted the Tokyo trial as it was now conceived. He had been in favor of a short court-martial concerning Pearl Harbor, a treacherous attack in an undeclared war.'[30] As early as November 1946, F. F. Garner of the Foreign Office noted accelerating weariness with war crimes trials: 'At a recent meeting, the cabinet expressed the strong wish that we should advocate a policy of discontinuing war crimes trials and I am sure that they would not favour our participation in any further trials of Japanese major or "sub major" war criminals.'[31] Towards the end of the following month, Gascoigne reported from Tokyo that Truman and MacArthur were both embarrassed at the slow advancement of the trial. MacArthur told Gascoigne that the IMTFE would defeat itself by occupying so much time. Interest in the trial in the United States was waning.[32]

Progress was bound to be slow for the reasons indicated earlier. Matters were exacerbated by sharp differences of opinion among the judges. Again, with a total of eleven judges from different countries, some disagreement was to be expected. Webb's cavalier behaviour and lack of diplomacy accounted for much of the difficulty. The stifling heat of the summer in Tokyo could lead to frayed tempers. Christmas Humphreys, KC, who assisted Comyns Carr in the early stages in Tokyo, wrote in a private letter in July 1946: 'The judges are fighting among themselves and have now struck work altogether at the heat in Court and the whole Trial is dragging along at a slower tempo than even I, always the pessimistic prophet, thought possible. In the Legations we play tennis at 85 and just drip placidly.'[33] The reference to the judges having gone on strike alluded to the breakdown of air conditioning. Relations between Webb and his fellow judges were at their worst in the first few months of 1947. Patrick told Gascoigne in October 1947 that the position had been so serious six months before that the New Zealand judge, Northcroft, had notified his government. The Prime Minister of New Zealand, Peter Fraser, raised the subject personally with the Australian Prime Minister, Ben Chifley, and urged that Webb should be recalled. It appeared that Fraser had received representations about Webb's conduct from another source, in addition to Northcroft. Patrick thought that Webb might be withdrawn by his government: since it would be too late to send another Australian, Northcroft would probably assume the chair as the next most senior judge. In fact, Webb returned to Australia for only a short period and then went back to Tokyo to resume the presidency. Patrick also remarked on the fact that Pal, who had arrived late, had gone back to India and might not return.[34]

Some of the most mordant comments on the atmosphere of the trial were provided by Comyns Carr in letters to the British Attorney General, Shawcross, which were communicated to the Foreign Office. Carr wrote on 6 October 1947 that Keenan had at first behaved better upon returning from a visit to the United States but that he had then displayed 'the cloven hoof'. Keenan was trying to change arrangements so that he could prosecute Kido Koichi instead of Comyns Carr doing so. The reason was that Keenan was involved in a dispute with Webb over the Emperor's responsibility, and Keenan wished to outmanoeuvre Webb. Carr criticised both: each had made unwise comments and could be relied upon to make further such comments, both being indiscreet. Keenan was making other changes in the allocation of work that would diminish the effectiveness of the prosecution. Keenan also wished to organise another major trial of Japanese leaders, presumably on an all-American basis. Comyns Carr added, 'anyway, don't ask me to take part in it'.[35] Keenan appeared to be abstaining from alcohol, after earning a reputation for heavy drinking. Comyns Carr wrote to Shawcross: 'Do you still want me to stick this one to the end? I may be able to be of use behind the scenes in keeping it more or less on the rails. . . .'[36] Matters clearly deteriorated for, on 21 October Comyns Carr noted that developments had been more disastrous than he had expected. Keenan was utterly hopeless, and his staff was inefficient. Carr added: 'When you agreed that the Nuremberg system should be replaced by having one "Chief of Counsel", I supposed you had no idea of the kind of man under whose heel I was to be placed. If I had known I would never have come'.[37]

The climax to court proceedings occurred at the end of December 1947 and beginning of 1948 when General Tojo Hideki, Prime Minister from 1941 to 1944, gave evidence. This was the most important phase so far, since Tojo had been central to key decisions within the War Ministry and the Cabinet which had culminated in the Japanese attacks on Malaya and Pearl Harbor. The transcript of the IMTFE makes fascinating reading for the respective contributions of Keenan, Tojo, and Webb.[38] Contrary to what had been agreed beforehand, Keenan decided to conduct the cross-examination of Tojo himself. In his affidavit Tojo emphasised his determination, upon becoming war minister in 1940, to achieve improved co-ordination between the armed forces and the government; to maintain firm discipline in the army so as to control factionalism; and to make every effort to resolve the undeclared war against China, which had begun in July 1937 and was known as the 'China incident'. Tojo commented on his meetings with the Emperor. Hirohito had expressed a strong desire for peace, while accepting preparations for war. Occasionally the Emperor had expressed his own opinions but these had been uttered following prior consultation with the Lord Keeper of the Privy Seal – the Emperor had followed the recommendations of his advisers.[39] Pressure was put on Tojo by Keenan, outside the courtroom, to modify his evidence, since he had implicated the Emperor too directly in the approval of decisions leading to war: Tojo did so. The cross-examination is interesting not only for the duel between Keenan and Tojo but also for the sparring between Keenan and Webb. At one point Keenan, probably aware that the cross-examination was not going satisfactorily, asked if an associate, John W. Fihelly, could assist him in conducting the next phase. There was no objection from the defence but the court denied the request, and Keenan had to continue.[40] Keenan asked Tojo if his statement was envisaged as an extension of imperialistic, militaristic propaganda. The defence objected, and Webb overruled the question. Keenan then inquired if Tojo would agree that aggressive war was a crime. The defence again objected on the grounds that this was a matter for the Tribunal to decide. Webb agreed and remarked, 'But I can assure counsel that we are getting no help from this type of cross-examination'.[41] A brief argument between Keenan and Webb ensued.

Comyns Carr wrote to Shawcross on 2 January 1948 that matters had gone from bad to worse. Keenan had proved disastrous in confronting Tojo: in the words of one of the employees of the British mission, 'Tojo had a good morning hanging Keenan'.[42] Carr added that Tojo's evidence was revealing in more ways than one:

> Tojo's evidence is really a plea of guilty but a very fine performance, accepting responsibility for everything and seeking to justify it. Incidentally the defendants if they have done nothing else, have proved the guilt of the Emperor pretty conclusively, which, in view of the decision not to prosecute him, we had been trying to keep in the background, and K[eenan] has been going out of his way, quite unsuccessfully to disprove. Of course, they have all been parading their loyalty to him, but that is the practical effect of their evidence.[43]

Later in January Gascoigne confirmed Comyns Carr's assessment and illustrated how MacArthur sought to intervene at times in the conduct of the trial. Tojo had handled his defence skilfully, outmanoeuvred Keenan, and made clear his standing in the eyes of the Japanese people. MacArthur demonstrated his anxiety at the blundering manner in which Keenan had acted:

> He [MacArthur] had arranged with Chief Prosecutor Keenan that there should be no cross-examination of Tojo and that after Tojo had made his affidavit, he should be told to 'stand down'. But in the excitement of the moment Keenan had persisted with his examination of the defendant and the results had reflected extremely badly upon the Prosecution.[44]

As regards the accused, the greatest controversy surrounded Tojo and Shigemitsu Mamoru. In the case of Tojo, this arose from his unusually prominent role in directing war preparations and then Japan's pursuance of a vast war in Asia and the Pacific until he was compelled to relinquish the office of prime minister in 1944. In the case of Shigemitsu, the controversy resulted from the contention of some, including influential British acquaintances, that he had worked for peace and that he had erroneously been accused of sharing responsibility for advocating aggressive war. Shigemitsu had served as ambassador in London between 1938 and 1941, a crucial period in Anglo-Japanese relations due to the heightening of tension provoked by the 'Undeclared War' in China.[45] Shigemitsu was adroit in fostering contacts with significant figures in the British establishment, notably with Lord Hankey, secretary to the British Cabinet from 1916 to 1938 and subsequently a Cabinet minister under Neville Chamberlain and Churchill; and R. A. Butler, a leading Conservative politician who had served as parliamentary under-secretary in the Foreign Office from 1938 to 1941. In the light of their meetings with Shigemitsu, Hankey and Butler were convinced that the ambassador had done his best to avert war, and they argued that he should not have been prosecuted. Hankey waged a brave campaign in support of Shigemitsu in the House of Lords and outside it.[46] Sir George Sansom, a distinguished Japanologist and a former member of the staff of the British embassy in Tokyo, provided a succinct, balanced assessment of Shigemitsu in December 1946:

> Personally, I think it is a mistake to try Shigemitsu, and I understand that it is being done under Russian pressure because Shigemitsu was known to be very strongly anti-Communist and was in office at the time of the Chang-ku-feng incident [in 1938]. Shigemitsu was, of course, a strong nationalist and believed that the Japanese ought to dominate China. As you will recollect, when we were in the Foreign Office together in 1939–40, we felt that Rab [R. A. Butler] and his friends were too friendly with Shigemitsu, whereas Rab thought that we were 'too rigid'. Certainly, Shigemitsu was not the friend of Britain that some alleged him to be, but I do think that he was definitely not in the same category as the hard-boiled military extremists; he had too much sense for that.[47]

Comyns Carr believed that it was correct to prosecute Shigemitsu because of the need to establish a principle not consolidated at Nuremberg:

> Namely that the civilian government, not the soldiers, were responsible for the fulfilment of the terms of the Geneva Convention, for the proper treatment of prisoners-of-war, etc. Shigemitsu, as Foreign Minister, had received from the Swiss all the reports of the Japanese ill-treatment of prisoners and had done nothing more than pass them on to the War Office 'for comments'. The War Office very seldom bothered to comment and when they did their explanations were very lame. Shigemitsu showed no concern and, again, simply passed the War Office reports to the Swiss.[48]

At last, in the summer of 1948, the daily grind of the deliberations in court drew to a close, and the time had come for the judges to determine their verdicts. Röling believed that bias was often shown towards the prosecution and against the defence but that in total the trial had been reasonably fair and certainly necessary.[49] Röling was, however, critical of the way in which the judgement of the court was decided. Seven judges (from the United States, Britain, China, the Soviet Union, the Philippines, Canada, and New Zealand) organised the drafting and communicated the results to the other four judges (from Australia, France, the Netherlands, and India) as a *fait accompli*. Röling contended that this was not appropriate and that the procedure followed at Nuremberg was correct, whereby a draft was produced on the basis of consensus: the general line of approach should have been discussed in chambers.[50] With respect to the judgement itself, Röling noted that in making the defendants responsible for crimes against peace, the court was applying *ex post facto* law. He concluded, however, that this was ultimately a political, rather than a legal, decision, and the authority granted to the IMTFE in the charter was clear. Röling also supported 'negative criminality' – the failure to prevent crimes committed by others. The judgement ran to 664 pages. Dissenting opinions were also submitted by Jaranilla, Bernard, Webb, and Röling, and Pal published what he described as a dissentient judgement. These will be considered below.

The court found that a criminal conspiracy, as alleged in Count 1, had been proved:

> The conspiracy existed for and its execution occupied a period of many years. Not all of the conspirators were parties at the beginning, and some of those who were parties to it had ceased to be active in its execution before the end. All of those who at any time were parties to the criminal conspiracy or who at any time with guilty knowledge played a part in its execution are guilty of the charge contained in Count 1.[51]

The fundamental importance of the charge of 'conspiracy' is demonstrated in that twenty-three out of twenty-five defendants were found guilty of participating in the conspiracy. Matsui Iwane and Shigemitsu were acquitted, but Matsui was convicted of disregard of duty to secure the observance and prevent breaches of the laws of war (Count 55), and was sentenced to death. Of the other defendants, twenty-two out of twenty-five were found guilty of waging war against China (Count 27), and eighteen were found guilty of waging war against the United States, the British Commonwealth, and the Netherlands (Counts 29, 31, 32). Only two were found guilty of waging war against France (Count 33) and against the Soviet Union at Lake Khassan in 1938 (Count 35); three were found guilty of waging war against the Soviet Union at Nomonhan in 1939 (Count 36); five were found guilty of ordering, authorising, or permitting atrocities (Count 54), and seven were found guilty of Count 55.

Seven of those found guilty were sentenced to death by hanging. These were Doihara Kenji, Hirota Koki, Itagaki Seishiro, Kimura Heitaro, Muto Akira, Matsui, and Tojo. Deep controversy surrounded the death sentence against

Hirota, a former Prime Minister and Foreign Minister who was awarded a death sentence by six out of eleven judges. Among the dissentients, Webb was opposed to the passing of any death sentences, and Röling held that Hirota was definitely not guilty of Count 1.[52]

Five of the judges produced separate dissents. The Philippines judge, Jaranilla, dissented on the grounds that the sentences were too lenient, but this was a rather minor statement in comparison with the others. The French judge, Bernard, produced a convoluted statement. He believed that aggressive war was a crime but that sufficient proof against certain of the defendants was lacking. His most trenchant observation concerned the exclusion of Emperor Hirohito from the trial. 'It cannot be denied, it had a principal author who escaped all prosecution and of whom in any case the present Defendants could only be considered as accomplices.'[53] Pal produced an extremely lengthy dissent, which was published in Calcutta in 1953. This was cleverly argued and criticised the considerable weakness in the functioning of the IMTFE. Pal made the most of the vagueness and uncertainty within international law. While not excusing Japanese atrocities, he revealed sympathy for the dilemmas facing Japanese leaders and concluded that it was not appropriate to convict the accused.

Webb stated that as he had been unable to agree with a majority of the Tribunal on the law and on the method of ascertaining the facts, he had proposed that judges should, if they wished, draft their own judgements. Subsequently, if any judge found himself to be in essential agreement with the majority, his judgement could be withdrawn. As matters turned out, Webb concluded that in most, if not all, respects, his judgement was close to that submitted by the majority, and therefore he had withdrawn his judgement except for a short statement. Here Webb argued that aggressive war was clearly a crime and that no one involved could escape responsibility, whatever his rank and status. Moreover, the charge of 'conspiracy' was permissible in the British Commonwealth, although some judges disapproved of it. Webb was opposed, however, to the imposition of death sentences. It was not wise to hang elderly men, and it would be preferable to imprison them for a prolonged period, probably outside Japan. Webb agreed with Bernard that the Emperor should not have been removed entirely from the trial. Whatever the precise role fulfilled by Hirohito, it could not be denied that he occupied a central position in the Japanese state.[54]

The most balanced and cogent dissenting opinion was compiled by Röling from the Netherlands. Röling was deeply sceptical of the merits of pursuing 'crimes against peace' in the Tokyo trial. The Pact of Paris (the Kellogg–Briand pact) of 1928, upon which the prosecution had placed strong emphasis, contained the significant reservation that each state was able to determine when circumstances justified recourse to war in self-defence, and Röling noted appreciable differences of opinion among those authorities active in the sphere of international law when it came to ascertaining the meaning of the Pact of

Paris. Röling emphasised, however, the responsibility of the military for stimulating aggression:

> It may be stated at this point that, unlike other crimes, the crime of aggression is such that the emphasis falls upon the activities in preparation. He who propagates, or plans, or starts the aggression takes upon himself heavier responsibility than the statesman who cannot but accept the consequences of previous events, or who carries on an established policy.[55]

Röling also defined the criteria by which it was possible to impose criminal responsibility upon an official for certain acts which he had not directly ordered or permitted. These were first, that the official knew, or should have known, of the acts committed. If he *should* have known, lack of actual knowledge could not be claimed in self-defence. Second, he must have possessed the power to prevent the acts: atrocities would be committed in all wars and could not be prevented absolutely. Criminal responsibility arose only where all possible steps to avert war crimes had not been adopted. Finally, he must have had the duty to prevent these acts: a specific obligation had to be investigated, placing on officials or military commanders, criminal responsibility for some 'omissions'.[56]

Röling argued that as the law presently stood, it was not so much the end that counted but rather the means. This arose because of the difficulty in defining ultimately aggressive aims by means that were not illegal in themselves. In the case of Tojo, Röling discerned a very high degree of responsibility, amounting to deception, in the pursuance of aggression. Tojo had deceived the Emperor. He had been nominated for the office of minister of war and subsequently prime minister because it was believed that he could maintain effective discipline and possibly persuade younger army officers to accept a negotiated diplomatic solution to the crisis in Eastern Asia and the Pacific. In contrast, Hirota's responsibility was more limited. He had followed a devious, subtle policy of securing a gradual Japanese domination of Eastern Asia, including the non-violent expulsion of Western interests from Asia. Decisions taken in August 1936 had been fundamental to expansion, although the most vital time for decision had occurred in September 1940 with the conclusion of the tripartite pact comprising Japan, Germany, and Italy. Hirota had been partly responsible for the former but not the latter.

In keeping with his scepticism about prosecuting 'crimes against peace' Röling opposed death sentences for those convicted solely of such offences. Internment for life was the correct punishment. Thus, he agreed that Araki Sadao, Hashimoto Kingoro, Hiranuma Kiichiro, Hoshino Naoki, Minami Jiro, Kaya Okinori, Oshima Hiroshi, Shiratori Toshio, and Suzuki Teiichi, who had been found guilty of conspiracy to wage a war of aggression or of waging a war of aggression, but not guilty of any conventional war crime, should suffer life imprisonment – the same punishment had been also been awarded to Koiso Kuniaki and Umezu Yoshijiro. By contrast, the majority judgement had sentenced Oka Takasumi, Sato Kenryo, and Shimada Shigetaro to life imprisonment; Röling argued that they should have been found guilty of conventional war crimes and received death sentences. Röling approved the death sentences for Doihara, Itagaki, Kimura, Matsui, Muto, and Tojo, but he considered that Hirota, whom the majority had sentenced to death, Hata Shunroku, Kido, and Hirota, who had received life imprisonment, and Togo Shigenori, and Shigemitsu, who had been awarded prison terms of twenty and seven years, respectively, should have been acquitted.[57] With respect to Hirota, Röling felt that while he might have been guilty of political immorality he did not belong to 'those arch-aggressors who are judged by this Tribunal to deserve the death penalty'.[58]

In essence, therefore, Röling sought to dissociate himself from the more sweeping, and perhaps biased, decisions of the majority, and yet to recognise the enormity of the atrocities committed by the forces of the Japanese state. In the main, he believed that the military was responsible for these atrocities, and that generals who came within the criteria he had established should be punished severely. Röling did not object to the imposition of the death penalty, as did Webb, nor did he accept the critical view of Emperor Hirohito expressed by Webb and Bernard. He also rejected the interpretation of Pal, which failed to recognise the necessity of punishing those Japanese leaders bearing responsibility for the shocking conduct of the armed forces.

Once the judgement and verdicts had been announced, the Allied governments had to determine their responses to the submission of appeals by the condemned. Gascoigne, head of the British liaison mission, reported on 12 November 1948 that MacArthur intended to convene a meeting of all heads of missions in Tokyo, representing all countries attending the Far Eastern Commission (FEC), to request their opinions as to whether sentences should be 'approved, reduced or otherwise altered'. Gascoigne recommended that he (Gascoigne) should make no observations.[59] MacArthur was bound to consult the Allied Council for Japan (ACJ) and the FEC before deciding whether to approve or reject sentences. MacArthur could not increase the severity of sentences. The consensus in the British Foreign Office was that despite some unsatisfactory features, such as the incompetence of the chief counsel for the prosecution and some divergences between the judges, the trial had been conducted fairly. It would be most sensible not to offer any comments and not to intervene on behalf of any of the accused – to do so 'might well involve us in press and parliamentary criticism of a very disagreeable nature'.[60] The Attorney General was consulted, and Shawcross expressed agreement with the response proposed by the Foreign Office.[61]

Surprise was expressed in the Foreign Office at the dissenting opinions submitted by Webb and Pal.[62] Webb's remarks concerning the Emperor were deplored, as casting doubt over the equity of the trial presided over by Webb himself.[63] Rumours circulated in Tokyo that the Australian government might support Webb's opposition to the implementation of death sentences.[64]

MacArthur met representatives of the FEC countries on 22 November. He invited observations on the sentences handed down. The representatives of Australia, Canada, China, France, New Zealand, the Philippines, the United Kingdom, the United States, and the Soviet Union indicated no objection to the implementation of sentences. The Canadian representative added that he would not object in principle to any proposal for clemency. The representative of the Netherlands urged changes comprising reduction in the terms of imprisonment imposed on Hata, Togo, and Umezu to ten years each, and commutation of Hirota's death sentence to imprisonment for life. The Indian representative drew attention to Webb's opposition to death sentences and observed that unanimity among judges should be required for the imposition of a death sentence. MacArthur stated his opinion that all sentences should be carried out.[65]

Gascoigne summarised Japanese press reactions. In essence these concluded that the Japanese people must accept condemnation for pursuing a war of aggression and must ensure that such a situation did not recur; a few reservations were stated regarding the application of *ex post facto* law.[66] Sir Robert Craigie, the last British ambassador to Japan before the outbreak of war, wrote to the Foreign Office criticising certain of the sentences and castigating the death sentence passed on Hirota. Dudley Cheke minuted that Craigie had offered no evidence, and that Comyns Carr had expressed the opinion that Hirota was the first Japanese leader to outline a programme of comprehensive aggression.[67] Comyns Carr had returned to London by mid–November and was consulted by the Foreign Office. He was opposed to any reduction in sentences.[68] Hankey and his associates were vocal in censuring the prison sentence passed on Shigemitsu, but Comyns Carr believed it was justified. 'The Tribunal had seen evidence that, at a time when Shigemitsu was protesting about his friendship to Britain and America, he had in fact advised the Japanese Foreign Office not to attack Britain and America "because they were too strong" but to attack France, Holland and Portugal "because they could do nothing about it." '[69] Comyns Carr added that it was incorrect to state that it was only on Soviet insistence that Shigemitsu had been brought to trial. As regards the position of Emperor Hirohito, Comyns Carr modified an opinion he had expressed previously and guessed that, if the Emperor had been tried, he would probably have been acquitted by a fair-minded tribunal.[70]

MacArthur wished to terminate the proceedings as quickly as possible. He rejected a passionate appeal submitted by the American Ben Bruce Blakeney on behalf of all the defence counsel[71] and ordered that the death sentences should be carried out swiftly. The condemned were hanged on 23 December 1948 in the presence of representatives of each of the countries belonging to the ACJ.

One of the enduring controversies of the trial surrounded the role of the Emperor, and this was stimulated by Webb's dissenting opinion. In Britain the *Manchester Guardian* described the outcome of the IMTFE as somewhat disappointing. Dissatisfaction was accentuated by the exclusion of the

Emperor from the trial. Using wartime terminology, the newspaper commented a little sardonically, that the Emperor was in a 'reserved occupation'. This was understandable in the context of MacArthur's reform programme, which was aimed at enlisting the positive support of the Japanese people 'but it had a lamentable effect upon the legal fabric of the case'.[72] Sansom, the British diplomat who was then in Tokyo, stated in January 1946 that it would be 'a major blunder' to indict the Emperor and added that Keenan concurred.[73] In strict legal terms the objection of the *Manchester Guardian* was justified. Whatever power the Emperor did or did not exercise, he had occupied a central symbolic position in the state and was conversant with many secret aspects of the functioning of the government. Full defence of the accused was handicapped by the total exclusion of the Emperor from the trial. Political realities, however, dictated exclusion: the Truman administration and the Attlee government were suitably convinced.

There were undoubtedly numerous weaknesses in the structure and development of the Tokyo trial. Richard Minear made the most of these defects in his lively, concise survey of the trial.[74] Minear was deeply influenced by revulsion against the contemporary war in Vietnam, and this led him to a rather unbalanced treatment of the subject. At this point I must indicate that as a result of preparing this chapter, I have changed my mind on the necessity for a trial of Japanese leaders. For many years I was largely persuaded by the arguments advanced by Minear that the trial was an excessive, distorted version of 'Victors' Justice', which did little, if anything, to advance the cause of international justice. Three aspects have led me to modify my view – the scale and savagery of the atrocities committed by the Japanese armed forces during the conflicts in Asia and the Pacific; examining more closely the arguments advanced by Röling; and reflecting on the impact of the shocking atrocities committed in Rwanda and the former Yugoslavia in the 1990s, to which must be added the mass murder pursued by the Khmer Rouge regime in Cambodia in the 1970s and the situation in East Timor in 1999. John Dower has rightly pointed out that racism, often of a virulent nature, affected all states which participated in the wars in Asia and the Pacific. Atrocities were committed by both sides or all sides in the war.[75] However, Japanese forces were responsible for the most widespread, revolting crimes, affecting all races and both sexes. These comprised POWs and civilians equally. As regards the latter, evidence from every war theatre involving the Japanese armed forces reveals the systematic resort to torture, rape, and murder against men, women, and children: the most extreme examples were seen in Nanking (China) in December 1937 and in Singapore in February 1942. On both occasions, Chinese were the victims of extreme cruelty. Abundant evidence of a terrible character was submitted to the IMTFE, and the transcript of the trial is often occupied with the details of these terrible events and of similar acts committed throughout Asia and the Pacific. Yuki Tanaka has attempted an analysis and explanation of how such atrocities could occur in his study published in

English in 1996.[76] In essence Tanaka attributes the conduct to the unhealthy fostering of militarism within the framework of narrow emperor-centred nationalism. The original cult of *bushido* was perverted in the twentieth century, and the chivalrous attitudes shown during the Russo-Japanese war of 1904–5 were replaced by the extreme brutality encouraged in the armed forces during the 1930s.[77] Japanese officers were usually rather ignorant, if not wholly ignorant, of international law: it had not figured very prominently in their military education. Tojo, as Prime Minister, stated in 1942 that POWs should be made to work hard in the interests of assisting the consolidation of the Greater East Asia Co-Prosperity Sphere.[78] When cross-examined in the trial, Tojo replied that his remarks were consistent with the Geneva Convention (1929) but that he had never sanctioned the atrocities revealed in the IMTFE, and they could not possibly be defended.[79]

Atrocities of such magnitude cannot simply be attributed to those who carried them out. The army, naval, and certain civilian leaders must accept at least some of the responsibility for such a catalogue of revolting war crimes. Here I am persuaded by Röling's opinions. He and Minear participated in a symposium in Japan in 1983. Each was critical of the conduct of the IMTFE, but Röling argued that, despite its significant defects, the trial was worth while and it had significant accomplishments to its credit.[80] Röling was a courageous man of progressive views: his experience in Tokyo convinced him to become a vigorous campaigner for international peace and for the extension and enforcement of international law. He was the most impressive and cogent of the judges who participated in the IMTFE.

Both the American and British governments came to regard the Tokyo trial as an embarrassment which should be brought to an end as soon as feasible and not repeated. Shawcross, the British Attorney General, wrote to W. E. Beckett, the senior legal adviser in the Foreign Office, in September 1947 opposing the holding of further war crimes trials in Tokyo. 'I am quite sure that any repetition of the present proceedings at Tokyo would be disastrous.'[81] Disillusionment was the consequence of lack of sufficient preparation in the United States and Britain for a trial of the complexity of that held in Tokyo between 1946 and 1948. Nevertheless, I am persuaded by Röling that the importance of the Tokyo trial is that it has contributed, despite its serious flaws, to the consolidation of international law and to holding the leaders of states responsible for the grave crimes committed under the authority of the regimes they have led.

Notes

Transcripts/translations of Crown copyright in the Public Record Office, Kew, appear by permission of the Controller of HM Stationery Office. During the preparation of this chapter, I have gained from reading Catherine Whiteside, 'Arbitrary justice: the establishment, defendants, and controversy of the Tokyo war crimes trial', unpublished BA dissertation, University of Manchester, History Department, 1997.

1 For a valuable reassessment of the significance of the use of the atomic bomb against Japan, see Sadao Asada, 'The shock of the atomic bomb and Japan's decision to surrender – a reconsideration', *Pacific Historical Review* 67: 4 (November, 1998), 477–512.

2 For a balanced discussion of the reign of Hirohito, see Stephen Large, *Emperor Hirohito and Showa Japan* (London: Routledge, 1992). For a longer and more critical study, see H. P. Bix, *Hirohito and the Making of Modern Japan* (London: Duckworth, 2001).

3 For a wide-ranging, fascinating re-evaluation of the occupation, see John Dower, *Embracing Defeat: Japan in the Aftermath of World War II* (London: Allen Lane/ Penguin Press, 1999). Dower discusses the nature of the Tokyo trial and its concomitants in ch. 15 (pp. 443–84). See also R. E. Ward and Sakamoto Yoshikazu (eds), *Democratizing Japan: the Allied Occupation* (Honolulu: University of Hawaii Press, 1987).

4 For a balanced sympathetic study, see A. L. Hamby, *Man of the People: a Life of Harry S. Truman* (Oxford: Oxford University Press, 1995). The tide may now be turning in the opposite direction, as far as some historians are concerned. See the critical presidential address to the Society for Historians of American Foreign Relations by Arnold A. Offner, 'Another such victory', *Diplomatic History* 23: 2 (1999), 127–55.

5 The most comprehensive biographical discussion of MacArthur's role in Japan is found in the concluding volume of the study by D. Clayton James, *The Years of MacArthur*, vol. 3 *Triumph and Disaster, 1945–1964* (Boston: Houghton Mifflin, 1985).

6 See Dower, *Embracing Defeat*, which contains many astute observations on how MacArthur viewed the challenges facing him in directing the reconstruction of postwar Japan.

7 For a discussion of Anglo-American relations as concerned Japan, see Roger Buckley, *Occupation Diplomacy: Britain, the United States and Japan, 1945–1952* (Cambridge: Cambridge University Press, 1982); and Peter Lowe, 'Sir Alvary Gascoigne in Japan, 1946–1951', in Ian Nish (ed.), *Britain and Japan: Biographical Portraits* (Folkestone: The Japan Library, 1994), pp. 279–94, 340–2.

8 Buckley, *Occupation Diplomacy*, p. 108.

9 Public Record Office, Kew (hereafter PRO), LCO2/2983, letter from Patrick Dean, Foreign Office (hereafter FO) to Major General the Viscount Bridgeman, War Office, 14 November 1945.

10 PRO, LCO2/2983, telegram from the Dominions Office to Canada, Australia, New Zealand, and South Africa, 4 December 1945.

11 *Ibid.*, letter from Dean to Sir Hartley Shawcross, 14 December 1945.

12 PRO, FO371/57423/9642, despatch from the Secretary of State for Burma to the Governor of Burma, 18 January 1946.

13 PRO, FO371/57427/5116, Minute by R. G. J. Scott-Fox, 4 May 1946.

14 For a useful, brief biographical essay on Arthur Comyns Carr, see the entry by Roy Douglas in Duncan Brack (ed.), *Dictionary of Liberal Biography* (London: Politico's Publishing, 1998), pp. 84–5.

15 PRO, FO371/57423/1177, telegram from Washington [the Earl of Halifax] to FO, 29 January 1946. Here the British ambassador reported that the American State Department declined to approve the appointment of an Indian judge.

16 R. H. Minear, *Victors' Justice: the Tokyo War Crimes Trial* (Princeton, N.J.: Princeton University Press, 1971). For a helpful, concise survey of war crimes trials since 1945, see Yves Beigbeder, *Judging War Criminals: the Politics of International Justice* (London: Macmillan, 1999).
17 PRO, FO 371/57423/1620, telegram from Tokyo [Oscar Morland] to FO, 8 February 1946.
18 *Ibid.*, minute by Foulds, 12 February 1946.
19 *Ibid.*, telegram from FO to Tokyo [the British liaison mission], 15 February 1946.
20 See B. V. A. Röling, *The Tokyo Trial and Beyond: Reflections of a Peacemonger*, ed. and intro. by Antonio Cassese (Oxford: Polity Press/Blackwells, 1993), p. 87.
21 PRO, FO371/57423/1620, telegram from Tokyo [Alvary Gascoigne] to FO, 10 November 1947.
22 Ann Tusa and John Tusa, *The Nuremberg Trial* (London: BBC Books, repr. with new intro. 1995), p. 112.
23 Röling and Cassese, *The Tokyo Trial and Beyond*, pp. 29–30.
24 PRO, FO371/63820/15007, telegram from Tokyo [Gascoigne] to FO, 11 November 1947.
25 Röling and Cassese, *The Tokyo Trial and Beyond*, pp. 19–91; and R. J. Pritchard and S. B. Zaide (eds), *The Tokyo War Crimes Trials*, 22 vols (New York and London: Garland Publishing, 1981), vol. 21, pp. 1–249 (dissenting opinion of Röling). See also the interesting comments by Röling when he participated in a symposium held in Tokyo in 1983, as recorded in C. Hosoya, N. Ando, Y. Onuma, and R. Minear (eds), *The Tokyo War Crimes Trial: an International Symposium* (Tokyo: Kodansha International, 1986). I am most grateful to Professor Ian Nish for drawing the latter to my attention.
26 Röling and Cassese, *The Tokyo Trial and Beyond*, p. 29.
27 Röling's comments, as recorded in Hosoya *et al.*, *The Tokyo War Crimes Trial*, p. 190.
28 See Minear, *Victors' Justice*, pp. 183–4, where the text is reproduced.
29 *Ibid.*, pp. 185–92 for the text of the charter.
30 Röling's comments, as recorded in Hosoya *et al.*, *The Tokyo War Crimes Trial*, p. 190.
31 PRO, FO371/57428/7983, minute by F. F. Garner, 13 November 1946.
32 *Ibid.*, telegram from Tokyo [Gascoigne] to FO, 26 December 1946.
33 *Ibid.*, FO371/54728/6601, letter from Christmas Humphreys to Scott-Fox, 16 July 1946.
34 *Ibid.*, FO371/63820/13703, telegram from Tokyo [Gascoigne] to FO, 9 October 1947.
35 *Ibid.*, FO371/63820/15007, copy of a letter from Comyns Carr to Shawcross, 6 October 1947.
36 *Ibid.*
37 *Ibid.*, copy of a letter from Comyns Carr to Shawcross, 21 October 1947.
38 Pritchard and Zaide (eds), *The Tokyo War Crimes Trial*, vol. 15, pp. 36170–36840.
39 *Ibid.*, vol. 15, pp. 36180; 36327–8; 36381.
40 *Ibid.*, vol. 15, pp. 36534–5.
41 *Ibid.*, vol. 15, p. 36570.
42 PRO, FO371/69831/1566, copy of a letter from Comyns Carr to Shawcross, 2 January 1948.

43 *Ibid.*
44 *Ibid.*, FO371/69831/2130, telegram from Tokyo [Gascoigne] to FO, 25 January 1948.
45 See the references to Shigemitsu in Peter Lowe, *Great Britain and the Origins of the Pacific War* (Oxford: Clarendon Press, 1977); and Antony Best, *Britain, Japan and Pearl Harbor: Avoiding War in East Asia* (London: Routledge, 1995).
46 See Lord Hankey, *Politics, Trials and Errors* (Oxford: Pen-in-Hand, 1950), for an account of his campaign.
47 PRO, FO371/57428/8209, letter from Sir George Sansom to M. E. Dening, 4 December 1946.
48 *Ibid.*, FO371/69833, minute by D. J. Cheke, based on a discussion with Comyns Carr, 16 November 1948.
49 Röling and Cassese, *The Tokyo Trial and Beyond*, pp. 51–4.
50 *Ibid.*, p. 63.
51 Minear, *Victors' Justice*, p. 198.
52 Röling and Cassese, *The Tokyo Trial and Beyond*, p. 45. See also Hosoya *et al.*, *The Tokyo War Crimes Trial*, p. 131.
53 Pritchard and Zaide (eds), *The Tokyo War Crimes Trial*, vol. 21, p. 22 (dissenting opinion of Bernard).
54 *Ibid.*, vol. 21, pp. 3–4, 7–8, 17 (dissenting opinion of Webb).
55 *Ibid.*, vol. 21, p. 52 (dissenting opinion of Röling).
56 *Ibid.*, vol. 21, pp. 59–60.
57 *Ibid.*, vol. 21, pp. 67, 81–2, 124, 178.
58 *Ibid.*, vol. 21, pp. 197–8.
59 PRO, FO371/69833/15910, telegram from Tokyo [Gascoigne] to FO, 12 November 1948.
60 *Ibid.*, FO371/69833/15911, minute by E. J. F. Scott, 15 November 1948.
61 *Ibid.*, letter from M. E. Reed (Law Officers Department) to Sir O. Sargent, 18 November 1948.
62 *Ibid.*, FO371/69833/15996, minute by Scott, 15 November 1948. For Pal's views, stated at great length, see R. B. Pal, *International Military Tribunal for the Far East: Dissentient Judgment of Justice R. B. Pal* (Calcutta: Sanyal, 1953). Note also the observations by Dower, *Embracing Defeat*, pp. 469–74.
63 *Ibid.*
64 PRO, FO371/69833/16062, telegram from Tokyo [Gascoigne] to FO, 16 November 1948.
65 *Ibid.*, FO371/69833/16062, despatch from the Commonwealth Relations Office to the Government of New Zealand, 28 November 1948.
66 *Ibid.*, FO371/69833/16149, telegram from Tokyo [Gascoigne] to FO, 17 November 1948.
67 *Ibid.*, FO371/69833/16327, letter from Sir Robert Craigie to Sargent, 18 November 1948 [wrongly dated 'December'], with minute by Cheke.
68 *Ibid.*, letter from Sargent to Craigie, 24 November 1948.
69 *Ibid.*, minute by Cheke, 16 November 1948.
70 *Ibid.*, minute by Cheke, 17 November 1948.
71 For the text, see Minear, *Victors' Justice*, pp. 204–8.
72 *Manchester Guardian* (13 November 1948), enclosed in PRO, FO371/69834/16646.

73 PRO, FO 371/57423/1194, telegram from Tokyo [Gairdner] to FO, 30 January 1946.
74 Minear, *Victors' Justice.*
75 See John Dower, *War Without Mercy: Race and Power in the Pacific War* (New York: Pantheon, 1986) and *Embracing Defeat.*
76 Yuki Tanaka, *Hidden Horrors: Japanese War Crimes in World War II* (Oxford: Westview Press, 1996), p. 3.
77 *Ibid.*, pp. 206–9.
78 *Ibid.*, p. 18.
79 Pritchard and Zaide (eds), *The Tokyo War Crimes Trial*, vol. 6, p. 14576, vol. 17, p. 42017.
80 Note the contributions and answers to questions contained in Hosoya *et al.*, *The Tokyo War Crimes Trial*, pp. 56–67, 105–21, 152–8, 170–208; and also Röling and Cassese, *The Tokyo Trial and Beyond*, p. 86.
81 PRO, FO371/63820/12511, letter from Shawcross to W. E. Beckett, 9 September 1947.

8

The trial of Maurice Papon for crimes against humanity and the concept of bureaucratic crime

Robert Boyce

The trial of Maurice Papon in the assize court of Bordeaux over the winter of 1997–98 was noteworthy for several reasons. In the first place, the crimes for which he was charged had been committed more than half a century before the trial began. None of the three judges and only one of the nine jurors had even been born at the time the crimes occurred.[1] To assist the jurors to understand the circumstances surrounding the case, therefore, the state prosecutor as well as Papon's defence team were permitted to call upon a number of leading historians to describe the circumstances surrounding the events in question. This was a historic trial in more ways than one.

A second feature of the trial arose out of the nature of the charges. Papon, an official of the wartime Vichy regime, was charged with crimes against humanity for ordering the arrest and detention of nearly 1,600 Jews in Bordeaux where he was posted and their transfer to the transit camp at Drancy, north of Paris, from where they were deported to Auschwitz. He was thus charged not with one crime but with hundreds of crimes committed between June 1942 and May 1944. The *acte d'accusation*, a document of over a hundred pages, required two days of court time to read out, and between 8 October 1997 when the trial began and 2 April 1998 when the verdict was announced, 133 witnesses, dozens of depositions, and fifty thousand pages of documents were produced in court. This made it the longest and probably also the most expensive trial in French history.[2] It was also one of the most widely publicised. Every national newspaper and television channel provided regular coverage, and by the close Papon, Jean-Marc Varaut, Papon's chief counsel, Arno Klarsfeld, counsel for the children of the victims, and Jean-Louis Castagnède, the presiding judge, had become familiar names in France.[3]

A third feature of the trial was the status of the accused. This was not the first time a Vichy official had faced trial in France. Contrary to a still-popular myth that France has never faced up to its wartime record but preferred to sweep its crimes under the carpet, in the seven years after the Liberation over 124,000 Frenchman were brought to trial and more than 75 per cent of them were convicted of war crimes, mostly for collaboration with the occupying power or attacks against the Resistance. Marshal Philippe Pétain, head of the Vichy regime, was convicted of collaboration, although his death sentence was commuted to life imprisonment. Pierre Laval, twice Prime Minister under Pétain, was convicted and shot. Members of the prefectoral corps to which Papon belonged were purged with particular thoroughness. Of the approximately one hundred who had served Vichy, sixty were dismissed, two were shot, and a third was sentenced to death before having his sentence commuted to life; only six were kept in post, while the rest were transferred to other jobs.[4] Nor was that the end of it. In response to growing interest in France's role in the Holocaust, dossiers were re-opened and starting in 1975 several leading Vichy officials were charged with crimes against humanity.[5] Two were convicted, another died after charges were laid, and a fourth was assassinated by a deranged attacker prior to trial.[6] But in each of these cases the accused had been directly involved in wartime crimes as policeman, gaoler, or torturer, or as author of the policy that gave rise to the offence.[7] The same could not be said of Papon. At the time of the crimes for which he was charged, he was Secretary-General of the Prefecture in Bordeaux: a middle-ranking official who received orders from persons higher up the administrative chain and transmitted them to persons further below. His only weapon was his pen, and in most instances he never even saw his victims, who remained merely entries on his lists. For this reason, Papon could not be dismissed at his trial as the unacceptable face of Vichy. To all intents and purposes he was a representative figure of Vichy's administrative machine, a faithful executor of its policy. Despite Judge Castagnède's repeated protests that the trial was of one man, not of a whole political system, Papon was almost universally regarded as a proxy for the Vichy regime, and in the liberal media at least, his conviction was treated as the condemnation of Vichy as a whole.

A fourth feature of the trial was the remarkable range of hopes and fears attendant upon its outcome. To the surviving victims and their children, this was the opportunity long denied them of securing justice and obtaining some release from the frustration of watching terrible crimes go unpunished. To others not directly involved, it promised a salutary lesson for those tempted to support the extreme right-wing National Front, which shares a common heritage with Vichy and which had recently scored impressive election victories in several parts of France. Not all observers, however, were hopeful that good would come from the trial. Not a few, including several who were sympathetic to the victims, feared the result of relying upon the courts to improve public understanding of the past, when the actions of one age would inevitably be judged by the standards of another. This almost certainly was the reason why François Mitterrand was cool towards the prosecution of Papon and may have used his influence as president in the 1980s to delay the proceedings. 'Quand on n'a pas eu 20 ans en 1940, on n'a rien à dire sur Vichy',[8] he had once observed. As a former employee of Vichy who had known Papon since 1954 and been a close acquaintance of the Vichy chief of police, René Bousquet, it could be said that Mitterrand had a personal interest in letting sleeping dogs lie.[9] But Simone Veil, a Cabinet minister under Valerie Giscard d'Estaing, Mitterrand's predecessor, and an Auschwitz survivor, could in no way be described as a Vichy sympathiser. Yet she dissociated herself from the trial for similar reasons.[10] Another was Henri Rousso, Director of the *Institut d'Histoire du Temps Présent* and author of the highly regarded study of Vichy and modern memory *Le Syndrôme de Vichy*. He had been requested to appear as an expert witness by Papon's defence counsel, who evidently hoped to exploit Rousso's argument about the relativity of perceptions of the past to underline the dangers of convicting a man so many years after the crimes were committed. Rousso refused to be made use of for such partisan purposes.[11]

There were also those who feared that by raking over the coals of the Second World War the trial would damage Franco-German relations and in turn compromise French influence within the European Union.[12] And there were those who worried that the trial might undermine the reputation of contemporary conservatism in France itself because of Papon's post-war associations. At the Liberation in 1944, General Charles de Gaulle kept Papon in post, and upon returning to public office in 1958 he appointed Papon the Prefect of Police in Paris, a post he occupied in October 1961 when the police crushed a peaceful, if illegal, demonstration in favour of Algerian independence with extraordinary brutality and extensive loss of life.[13] When Papon retired from the prefectoral service in 1967, he received the plum job of President of Sud Aviation, a public sector company. The following year he was elected to Parliament as a member of the Gaullist Party, the *Union Democratique Républicaine* (UDR), replaced by the *Rassemblement pour la République* (RPR) after 1976. He ended his public career as Minister for the Budget in 1978–81 under Giscard d'Estaing, head of the liberal *Union Democratique Française* (UDF). Thus both wings of French conservatism were indirectly implicated by Papon, and for the sake of France's domestic harmony as well as its German and European relations, some observers would have preferred that the trial be indefinitely postponed.[14]

Despite the risks and inconvenience, however, the trial offered the possibility of squaring up to the past and exposing the real character of the Vichy state to a new generation that might not otherwise understand what it had done in France's name. In particular, it would provide insights into the motivations of the Vichy civil service: a means of explaining why a man like Papon should have participated in the systematic mistreatment of refugees and French citizens. Complete agreement on these issues was probably out of the question, but at the trial's conclusion most observers, witnesses, and even, it seems, jurors appear to have accepted that important new light had been shed upon this dark chapter in French history. Papon was widely portrayed as an arch-example of a bureaucratic criminal: one who from the remoteness of an administrative office had contributed to immoral or inhuman policies out of indifference or personal advancement.[15] This was a very different explanation from the older ones based upon assumptions that the French authorities had been forced into anti-semitic policies by the German occupiers or that the French had been inspired by their own anti-semitic prejudices. There are, however, grounds for doubting whether the images of Vichy or of Papon presented by the trial constitute an important advance in our understanding of the past.

I The peculiar origins of a bureaucratic criminal

The puzzle surrounding Papon's motives is illustrated by examining briefly his early life in order to see what values prevailed up to the time of Vichy. He was born in September 1910 into a middle-class and strongly republican family in Gretz-Armainvilliers, a town 25 kilometres east of Paris. His father, a notary by profession and founder of a thriving glass-manufacturing firm, was an active member of the local Radical Socialist Party. The largest party in the country, the Radicals presented themselves as the chief defenders of republican principles. Prominent in his father's circle were the two Radical Deputies for the Seine-et-Marne department, Jacques-Louis Dumesnil and François de Tessan, who were later to help the young Papon in his administrative career. Both men had long and highly successful political careers, culminating in a succession of ministerial posts in interwar governments, but in 1940 Dumesnil voted emergency powers for Marshal Pétain, for which he was banned from holding public office after the Liberation. De Tessan also voted for emergency powers, but soon joined the Resistance and died in the Nazi concentration camp at Dachau.[16] Their contrasting fates are illustrative of the dilemmas that confronted the liberal Third Republic and Papon himself after the outbreak of war.

A promising student, Papon graduated from the local primary school at Gretz-Armainvilliers and at the age of 11 went up to Paris to study for his *baccalaureat* at the *Lycée Montaigne*, and from there to the *Lycée Louis-le-Grand*, one of the great preparatory schools of Paris, to prepare for university. In 1929 he entered the faculty of law at the University of Paris. Upon gaining his *licence*, he spent two years at the military academy of Saint-Cyr, where he obtained a commission as a sub-lieutenant in the colonial infantry, before returning to complete his studies. At this point he took up political economy and public law, and entered the *Ecole des sciences politiques* to study public finance. Having obtained diplomas in law (*mention bien*) and political economy (*mention très bien*), and narrowly failing the *concours* for the *Inspection générale des finances*, he sat the civil service examinations in July 1935 and gained a post in the Ministry of the Interior. For eighteen months, from June 1936 to January 1938, he was seconded to assist de Tessan, first at the *Présidence du Conseil* and then the Foreign Ministry when de Tessan served as a secretary of state in the Popular Front governments. Thereafter he returned to the Ministry of the Interior until August 1939, when his request to rejoin the army was approved.

This was, by and large, a conventional trajectory for an entrant to the upper civil service of Papon's day, yet there are at least two features of his path that deserve mention. The first is his cultural and intellectual maturity. Papon demonstrated this during his student days in several ways, including his close interest in the theatre and his pursuit of diploma courses in psychology and sociology in addition to political economy at the *Ecole libre des sciences politiques* and his legal studies at the Sorbonne. The second is his intense patriotism, expressed through active commitment to liberal and republican causes. One example was his decision to join the *Ligue d'Action Universitaire Républicaine et Socialiste* (LAURS). Throughout his time as a student both the law faculty at the *Sorbonne* and the *Sciences Pô* were strongholds of right wing, anti-parliamentary *ligues*, notably the *Camelots du Roi*, the youth movement of *Action Française*. Indeed, only three years before Papon's arrival, the law faculty had erupted in rioting after a professor associated with the Radical-Socialist Party was nominated to an empty chair.[17] LAURS specialised in countering *ligue* demonstrations and their nationalist, anti-semitic policies, and later leading LAURS members were to become prominent in the wartime Resistance and post-Liberation politics. During Papon's student days its secretary was Pierre Mendès France, a Jew and future premier of France. Membership in LAURS was a notable act of independence on Papon's part, and a reflection of the seriousness with which he confronted public affairs. Nor did his commitment to republicanism and human rights end with his formal studies and entry into the civil service. Significantly, de Tessan, his political mentor, published a book entitled *Voici Adolf Hitler*, an early warning against the menace from the east. Between 1937 and 1939 Papon himself wrote occasionally for *Le Jacobin*, a small radical publication financed by a Jewish businessman, which distinguished itself by its stand against the policy of appeasement.[18] In 1938, by now married with a young family and living in somewhat cramped quarters, he provided shelter for some months to a Jewish friend from student days, who had been forced to flee Vienna after the *Anschluss*.[19] These episodes in Papon's early life were described at his trial and went unchallenged. By common consent there had been nothing in Papon's life before the war that pointed towards bigotry, race hatred, sympathy for fascism, or narrow, self-serving ambition; rather the contrary.[20]

On 10 May 1940 German armies invaded the Low Countries and France. The attack had long been anticipated but not the location of its *Schwerpunkt* nor its massive armoured follow-through. French forces that had advanced into Belgium were cut off and obliged to surrender. The rest of the army was thrown back in disarray, the British expeditionary force was hastily withdrawn to Dunkirk, and within six weeks the Battle of France had turned into a rout. The President of the Council, Paul Reynaud, resigned on 16 June, handing over to Pétain, the First World War hero and recently appointed Vice-President, who immediately requested an armistice. Humiliated, deputies and senators of the two Houses of the French Parliament retreated to Bordeaux, then to Vichy when Bordeaux was placed under direct German control. They met on 10 July in Vichy's municipal casino – the only building large enough to hold them – and voted overwhelmingly to accord Pétain exceptional powers. Within days, he began to implement his so-called National Revolution. This was, in fact, a counter-revolution: the revenge of the anti-dreyfusards, the adherents of the interwar *ligues*, the devotees of Charles Maurras, and all the enemies of the Popular Front, who sought to sweep away a century and a half of liberalism and to erect in its place a narrowly nationalist and authoritarian state. Called *l'Etat Français*, the very word republic was effaced and the motto *liberté, égalité, fraternité* was replaced by the triad *travail, famille, patrie*, borrowed directly from Maurras's *Action Française*, the most influential of the right-wing anti-parliamentary associations. The Vichy regime, as it has come to be known, gave expression to an exclusive view of French society, targeting freemasons, Protestants, the foreign-born, and Jews – particularly Jews – for exclusion. Days after emergency powers were voted, Vichy introduced the first orders restricting Jewish rights and freedoms. In August it lifted legal restrictions on anti-semitism in the media. And on 3 October it adopted the first of three *statuts des juifs*, which employed for the first and only time in French history the criterion of race as the basis of citizenship in order to exclude Jews from civil society.[21]

Papon was still at his army post on the Syrian frontier with Turkey when the first *statut* was introduced and may not have been fully aware of the racist foundations of the National Revolution. But he was soon demobilised, and before the end of October 1940 he was back at the Ministry of the Interior in Vichy, where he came under the wing of Maurice Sabatier, a senior colleague who had taken an interest in his career since 1936. With many officials either prisoners of war or dismissed as a result of the anti-semitic laws and the work of the Ministry increasing, Sabatier had rapidly ascended the administrative ladder. In 1940 he had become responsible for Algerian affairs, thus participating in the preparation and distribution of anti-semitic orders in North Africa. When the Ministry was reorganised into three main sections in October of that year, Sabatier became chief of the section responsible for departmental and local affairs. In February 1941 Admiral Jean-François Darlan, the head of government, appointed him to the newly created post of Secretary-General for Administration. Two months later the Germans replaced Darlan with Laval, who conducted a further shake-up of the Ministry, promoting officials prepared to support his policy of more active collaboration while relegating those who seemed less enthusiastic. The post of regional prefect – with executive authority for two or more departments – had recently been created, and Sabatier became Regional Prefect for the Aquitaine with authority for the Gironde, the Landes, and the Basses-Pyrénées departments, and centred on Bordeaux.

Papon's career advanced in lockstep with Sabatier's, including no less than five promotions in eighteen months. The last was his nomination as Secretary-General of the Prefecture of the Gironde in May 1942. In effect, he became Sabatier's deputy, and indeed on 20 June Sabatier delegated to him authority over a number of the most sensitive issues, including dealings with German occupation officials and the Jewish question.[22] The documents presented at Papon's trial confirmed that he wasted no time fulfilling his expanded duties. Within four days, his signature appeared on orders for the mass arrest of enemy aliens and the enumeration of foreign Jews. On 18 July the first convoy of 171 detainees left Bordeaux for Drancy, and thence to 'the East'. Over the next two years ten more convoys followed, carrying altogether 1,560 individuals including infants, elderly, and seriously ill victims. Through the efforts of Papon and the local gendarmerie, Bordeaux yielded up relatively more Jews to the Holocaust than the French average.[23]

II Papon's defences analysed

While not denying involvement in the deportations, Papon and his lawyers presented an elaborate rationale for his denial of responsibility for the tragic outcome. He claimed that he and French colleagues had had little choice but to act as they had done, because German authorities had closely monitored their actions and possessed their own sources of information on the local Jewish and refugee population.[24] With the Germans looking over their shoulders, French administrators had been bound to give the impression of diligence in following up orders.[25] This informed much of the documentation presented in the court. Since it had been produced with the German occupiers in mind, it could not be taken at face value and did not support the construction the prosecution placed upon it. In fact, French administrators had had an unwritten rule to go slow, and whenever possible Papon himself had sought to mitigate the harshness of the anti-Jewish policies, including the removal of over a hundred Jews from the deportation lists.[26] Moreover, while still in Vichy he had entered into contact with the Resistance, on several occasions risking his life to render them assistance.[27] He also claimed that, as a matter of principle, French administrative tradition allowed the delegation of authority but not of responsibility.[28] Hence it was Sabatier, his superior, who bore responsibility for the deportations that Papon had helped to organise.[29] He further insisted that he had not exercised authority over the police who carried out the mass arrests or over the detention camp from which victims were deported.[30] More emphatically, he claimed that he had not known, and could not have known, the fate of his victims: his task had been to detain them and have them transferred to Drancy. What had happened to them after they passed into German hands had only become known after the war.[31]

Certain elements of Papon's defence were by no means implausible. It is true that in France generally, as Robert Paxton, a Columbia University historian, explained to the court, the German occupiers were too few in number to carry out their repressive policies without the collaboration of French officials, who hence bear a heavy responsibility for the consequences. But Bordeaux itself was strongly held and the local French administration closely monitored on account of the city's strategic importance as an Atlantic port and naval base. Evidence also existed to show that Papon did render limited assistance to individual members of the Resistance in 1943 and 1944. His claim to have made contact with the Resistance as early as 1940 and to have actively worked for the Resistance almost from the moment he arrived at Bordeaux, however, was heavily suspect.[32] As proof, Papon produced his attestation of Resistance membership along with four witnesses prepared to corroborate his claim. However, the court also heard that his request to be regarded as a Resister had been refused several times after the war, and only when he obtained the influential post of prefect of police in Paris in 1958, had his claim been registered.[33] As for those called to testify on his behalf, all of them admitted that they had no direct knowledge of his Resistance exploits, while other Resistance leaders in a position to judge his claims had little or nothing to say in his favour. Papon thus appeared to have been '*un résistant du débarquement*', as one of the counsel for the victims put it: an eleventh-hour Resister, who had sought to create an alibi for himself when the course of the war turned decisively in the Allies' favour.[34] The German penetration and near-total destruction of the Resistance organisation in the Bordeaux region makes it more than usually difficult to be certain about the wartime events. But the evidence presented in the courtroom left little room for doubt that until the liberation of Bordeaux, Papon's first loyalty had been to the Vichy state, which had mounted a sustained campaign to crush the Resistance.

Other elements of his defence were comprehensively challenged. His claim that delegated authority carried with it no responsibility for the outcome, for instance, found support from only one other witness while being strongly disputed by others.[35] The prosecuting counsel pointed out that Papon's theory, if carried to its logical extreme, would leave Pétain to bear sole responsibility for all acts committed in Vichy's name.[36] Papon's own testimony revealed him to be far from consistent in applying the theory. Sometimes he insisted that his superior Sabatier had been to blame, while at other times he exonerated Sabatier on the grounds that he too had been under orders, and not infrequently Papon sought to deflect responsibility from himself onto his own subordinates, in particular the local police official in charge of arresting Jews. As for Papon's claim to have mitigated the worst consequences of the deportation policy, this was largely contradicted by the frequently chilling testimony of the surviving victims and other witnesses.

For example, it was shown that one of Papon's first acts on becoming Secretary-General of the Prefecture in Bordeaux had been to order ('*très urgent*') the arrest of four 'foreigners' and their transfer to Drancy. According to a police report in his possession, two of the four were foreigners and two

French citizens, and of the four two were Catholic, one was 'without religion', and the fourth was Jewish. But in the report Papon subsequently prepared they appeared quite differently: instead of nationalities only their birthplaces were given, which made them all appear to be foreign, one of the Catholics and the individual 'without religion' became Jewish, and the second Catholic became 'without religion'. Why Papon, usually a stickler for detail, should have misrepresented them is unclear. But the practical consequence was to make them all liable to be seized by the Germans and deported to concentration camps.[37] Another of Papon's early acts had been to instruct prefectoral officials to update and expand their records of Jews and refugees living in their departments, and this information was passed to the German authorities. Two months later, as plans were being made for a second convoy from Bordeaux, Papon confirmed to Sabatier's secretary that the German authorities were prepared to exclude children under 16 years of age. Nevertheless, among the 443 detainees aboard the train on 26 August 1942 were numerous under-age victims, including two aged 4 and 9 whose names appear to have been added hastily to the list. Some of the children had been placed in the care of non-Jewish families when their parents were arrested. The Bordeaux police had been sent out to arrest them.[38]

The Bousquet-Oberg agreement of July 1942, which paved the way for Vichy collaboration in the mass arrest and deportation of Jews from France, made an exception for French nationals and Jewish spouses of Aryans. Yet on several occasions Papon appears to have casually disregarded this dispensation. Thus in April 1943 Sabatino Schinazi, a French Jew married to a non-Jew, was arrested and detained along with the two eldest of the couple's nine children on the orders of Papon's section for Jewish affairs. Madame Schinazi repeatedly sought to secure their release, and eventually she succeeded in having the two children removed from the Jewish lists. Nevertheless for eighteen months they were detained and on 7 December 1943, despite Madame Schinazi's appeal to Papon, they found themselves on a train bound for Drancy and Auschwitz. It was only by luck that one of two children, Daniel, managed to escape. He and his brother, Samuel, arrested separately for acts of Resistance and later deported to Buchenwald, appeared before the court to recount the family's story.[39] Marie Reille, the Catholic wife of a French Jew, was also detained in Bordeaux and, despite the willingness of the Germans to allow her to remain behind, she was forced on board a convoy to Drancy on 21 September 1942 by one of Papon's officials. Her journey eventually took her to Poland and through the gates of Auschwitz before the German authorities pulled her from the crowd of women and children awaiting the short march to the gas chambers. With passage provided by the Germans, who apologised for the mix-up, she returned to Bordeaux where she marched to the prefecture to protest to the Director of the *Commissariat général aux questions juives* at this near-fatal mistake.[40]

As Papon's trial continued the court heard numerous other stories of Papon's conscientious and ostensibly enthusiastic efforts in support of Vichy's exclusionist policies. For example, in early July 1942, his order for improved records of Jews and refugees had gone out even though Jean Leguay, the Vichy official responsible for police operations against Jews, was still requesting his colleagues to sit tight and do nothing.[41] In November 1942, Papon sought and received permission from Darquier de Pellepoix, the Commissioner-General for Jewish questions, to cover the shortfall in his budgetary allocation for local anti-Jewish activity by charging expenses to the *Union générale des Israélites de France*: in other words, charging Jews for their own arrest, detention, sequestration of their property, and the destruction of their community.[42] As the *acte d'accusation* noted, when it came to anti-Jewish operations, Papon had displayed a zealous regard for the public purse while 'reacting like a good technocrat, seeking to demonstrate at all times his competence and efficiency.[43]

The Bousquet-Oberg agreement of 1942 called for the deportation of 40,000 Jews, 75 per cent from the German occupied zone and 25 per cent from the 'free' (Vichy) zone, with French Jews making up 40 per cent of the total. Initially only those aged between 16 and 45 years were to be selected, to maintain the fiction that they were destined for resettlement and hard labour in 'the East'. However, German demands for more victims led to the inclusion of the young and old, including the seriously ill, which undercut claims about their eventual fate. Meanwhile, the BBC and other agencies had begun to broadcast the emerging truth about the systematic liquidation of Jews in Poland and elsewhere.[44] The effect was to diminish public support for Vichy and, with the war turning against the Axis in 1943, the French police became increasingly reluctant to participate in anti-Jewish operations. In 1942, 42,000 Jews had been deported from France; in 1943, the total declined to 16,000.[45] Papon nevertheless did his best to fulfil his quotas. On his instructions, a convoy of 92 victims was despatched to Drancy on 25 November 1943, another of 136 victims on 30 December, and another of 317 victims on 12 January 1944. The final convoy of 50 victims left Bordeaux on 13 May 1944, barely more than two weeks before the long-awaited Allied landings in Normandy.[46] By then, Papon had been instrumental in deporting children as young as 6 months and men and women as old as 87 years, some of them dragged from their hospital beds.[47]

At his trial, Papon's repeated claim that he had not known the terrible fate awaiting the victims rang hollow in face of the evidence presented about contemporary awareness of the Holocaust. As early as the summer of 1942, the court heard, Jews incarcerated in Bordeaux had received word that the Germans had camps where they were systematically exterminating Jews, and by early 1943 reports had circulated that the Germans were using poison gas.[48] One victim testified that as he was being forced on board the convoy of 26 August 1942, a French police inspector demanded his ration card on the grounds that, 'Là où vous irez, vous n'en aurez plus besoin'.[49] Papon himself, Judge Castagnède pointed out, had betrayed an awareness of their fate by employing the term 'deportation' as early as July 1942. Papon lamely denied that the word had carried its current connotation during the war, and suggested that he should have written 'arrest'.[50] He persisted in claiming that no one, not even the Jews in France, had known of the existence of the extermination camps at that time, as evidenced by the shock and disbelief expressed when the camps were liberated in 1944. Prosecuting counsel argued that perhaps he had not known precisely how the Germans would dispose of the Jews, but it had been obvious that, once in German hands, they would be in danger. This alone had been contrary to Papon's duties as a public servant, and made his actions a crime.

III Results of the trial

The trial ended on 1 April 1998, and on 2 April the jury found Papon guilty on 430 of the 768 counts. For this he was sentenced to ten years' imprisonment suspended pending appeal.[51] Some of the victims or descendants expressed disappointment that the court and jury had stopped short of convicting him of complicity in murder and had sentenced him to less than life imprisonment since, in their opinion, he must have known the fate awaiting those deported from Bordeaux.[52] But by and large the outcome of the trial met with approval from those directly involved. Judge Castagnède was widely praised for the fairness of the proceedings. Most of the representatives of the Jewish and other deportee organisations affirmed that the verdict provided some release from the terrible sense of disregard they had suffered for so many years. And several of them acknowledged that Pétain's sentence reflected the essential need to distinguish between degrees of complicity. Théo Klein, former president of the *Conseil représentatif des institutions juives de France* (CRIF) observed that a life sentence might have transformed Papon into an object of sympathy. With the moderate sentence handed down, 'Les juifs ne sont plus en danger, il n'y a pas à avoir peur'.[53]

Most of the fears expressed at the outset of the broader political consequences also turned out to have been unfounded. It had seemed possible that the trial might revive anti-German sentiment in France, but the trial had turned out to be an almost purely *franco-français* affair. With Papon in the dock and Vichy's reputation under scrutiny, the chief emphasis was on crimes committed by Frenchmen against French men and women. If anything, the trial contributed to a moral levelling of France and Germany, which was more likely to reduce their current differences than increase them. The reputation of the conservative parliamentary parties of France, which also appeared threatened when the trial opened, emerged not merely unaffected but probably enhanced. Several embarrassing references were made during the proceedings to the indifference shown by de Gaulle, Giscard d'Estaing, and other post-war conservative leaders to the fate of Jews in France during the war.[54] But the trial focused considerably more attention upon the obscure wartime activities of Mitterrand, the Socialist leader, whose record as a Vichy official and receipt of Vichy's *francisque* medal at the hands of Pétain prior to joining the Resistance had aroused a storm of controversy when it became the subject of a recent best-seller.[55] Until the end of his life Mitterrand betrayed a deep ambivalence about Vichy's record. In contrast, Jacques Chirac, the Gaullist leader and Mitterrand's successor as president of France, had issued a forthright apology for crimes committed by Vichy, in a speech two years before the trial, marking the fifty-third anniversary of the first mass arrest of Jews in Paris in the *rafle du Vel d'Hiv*. Reference to the speech appeared repeatedly inside and outside the Bordeaux courtroom. At the very least, the trial went some way to reduce the perception of Vichy as a purely right-wing affair. On the other hand, the lengthy presentation of crimes committed against innocent Jews may have contributed to the break-up of the Front National shortly after the trial and its abrupt decline in electoral support.

As for greater public understanding of the past, however, the results of the trial were at best mixed. On the positive side, there is no doubt that the proceedings shed a harsh light on the reactionary and racist character of Vichy, as embodied in its National Revolution. Pétain's claim, made in his own defence after the Liberation, that he had been France's shield while de Gaulle had been its sword, has long been out of favour among academic historians while still widely accepted by the French public. The trial may thus have done something to chip away at the central myth of the Vichy regime, although one cannot be sure. In his final pleading, Alain Jakubowicz, counsel for the *Consistoire Israélite de France* and the B'nai B'rith, declared it a victory for the Davids over the Goliath of the state.[56] This, no doubt, is how the surviving victims and their relatives felt, having waited so long for the opportunity to air their grievances. But as Papon's chief counsel was wont to point out, the theatre of the courtroom lent itself to a different interpretation, with one old and physically ailing man in the dock, defending himself against accusations by a small army of lawyers for the interested parties, the state prosecutor, and three judges. For some observers at least, Jakubowicz's biblical analogy must have seemed hopelessly muddled.[57]

The trial almost certainly reinforced a number of other equally ill-founded beliefs, including the popular assumption that support for Vichy and the Resistance had been mutually exclusive. Evidence suggests loyalties and prejudices had not divided on such straightforward lines, and that not a few members of the Resistance may have shared with Vichy a narrow and anti-semitic view of the nation. The complexity of the situation is well illustrated by the wartime experience of Georges Kiejman, the former minister and celebrated trial lawyer. Kiejman and his mother, Jewish refugees from Poland, had sheltered in the town of Berri, a small town south of Paris, after the German invasion. Berri being in the German occupied zone, Jews were obliged to wear a yellow star of David, and one day Mrs Kiejman was arrested by a gendarme because her identity card did not identify her as a Jew. Mrs Kiejman was haled before a magistrate who, for reasons never made clear, accepted her story that she was not a Jew. The following year, the same gendarme who had arrested Mrs Kiejman was killed while engaged in Resistance activity.[58] Vichy agent and enforcer of Vichy's anti-semitic laws by day, the gendarme had been a Resistance hero by night. Papon sought to present himself in the court in similar guise, as a Vichy employee who had surreptitiously supported the Resistance throughout the German occupation. But as doubts were cast on his claim to have been an active Resister, the effect was to reinforce the old myth that one could not have been both a Vichyite and a Resister or a Resister and an anti-semite.

Nor was this the only way the trial tended to muddy the historical waters. Because it dwelt almost exclusively upon the wartime persecution of the Jews, it may also have helped to perpetuate the myth of pervasive anti-semitism in pre-war and wartime France. Among the French people, a small but vociferous minority did support Pétain and his anti-semitic, nativist National Revolution to the bitter end. But the great majority displayed almost none of the race hatred that characterised the peasant populations of, for example, Poland, Lithuania, or Hungary. Recent research indicates that from the start of the century and even in the 1930s, amidst almost unprecedented crises and increasing anti-semitism elsewhere, anti-semitism in France continued to decline.[59] The French population acquiesced in Vichy's policies because they looked to Pétain for protection, but they soon became disaffected when Hitler disregarded Pétain's efforts to secure a peace settlement and the return of prisoners of war. Prefects reported widespread public dismay and outrage once the mass arrests of Jews began.[60] Suffice it to note the observation of Serge Klarsfeld, Europe's leading Nazi hunter, which was repeated during the trial in response to Papon's claim that Vichy saved proportionately more Jews than other governments in occupied Europe. The one-quarter of France's Jews who perished during the war passed through Vichy's hands. The three-quarters of France's Jews who survived did so because of the Resistance and the many unrecorded acts of humanity by individual French men and women.[61] Nevertheless, with the trial devoted exclusively to French collaboration in the Holocaust, the almost inevitable impression created was of a wartime France fixated by anti-semitism.

As for Papon's motives, it may be that the trial was equally misleading, notwithstanding the mountain of evidence presented about his wartime activities. At first glance, it must seem obvious that he was motivated by anti-semitism, since so many Jews suffered and died as an indirect result of his actions. Certainly the policies he so vigorously implemented were monstrous and their consequences horrifying. Yet, as the court heard, the charge of anti-semitism did not square with his prewar record of liberal, anti-racist activity. Nor did the conflicting evidence end with the outbreak of war. Among his contemporaries within the Ministry of the Interior, Papon's closest friend was Maurice Lévy. Although a Jew, Lévy had been exceptionally allowed to remain in post after the introduction of the *statut des juifs* because of his distinguished war record in 1939–40, which included decorations for bravery. In 1942 Lévy sought to accompany Papon when he went to Bordeaux, and was dissuaded by Sabatier who pointed out that the Germans would not accept Jews in the Prefecture there.[62]

Marc-Olivier Baruch, the author of a widely praised history of the higher civil service under Vichy and one of the historians who appeared as an expert witness at Papon's trial, referred to the existence of latent anti-semitism within the higher civil service. But, as he explained to the court, it had not been anti-semitism that had driven them to participate in the Holocaust, but rather their loyalty to the state and the logic of Vichy's National Revolution.[63] According to his published account, no more than a handful of senior functionaries had been enthusiastic about the National Revolution itself.[64] One imagines that Sabatier, Papon's superior, had not been among them since, the court heard, his wife was a Jew.[65] There are abundant grounds for doubting that Papon had been any more enthusiastic. Arno Klarsfeld forthrightly acknowledged towards the end of the trial that, in his view, Papon had not acted out of personal animus against the Jews and hence was not to be regarded as anti-semitic.[66] Jakubowicz and Gérard Boulanger, two other leading counsel for the interested parties, echoed Klarsfeld's view. So, too, did Serge July, editor of the national liberal daily, *Libération*, whose leading article at the conclusion of the trial affirmed:

> Maurice Papon ne fut ni un partisan de la révolution nationale, ni un militant de la collaboration avec l'Allemagne, il n'était même pas anti-sémite. A cet égard, it était exemplaire d'une caste qui a compté aussi, à cette époque, ses héros emblématiques.
>
> Maurice Papon était simplement sécrétaire général de la préfecture. Il vient d'être condamné non pour un militantisme tragique en faveur d'une idéologie monstreuse, mais pour son activité de haut fonctionnaire autoritaire, efficace et indifférent à la portée de ses actes . . .
>
> L'idéologie administrative, lorsqu'elle est laissée à elle-même, peut engendrer des criminels de bureau. Il n'en sont pas moins criminels. C'est ce que vient de rappeler opportunément le verdict de Bordeaux.[67]

The view that Papon's crimes represented the behaviour of a man driven by personal ambition and working within a bureaucracy jealous of its authority, strongly hierarchical, and remote from the citizens whose lives were damaged or destroyed by its actions, found favour among a remarkable number of observers as the trial ended. Caroline Daigueperse, respresenting the *Consistoire central*, the *Union des communautés juives de France*, B'nai B'rith, and the Jews of Bordeaux, described Papon as having acted 'comme un fonctionnaire, un bureaucrate qui se retranche derrière un organigramme administratif, la hiérarchie, l'obéissance aux ordres'.[68] Bertrand Favreau, representing the *Ligue des Droits de l'homme*, spoke of Papon's 'crime de papier . . . anonyme, segmenté, froid . . . le fruit d'une chaîne de services'.[69] Michel Zaoui, representing the *Association amicales des déportés d'Auschwitz et des camps de Haute-Silésie* and other deportees' groups, spoke of 'ce crime administratif, ce crime de bureau, se distingue par l'éloignement du bureaucrate de sa victime', and he quoted Franz Kafka that 'les chaînes de l'homme torturé sont faites en papiers de ministères'.[70] Boulanger described Papon as a bureaucratic criminal, 'un technicien de commandement de la morgue'.[71] *Le Monde*'s chief diarist, the distinguished author Bertrand Poirot-Delpech, entitled his account of the trial *Papon: un crime de bureau*. In his view, the trial revealed Papon to have been a selfish authoritarian type, deferential to his superiors, coldly indifferent to his inferiors, a typical product of a higher civil service that had become indifferent to the nation it was supposed to serve and that served only itself. For him and like-minded critics, the lesson of the trial was that the upper civil service must be sensitised to its actions and encouraged to dissent on moral grounds whenever policies breached principles of republican justice.

It is no doubt true that the higher civil service in pre-war and wartime France was an exclusive and self-consciously elitist institution, that Papon, at least by the time of the trial in Bordeaux, appeared arrogant and indifferent to the fate of the victims, and that his wartime office occupied an intermediate place in a long and extremely complicated chain of command. Yet, even granting these points, the common view of his behaviour that emerged at the end of the trial seems unconvincing. One reason for his dissembling and cold, almost repellent, manner in the Bordeaux courtroom may be attributable to his advancing years and resentment at being made the scapegoat for the whole Vichy state. It was almost certainly due in part to the adversarial character of the trial, which led him to adopt the strategy of denying responsibility for everything and apologising for nothing.[72] It was further coloured by the image presented by Varaut, his chief legal counsel, whose confidence, apparent disdain for the victims, and royalist politics made him seem a throwback to the *Pétainiste* circles of the 1940s.[73] Added to this was the fact that, as Papon aged, he had moved increasingly in conservative circles, becoming remote from his youthful self. A tall, handsomely turned out octogenarian whose memory and repartee were often remarkably acute, it was all too easy to forget that the court was trying a young man who had arrived in Bordeaux fifty years earlier to assume responsibilities that in ordinary circumstances were well beyond those imposed on a 32-year-old.

As for the peculiarities of the French higher civil service as a whole, criticism of its remoteness and indifference to the consequences of its actions must be put into context. Not just France, but every country that has succeeded in establishing responsible government and the rule of law, has had to create a disciplined civil service, willing to resist the temptations of financial gain or political favouritism, and to subordinate itself to the will of its political masters. The French civil service was a Napoleonic creation, which bore a close resemblance to the military in structure and ethos. It took time to become professionalised and depoliticised, but the process was largely completed by the last quarter of the nineteenth century if not before. Like the French army, which was popularly known as *la grande muette* (the silent service), the higher civil service existed to do the bidding of the legally constituted government, whether of empire, monarchy, or republic, and whatever its political stripe.

This was the service that Papon joined in 1935: a time when France faced acute threats of internal social and political strife as well as possible attacks from Italy and Germany. Civil service tradition required him to set aside partisan politics, which he appears to have done more or less. But it did not require the suppression of the Jacobin patriotism which formed the core of his political beliefs. By then the French higher civil service had come to be regarded not merely as a source of secure employment but as a calling, 'something noble', in the words of two of the leading post-war officials who entered the service at virtually the same time as Papon.[74] Devotion to duty became all the more compelling when the French army was defeated in 1940 and the civil service found itself standing alone between the nation and the German occupiers, who proceeded to partition the country, detaching several parts from French control, handing over another to Italy, and absorbing one completely into the Reich. The reaction of officials such as Papon was to serve with greater discipline than ever. As several observers were to point out scornfully, the same higher civil service that had served the public good under the previous seventy years of republican government became a highly effective instrument of injustice when the Vichy state was created. It was, therefore, all too easy to portray Papon's career as a case of opportunism or moral relativism, in which he had moved effortlessly from serving the liberal Third Republic to authoritarian Vichy, then the liberal Fourth Republic, and finally de Gaulle's and Giscard d'Estaing's conservative Fifth Republic.[75] But to Papon himself, no doubt, this was precisely the point: the duty of higher civil servants was to ensure the continuity of the state, whoever was politically in charge. In the same way, prosecuting counsel argued that Papon's ruthless efficiency and personal ambition were evidence of his flawed personality because of the tragic consequences of his actions. Yet it is only fair to note that capable, ambitious individuals are everywhere sought after to ensure the efficient running of state bureaucracies.

In the summer of 1939 Papon had requested permission to join the army, which was not the action of a coward. While he was overseas, the Third Republic gave way to the Vichy *Etat français*, an act whose constitutionality has been widely questioned since 1945, but which went largely unquestioned in wartime France. Practically no one in public life, not even de Gaulle, was prepared to speak up for the Third Republic, which appeared to have failed calamitously, and Vichy's legitimacy seemed established by the overwhelming vote of deputies and senators in favour of according Pétain emergency powers. Papon's decision to accompany Sabatier to Bordeaux in the spring of 1942 was consistent with his earlier behaviour. Bordeaux, southern anchor of Germany's Atlantic wall and a major submarine base, lay firmly inside the occupied zone. Vichy's decision to send such a senior civil servant as Sabatier reflected its determination to maintain French authority in the city and stop it slipping completely into Germany's New Order. Papon, it seems reasonable to assume, shared this preoccupation: a pressing and ostensibly vital one at a moment when Germany appeared to have won decisively in the West and was still on the offensive in the East. It is almost certainly for this reason that Sabatier, Papon, and Lévy were prepared to leave the relative comfort of Vichy to live under the constant surveillance of the Germans in Bordeaux, and for Sabatier and Papon to follow orders from Vichy despite their brutal consequences.

Viewed in this light, the motives that drove Papon to assume responsibility for the 'Jewish question' in Bordeaux were, to all intents and purposes, no different from those that prompted his compatriots to join the Free French in London or the Resistance within France. In each case the crucial impetus was patriotism. The difference between them lay not with personal ambition or moral blindness, but largely the circumstances in which they found themselves and the practical consequences of their actions. This in no way diminishes the awfulness of the crimes for which Papon was charged and convicted. It may be agreed that there is something particularly monstrous about participating in the arrest of innocent and vulnerable men, women, and children, and handing them over to an enemy manifestly bent upon abusing them, even if one did not know what would actually happen to them. Papon, having chosen to carry out these acts, bore some responsibility for the consequences and hence was guilty of crimes against humanity.[76] But it is perhaps too easy to forget the moral compromises required of all those who were prepared to defend France, including the Free French forces who carried out the systematic bombing of large civilian concentrations in German towns and cities, and the Resisters whose acts of sabotage enabled the Germans to present them as terrorists and provoked the execution of innocent hostages. In every case, love of country at a time of unprecedented crisis led people to behave as if the end justified the means. It is now widely accepted that Pétain and the Vichy regime were too little concerned with national liberation and too much preoccupied with their reactionary National Revolution to warrant comparison with the other two French wartime forces. This undercuts the moral legitimacy of a Vichy agent such as Papon. Yet his patriotism, however misdirected, seems to have been real enough.[77] For all its efforts to expose the truth about Papon's responsibility for the fate of the 1,560 deportees from Bordeaux, the assize court was ultimately not very helpful in establishing the motives for his acts. This was perhaps the greatest shortcoming of the trial. But in fairness to those involved, historians are seldom much better than lawyers in unravelling the conundrum of human volition.

Notes

1 The composition, occupation, and age of the jurors are given in J.-A. Fralon, 'Pendant l'attente: "La nuit est dure, mais c'est le bout du chemin"', *Le Monde* (3 April 1998), p. 6. See also *Le Procès de Maurice Papon*, tome 1, *8 octobre 1997–8 janvier 1998* (Paris: Albin Michel, 1998), p. 33. This is the most complete, albeit still far from comprehensive, transcript of the trial. Where appropriate, the author has drawn from other sources, notably the transcript compiled by Usha and Jean-Marie Matisson for the victims and interested parties and made available through the internet at *www.matisson-consultants.com/affaire-papon* (hereafter Matisson MS).

2 The Ministry of Justice estimated the cost at 15 million francs. P. Nivelle, 'Insolvable, Papon doit 4,6 millions de francs', *Libération* (4 April 1998).

3 'Parmi les records battus par le procès, il y aura eu celui de la couverture médiatique', B. Poirot-Delpech, *Papon: un crime de bureau* (Paris: Editions Stock, 1998), p. 68.

4 N. Weill, 'Le souvenir amer d'une répression parfois défaillante', *Le Monde Supplément* (1 October 1997), p. vii.

5 Aside from Germany, obviously a special case, France thus became the only country to put its own nationals on trial for crimes against humanity committed during the Second World War. R. O. Paxton, 'The Trial of Maurice Papon', *The New York Review* (16 December 1999), p. 32.

6 The charges and summaries of the court record of those facing trial since the 1970s are conveniently compiled in S. Chalandon and P. Nivelle (eds), *Crimes contre humanité: Barbie, Touvier, Bousquet, Papon* (Paris: Librairie Plon, 1997).

7 Statement by the *avocat général*, Marc Robert, 9 October 1997, *Procès*, t. 1, p. 45.

8 ('If you weren't twenty in 1940, you have nothing to say about Vichy.') Mitterrand had also described the law specifying crimes against humanity of 1964, which was to apply retroactively to the wartime period as 'a political settling of scores'. S. Denis, 'De Gaulle disait "Les fonctionnaires sont faits pour fonctionner." Toute la carrière de Papon le preuve. Sans états d'âme', *www.Parismatch.fr*, n.d.

9 Indications that Mitterrand may have discouraged the trials are summarised in Poirot-Delpech, *Papon*, pp. 453–4. See also P. Péan, *Une jeunesse française: François Mitterrand 1934–1947* (Paris: Fayard, 1994), pp. 313–20, 516–21; A. Klarsfeld, *La Cour, les nains et le bouffon* (Paris: Robert Laffont, 1998), pp. 80–1; 'La fin d'un marathon juridique', *Libération* (24 January 1997). However, Henri Nallet, *garde des Sceaux* (lord chancellor), and Georges Kiejman, the deputy minister of justice, categorically denied any interference by Mitterrand in Bousquet's trial and by implication other trials of Vichy officials. See J. Lacouture, *Mitterrand: une histoire d'un français*, t. 2: *Les vertiges du sommet* (Paris: Editions du Seuil, 1998), pp. 529–33.

10 *Procès*, t. 1, pp. 675–6 (statements by Jean-Marc Varaut and Jean Serge Lorach, 11 December 1997).

11 *Ibid.*, pp. 77–8 (letter read to the court by the presiding judge, Jean-Louis Castagnède, and statement by Varaut, 13 October 1997). Varaut did not fail to exploit Rousso's absence, see *ibid.*, p. 317 (31 October 1997), and t. 2, pp. 872, 875 (24 March 1998). On the dangers of merging the functions of historical investigation and courtroom, see J.-N. Jeanneney, *Le Passé dans le prétoire: l'histoire, le juge, et le journaliste* (Paris: Editions du Seuil, 1998); H. Rousso, *La Hantise*

du passé (Paris: Textuel, 1998); J. D. Bredin, 'A quel moment faut-il choisir de désobéir?'; and P. Nora, 'l'impossible imprescriptibilité', in Poirot-Delpech, *Papon*, pp. 455–8, 463–4.

12 See, for example, the testimony of Maurice Druon, *secrétaire perpétuel* of the *Académie Française*, *Procès*, t. 1, p. 297 (22 October 1997).

13 J.-L. Einaudi, *La bataille de Paris: 17 octobre 1961* (Paris: Editions du Seuil, 1991). At Papon's instigation, Einaudi was charged with criminal libel, but was acquitted after a weeklong trial in February 1998.

14 C. Chambraud, 'La droite est partagé sur l'analyse du régime de Vichy', *Le Monde* (23 October 1997). A useful survey of the hopes and fears aroused by the trial is set out by the documentary filmmaker M. Halter, 'Le désastre du procès Papon', *Libération* (29 December 1997).

15 See below, pp. 170–1.

16 G. Boulanger, *Maurice Papon, un technocrat français dans la collaboration* (Paris: Editions du Seuil, 1994), p. 28 and *passim*; P. Miquel, *Les quatre-vingts* (Paris: Fayard, 1995), p. 246.

17 E. Weber, *Action Française: Royalism and Reaction in Twentieth-Century France* (Stanford: Stanford University Press, 1962), pp. 157–9.

18 *Procès*, t. 1, p. 372, (testimony of Papon, 3 November 1997).

19 *Ibid.*, t. 2, p. 861, (statement by Francis Vuillemin, 23 March 1998).

20 *Ibid.*, t. 1, pp. 183–8, 371–2 and *passim* (testimony of Papon, 15 October and 3 November 1997); also Boulanger, *Maurice Papon*, pp. 26–30; B. Violet, *Le Dossier Papon* (Paris: Flammarion, 1997), *passim*; P. Nivelle, 'Jeune homme de cabinets', *www.libération.fr/papon/Procès/histoire1.htm.*

21 R. O. Paxton, *Vichy France: Old Guard and New Order, 1940–1944* (London: Barrie & Jenkins, 1972), p. 174; D. Peschanski, 'Exclusion, persécution, répression', in J.-P. Azéma and F. Bédarida (eds), *Vichy et les français* (Paris: Fayard, 1992), pp. 209–34.

22 *Procès*, t. 1, pp. 368–71 (testimony of Papon, 3 November 1997); Matisson MS, 'Attributions de Papon au Ministère de l'Intérieur entre 1940 et 1942: éléments de l'interrogatoire de l'accusé par l'avocat général Robert – audience du 3.11.1997'.

23 N. Weill, 'Bordeaux ou les délices de l'accommodation', *Le Monde Supplément* (1 October 1997), p. iii.

24 *Procès*, t. 1, p. 514 (cross-examination by Castagnède, 14 November 1997).

25 The claim was corroborated in the testimony of Marguerite Bonnecaze, *ibid.*, t. 2, pp. 8, 12 (9 January 1998).

26 *Ibid.*, t. 1, p. 712 (testimony of Papon, 12 December 1997); see also *ibid.*, p. 721 (15 December 1997); but see J. Amalric, 'Confondant', *Libération* (3 December 1997).

27 *Procès*, t. 2, p. 518 and *passim* (testimony of Papon, 14 November 1997). Papon's defence is summed up by Varaut at *ibid.*, pp. 869–945 (24, 30, 32 March and 1 April 1998).

28 *Ibid.*, t. 1, pp. 438, 613 (testimony of Papon, 6 November and 8 December 1997).

29 *Ibid.*, pp. 438–9 (6 November 1997).

30 *Ibid.*, p. 610 (8 December 1997).

31 *Ibid.*, p. 405 (4 November 1997), t. 2, pp. 432, 445 (11 February 1998).

32 *Ibid.*, t. 1, p. 393 (4 November 1997).

33 *Ibid.*, t. 2, pp. 524–5 (cross-examination by Castagnède, 18 February 1998).

34 'Me Blet passe au crible la défense de ce "résistant du débarquement"', *Le Monde* (13 March 1998).

35 Bernard Bergerot, director of personnel at the Ministry of the Interior from 1951 to 1958, concurred with Papon's interpretation, *Procès*, t. 1, p. 452 (7 November 1997); but see, for example, the testimony of Marc-Olivier Baruch, *ibid.*, p. 422 (5 November 1997). According to Alain Lévy, counsel for the *Fédération nationale des déportés et internés résistants et patriotes* (FENDIRP), Papon and his defence wilfully confused administrative law and penal law in their attempt to shift responsibility to superiors, Matisson MS, Maître Lévy, 'Klaus Barbie et Papon ont tous deux pris la vie des enfants', p. 13.

36 See, for example, the exchange between the *procureur général*, Henri Desclaux, and Papon, *ibid.*, t. 2, pp. 98–100 (15 January 1998).

37 *Ibid.*, t. 1, pp. 109, 162, 622–5, 630; Boulanger, *Maurice Papon*, pp. 82–4.

38 *Procès*, t. 1, p. 120 (*acte d'accusation*); *ibid.*, p. 882 (cross-examination by Castagnède, 23 December 1997).

39 *Ibid.*, t. 2, pp. 193–7 (cross-examination by Robert, 26 January 1998), pp. 204–9 (testimony of Samuel Schinazi, 27 January 1998), pp. 209–19 (testimony of Moïse Schinazi, 27 January 1998).

40 *Ibid.*, t. 2, pp. 38–44 (testimony of Yvette Silva, 12 January 1998).

41 *Ibid.*, t. 1, pp. 691–4 (cross-examination by Castagnède, 11 December 1997), pp. 743–50 (cross-examination by Robert, 16 December 1997).

42 *Ibid.*, t. 2, pp. 175–6 (cross-examination by Castagnède, 23 January 1998).

43 *Ibid.*, t. 1, p. 144 (*acte d'accusation*).

44 *Ibid.*, pp. 158–61 (*acte d'accusation*), p. 334 (statement by Bertrand Favreau, 31 October 1997).

45 *Ibid.*, pp. 310 (testimony by R. O. Paxton, 31 October 1997).

46 *Ibid.*, p. 108 (*acte d'accusation*).

47 *Ibid.*, t. 2, pp. 31, 439–41 and *passim* (evidence presented by Robert).

48 *Ibid.*, p. 205 (testimony by Simon Schinazi, 27 January 1998).

49 ('Where you're going, you won't need this any more'.) Chalendon and Nivelle (eds), *Crimes contre humanité*, p. 418.

50 *Procès*, t. 1, p. 696 (testimony of Papon, 11 December 1997). See also Chalendon and Nivelle (eds), *Crimes contre humanité*, pp. 398, 408.

51 In addition, the court demanded 4.6 million francs from Papon for costs and compensation to the victims, P. Nivelle, 'Insolvable, Papon doit 4,6 millions de francs', *Libération* (4 April 1998).

52 The disappointed included Alain Lévy, counsel for the *Fédération nationale des déportés et internés résistants et patriotes*, Bertrand Favreau, counsel for the *Ligue des Droits de l'homme*, Gérard Boulanger, counsel for several of the surviving victims, and Juliette Benzazon, the widow of one of the victims. Matisson MS, 'Les réactions au verdict', 15 April 1998.

53 ('Jews are no longer in danger, there is no more cause for fear'.) D. Licht, 'Quasi-unanimité autour du verdict: politiques et associations saluent la valeur pédagogique du procès', *Libération* (4 April 1998). Among others who welcomed the verdict were Dominique Delthil, counsel for *SOS-Racisme*, Joë Nordmann, counsel for FENDIRP, Caroline Daigueperse, counsel for the *Association cultuelle israélite de la Gironde*, the *Consistoire central*, the *Union des communautés juives de France*, and B'nai B'rith, and Arno Klarsfeld, counsel for the *Association des fils et filles des*

déportés juifs de France, Maurice-David Matisson, a surviving victim, Samuel Pisar, a leading member of the French Jewish community, Grand Rabbis Maman and Sitruck, and Henri Hajdenberg, President of the *Conseil représentatif des institutions juives de France* (CRIF), Matisson MS, 'Les réactions au verdict', 15 April 1998. See also J.-A. Fralon, 'Pendant l'attente: la nuit est dure, mais c'est le bout du chemin', *Le Monde* (3 April 1998), p. 6.

54 See, for example, *Procès*, t. 1, pp. 313, 412, 414, t. 2, p. 729.

55 In 1992 Mitterrand himself added to the controversy by placing a flower on Pétain's tomb. See *ibid.*, t. 1, p. 333 (cross-examination by Lévy, 31 October 1997), and t. 2, p. 698 (statement of A. Klarsfeld, 10 March 1998).

56 Matisson MS, 'Pour l'éternité', 12 March 1998.

57 On preliminary public reactions to the trial, see N. Weill, 'Une contribution ambiguë à l'historiographie de Vichy', *Le Monde* (3 April 1998), p. 9; also 'Réactions', *ibid.*, p. 9.

58 R. Bernstein, 'French collaborators: the new debate', *New York Review* (25 June 1992), p. 41.

59 R. Rémond, 'L'opinion française des années 1930 aux années 1940. Poids de l'événement, permanence des mentalités', in J.-P. Azéma and F. Bédarida (eds), *Vichy et les Français* (Paris: Fayard, 1992), pp. 490–1.

60 *Procès*, t. 1, p. 351 (testimony of J.-P. Azéma, 3 November 1997), t. 1, p. 409 (testimony of René Rémond, 4 November 1997).

61 *Ibid.*, t. 1, p. 357 (testimony of Azéma, 3 November 1997), p. 601 (statement by A. Klarsfeld, 8 December 1997).

62 *Ibid.*, p. 394 (testimony of Papon, 4 November 1997).

63 *Ibid.*, p. 420 (testimony of Baruch, 5 November 1997).

64 Baruch, *Servir l'état français*, pp. 168–9, 201 and passim.

65 *Procès*, t. 1, p. 290 (testimony of Mme Chapel, 22 October 1997).

66 *Ibid.*, t. 2, pp. 690, 703 (statement by A. Klarsfeld, 10 March 1998).

67 ('Maurice Papon was neither a partisan of the National revolution nor a militant of collaboration with Germany, he was not even anti-semitic. In this regard, he was exemplary of a caste which had, at this time, its emblematic heroes. Maurice Papon was simply secretary-general of the prefecture. He has just been condemned, not for a tragic militancy in favour of a monstrous ideology, but for his activity as a senior civil servant in which he was authoritarian, efficient and indifferent to the consequences of his actions . . . The administrative ideology, given free rein, can engender bureaucratic criminals. They are not less criminals. This is what the verdict in Bordeaux has opportunely signalled.') S. July, 'La fin des intouchables', *Libération* (4 April 1998).

68 ('as a coward, a functionary, a bureaucrat, who hid behind the organisation chart of the administration, the hierarchy, obeying orders'.) Matisson MS, 'Maître Daigueperse: "Vous proclamerez haut et fort l'alliance de la morale et de la justice"', 10 March 1998. Klarsfeld presented a similar explanation in his account of the trial, *La Cour*, p. 26.

69 ('crime by official documentation . . . anonymous, compartmentalised, callous . . . the result of a chain of command'.) Matisson MS, 'Maître Bertrand Favreau: "Mille cinq cent soixante fois une vie"', 13 March 1998.

70 ('this administrative crime, this bureaucratic crime, whose feature is the distance of the bureaucrat from his victim'), ('the chains of tortured humanity are made of

ministerial paper work'). *Ibid.*, 'Michel Zaoui "la spécificité du crime administratif" ', 16 March 1998.

71 ('a technician from the morgue'.) *Ibid.*, G. Boulanger, 'Le premier contre l'humanité est constitué dès que le premier homme a été tué parce qu'il est né' (9 March 1998).

72 *Procès*, t. 1, p. 69 (statement by Zaoui, 13 October 1997); *ibid.*, t. 2, pp. 854–5 (statement by Vuillemin, 23 March 1998).

73 Varaut had, in fact, written a sympathetic account of Pétain, *Le procès Pétain: 1945–1995*, and this was the object of a sustained attack by one of the prosecuting counsel. Matisson MS, Maître R. Blet, 'Ce numéro 41796 restera toujours sur le bras de monsieur Balbin, mais au moins il pourra lever son bras avec fierté,' 11 March 1998.

74 F. Bloch-Lainé and C. Gruson, *Hauts fonctionnaires sous l'occupation* (Paris: Odile Jacob, 1996), pp. 29, 130.

75 One counsel for the interested parties called him a chameleon, Klarsfeld, *La Cour*, p. 125, another 'une espèce d'ectoplasme qui peut vivre dans n'importe quel milieu' ('a sort of ectoplasm capable of living in any sort of condition'), Matisson MS, Maître Charrière-Bournazel, 'De ces âmes errantes vous êtes, comme moi, les petits frères inconsolés', 16 March 1998. See also P. Birnbaum, 'Les fonctionnaires contre la République', *l'Arche: le mensuel du judaïsme français*, www.col.fr/arche/arguments.htm

76 On Papon's guilt compared to that of Adolf Eichmann, Klaus Barbie, Paul Touvier, and René Bousquet, see the table of comparison in Klarsfeld, *La Cour*, pp. 230–1.

77 Baruch, almost alone among witnesses, affirmed this point, *Procès* t. 1, pp. 422–3 (5 November 1997).

9

The trial of Slobodan Milosevic: a twenty-first century trial?

Dominic McGoldrick

At 10.02 am on Tuesday, 3 July 2001, Slobodan Milosevic made an initial appearance before the International Criminal Tribunal for the former Yugoslavia (ICTY).[1] He wore a blue suit, a blue shirt, and a tie in the national colours of Serbia. He was the first former head of state in history to be prosecuted for war crimes by an international tribunal.[2] This image of international criminal justice was flashed across the world's media.[3] The humbling of a former head of state carried massive significance in terms of the power of law and institutions acting in the name of the international community. As many observers and the prosecution noted, the ghost of Nuremberg had finally risen. The trial proper began on 12 February 2002 and was expected to last up to two years.

This chapter considers the principal features of the first war crimes trial of the twenty-first century in terms of personnel and procedures, the alleged crimes, and issues of legality and legitimacy. It also speculates on the narratives or non-narratives of the trial and how these may impact on the professed aims and objectives of the litigation. This last aspect necessarily raises more questions than answers, but a trial of this magnitude justifies both preliminary analysis and speculation, not only to assist observation of the trial as it unfolds but also to challenge and provoke beyond mere observation.

I Slobodan Milosevic

Slobodan Milosevic was born on 20 August 1941 in Pozarevac, in present-day Serbia. In 1964 he graduated from the Law Faculty of the University of Belgrade. During a career in management and banking he held senior positions in a major oil company and in one of the largest banks in the Socialist Federal Republic of Yugoslavia (SFRY). Having joined the League of Communists of Yugoslavia in 1959, he held a succession of important party positions, culminating in the presidency of the Socialist Party of Serbia (SPS), an amalgamation of the League and the Socialist Alliance of Working People of Serbia. In 1989 he was elected President of the Presidency of the then Socialist Republic of Serbia (now the Republic of Serbia). In 1990, he was elected President of the Republic of Serbia in multi-party elections; he won re-election in 1992. Five years later he was elected President of the Federal Republic of Yugoslavia (FRY). He relinquished that position on 6 October 2000 following his defeat in the presidential election.

During the dissolution of the former Yugoslavia, Serbia fought successive conflicts with Slovenia, Croatia, and Bosnia to maintain the federal state.[4] It also engaged in a prolonged struggle to keep Kosovo as part of Serbia.[5] Milosevic rose to international prominence during this period and was surrounded by a cult of personality. He was demonised by Western media, being described as the 'Butcher of Belgrade'.[6] In relation to Kosovo, in April 1987 he famously told Serbs that the Kosovo Albanians would not beat them any more.[7]

In May 1999, Judge Hunt of the ICTY confirmed an indictment against Milosevic and four others[8] and issued an international arrest warrant. Two additional indictments followed. In January 2001, warrants to the FRY for the freezing of assets and surrender of Milosevic and the others were reissued. Milosevic was arrested on 1 April 2001 by the local authorities after a 26-hour siege of his presidential villa in Belgrade.[9] On 29 June 2001, he was transferred to the ICTY and detained on remand at the United Nations Detention Unit in Scheveningen, The Hague. He was kept in solitary confinement for a month. Throughout his incarceration he was been subject to constant electronic surveillance. His initial appearances in respect of the indictments took place on 3 July 2001 (the Kosovo indictment), 29 October 2001 (the Croatia indictment), and 11 December 2001 (the Bosnia indictment).

II Courtroom logistics

The case was set down for trial by Trial Chamber III, composed of three judges. The Presiding Judge is Richard May (United Kingdom), a specialist in criminal law and evidence.[10] The other two judges are Patrick Robinson (Jamaica) and O-Gon Kwon (South Korea). The working languages of the ICTY are English and French. Translation is provided into Serbo-Croat, but Milosevic has refused to use it. He is fluent in English but has spoken only Serbo-Croat at the trial. The trial is held in Court Number One, a small, modern, office space containing twenty-four computer monitors and an electronic projector (an ELMO). The three judges sit at the centre on a slightly raised dais and wear red and black gowns provided by the ICTY. To their immediate left the UN flag is draped on a pole. In front of the bench are the officials from the Registry. To the left is the prosecution team, to the right the three *amici curiae* (friends of the court). The lawyers wear their national legal costumes.[11] Milosevic sits on the far right, with two UN security officials close by. On each side of the courtroom is a series of booths for the translators. The Chamber is separated from the public by a bullet-proof glass wall, which creates a 'fish-bowl' effect. Participants and spectators are asked to rise when the judges enter and leave the courtroom.

The ICTY's internet site contains all of the essential documents related to the trial. These include the indictments and their amended versions, the transcripts of the hearings, and all of the Orders and Decisions. After press requests, the Chamber authorised still photography by three designated press photographers at the commencement of all proceedings and the release of the audio-visual record of the proceedings to the media. The ICTY films the proceedings and no independent filming is allowed inside the courtroom. Given the high media interest and limited space, only one person per media organisation has been admitted to the public gallery of the courtroom. For that same reason, and in order to accommodate as many media representatives as possible, media accreditation for the first week of the trial was on a daily basis, with different media representatives having access to the public gallery on each day. A media centre has also been established in the Netherlands Congres Centrum, opposite the ICTY, where the trial was relayed on a large video screen for the first week. On the first day, the opening statements were relayed with a simultaneous English translation. Subsequently, the relay and publication of public proceedings on the ICTY's website in English, Bosnian/Croat/Serb and Albanian has included a 30-minute delay. The delay is to prevent the disclosure of the identities of protected witnesses.

The prosecution team[12] is headed by the ICTY Prosecutor, Carla Del Ponte, a former Attorney General of Switzerland, and includes advocates from the UK and the Netherlands.[13] There is no defence counsel because Milosevic stated his wish to defend himself.[14] Part of his reasoning was that the ICTY was illegitimate, so he would not require lawyers to conduct a defence before it. The prosecution asked the Chamber to consider appointing a defence counsel, but the Chamber determined that such an appointment would breach international customary law. However, in August 2001, the Chamber requested the Registrar to designate *amicus curiae* for the proceedings.[15] While acknowledging that Milosevic was entitled to represent himself, the Chamber considered that it had the duty of ensuring that the trial was fair and that his rights were fully respected. On 6 September 2001, the Registrar designated Mr Steven Kay QC (London), Mr Branislav Tapuskovic (Belgrade), and Professor Michail Wladimiroff (The Hague) to act as *amici curiae*. The Chamber stressed that the *amici* did not represent Milosevic and could not put forward a positive defence case. Their role was to assist the Chamber in the proper determination of the case by making any submissions properly open to the accused by way of preliminary or pre-trial motion or by interventions during the trial. These could include objecting to evidence, cross-examining witnesses, and drawing the Chamber's attention to any exculpatory or mitigating evidence, but not calling witnesses or cross-examining on instructions. The Chamber later added that the *amici* should also point out any defences, for example, self-defence, which might properly be open to Milosevic and, significantly, make submissions as to the relevance, if any, of the NATO air campaign in Kosovo.[16] They are provided with copies of all the material provided to Milosevic and other specified documents, but they are not provided with any filings made on an *ex parte* basis. Milosevic protested at the appointment of the *amici*, regarding them simply as part of the ICTY and an expression of what he ironically termed the 'Hague fair play'. In October 2000, Wladimiroff's appointment was revoked after Milosevic complained that Wladimiroff had written articles that gave rise to a reasonable perception of bias.

Milosevic's failure to appoint defence counsel created two problems at the outset of the proceedings. First, the prosecution was uncertain what course to take on the disclosure of exculpatory material, that is, material which helps the accused's case. Normally, meetings on disclosure are held between the prosecution and defence counsel. In the absence of the latter, the Chamber advised the Prosecutor to review the material using a broad definition of 'exculpatory' and, if in doubt, to disclose it to Milosevic and to the *amici*. Second, Milosevic complained that his 'legal advisers' had not been allowed to visit and communicate with him. The rules on detention allowed legal visits only from a nominated lawyer and he had refused to nominate one.[17] Sensibly, the Chamber responded to this formalistic problem by ordering the two persons whom Milosevic had asked to meet, Ramsey Clark[18] and John Livingston, to be his lawyers, as distinct from defence counsel.[19] He was entitled to communicate with them 'fully and without restraint'.

III The indictments and charges

As noted, three separate indictments were issued against Milosevic. They contained a total of sixty-six counts, and conviction on any one count could attract life imprisonment. Each indictment concerned events in different parts of the former Yugoslavia and different types of military conflict. Kosovo was an internal civil war/terrorist situation; Croatia was a civil war and then an interstate war; and Bosnia was an international armed conflict/partial occupation and/or intervention in a civil war in another state. The classification has consequences for the applicable humanitarian law.

If the three indictments were tried separately, it was estimated that the case would run for least three years. The Chamber approved the prosecution's application to join the Croatia and Bosnia indictments, but considered that significant distinctions in time, place, and the nature of the alleged conduct precluded joinder of the Kosovo indictment.[20] Thus, the stage was set for two successive trials, with the first, on Kosovo, beginning on 12 February 2002. However, this decision was overturned on 1 February 2002, when the Appeal Chamber ordered joinder of all of the indictments and a single trial.[21] It did so on the basis that the acts alleged in the three indictments formed the 'same transaction'. The trial would still begin as scheduled although the prosecution would not be ready to proceed with evidence on the Croatia and Bosnia indictments until 1 July 2002 (that part of the case began in September 2002). For the purposes of the trial, the three indictments were deemed to constitute one indictment with a single case number.[22] The single trial allowed the prosecution to present a single historical narrative of events in the former Yugoslavia.[23]

The prosecution described the Kosovo indictment as essentially a deportation case.[24] It alleged that, between 1 January and 20 June 1999, forces of the FRY and Serbia acting at the direction, or with the encouragement or support, of Milosevic executed a campaign of terror and violence directed at Kosovo Albanian civilians.[25] The objective of the campaign was to remove a substantial portion of the Albanian population from Kosovo to ensure continued Serbian control over the province. The indictment described a series of well planned and co-ordinated operations by the above forces. Approximately 800,000 Kosovo Albanian civilians were expelled from the province by the forced removal from and subsequent looting and destruction of their homes, or by the shelling of villages. Survivors were sent to the borders of neighbouring countries, and, en route, many were killed, abused, or robbed. Furthermore, massacres took place in twelve stated locations, including the murders of 118 people in the village of Izbica on 28 March 1999.

Milosevic's alleged responsibility rested on his *de jure* authority as President of the FRY, Supreme Commander of the Yugoslav Army ('VJ'), and President of the Supreme Defence Council, and pursuant to his *de facto* authority. Thus, Milosevic was charged with individual criminal responsibility under Article 7(1) of the ICTY Statute, and superior criminal responsibility under Article 7(3), namely, one count of violations of the laws or customs of war (murder), and four counts of crimes against humanity (deportation, murder, and persecutions on political, racial, or religious grounds).

The Croatia indictment alleged that Milosevic participated in a 'joint criminal enterprise' between at least 1 August 1991 and June 1992. The purpose of this enterprise was the forcible removal of the majority of the Croat and other non-Serb populations from approximately one-third of the territory of the Republic of Croatia, in order to join it to a new Serb-dominated state. Serb forces, comprising Yugoslav People's Army ('JNA') units, local Territorial Defence ('TO') units, TO units from Serbia and Montenegro, local and Serbian Ministry of Internal Affairs ('MUP') police units, and paramilitary units, attacked and took control of towns, villages, and settlements in the territories. After the take-over, these forces, in co-operation with the local Serb authorities, established a regime of persecution designed to drive out the non-Serb civilian populations. This regime included the extermination, wilful killing, or murder of hundreds of civilians, including women and elderly persons, the deportation or forcible transfer of at least 170,000 civilians, and the arrest and unlawful confinement or imprisonment under inhumane conditions of thousands more. Virtually the entire non-Serb civilian population was forcibly removed, deported, or killed in a number of regions, and public and private property was intentionally and wantonly destroyed or plundered.

As with the Kosovo indictment, Milosevic's alleged guilt was based on individual and superior criminal responsibility. During the relevant period, he had been President of the Republic of Serbia and as such exercised effective control or substantial influence over the other participants of the joint criminal enterprise.[26] Thus, he was charged with nine counts of grave breaches of the 1949 Geneva Conventions (wilful killing, unlawful confinement, torture, wilfully causing great suffering, unlawful deportation or transfer, extensive destruction and appropriation of property not justified by military necessity and carried out unlawfully and wantonly); thirteen counts of violations of the laws or customs of war (murder, torture, cruel treatment, wanton destruction of villages or devastation not justified by military necessity, destruction or wilful damage done to institutions dedicated to education or religion, plunder of public or private property, attacks on civilians, destruction or wilful damage done to historic monuments, unlawful attacks on civilian objects); and ten counts of crimes against humanity (persecutions on political, racial, or religious grounds, extermination, murder, imprisonment, torture, inhumane acts, deportation inhumane acts (forcible transfers)). One of the specific allegations was that on 20 November 1991, Serb military forces dragged 255 Croats and other non-Serbs out of Vukovar hospital after the Serbs had taken control of the city. The victims were taken to a farm 5 km outside Vukovar, where they were beaten and tortured before being shot and buried in a mass grave.

Finally, the Bosnia indictment alleged that from 1987 until late 2000, Milosevic was the dominant political figure in Serbia and the SFRY/FRY, and that he acted alone and in a joint criminal enterprise whose aim was the forcible removal of the majority of non-Serbs, principally Bosnian Muslims and Croats, from large areas of Bosnia and Herzegovina. This enterprise was directly carried out by the JNA, the VJ, the Bosnian Serb Army ('VRS'), the special forces of the Serbian MUP, and Serbian irregular and paramilitary units. Milosevic exerted control or influence over certain of these groups, and provided financial, logistical, and political support to those outside his direct control. Moreover, he controlled, manipulated, or otherwise utilised the Serbian state-run media to spread exaggerated and false messages of ethnically based attacks by Bosnian Muslims and Croats against Serbs to create an atmosphere of fear and hatred among Serbs living in Serbia, Croatia, and Bosnia and Herzegovina which contributed to the forcible removals.

The indictment further alleged that Milosevic, while holding positions of superior authority, was responsible for the acts and/or omissions of his subordinates. Article 7(3) of the ICTY statute provides that a superior is responsible for the criminal acts of his subordinates, 'if he knew or had reason to know that his subordinates were about to commit such acts or had done so, and the superior failed to take the necessary and reasonable measures to prevent such acts or punish the perpetrators'. The Federal Presidency had direct control over the JNA as its 'Commander-in-Chief' and effective control over units supervised by the JNA. The generals who directed the JNA in Bosnia and Herzegovina were in constant communication and consultation with Milosevic. Furthermore, as a member of the Supreme Defence Council and as president of the FRY, Milosevic had *de jure* and *de facto* control over the JNA and later the VJ. In these capacities he also exercised control over key figures in the MUP as well as in the State Security ('DB'), which together directed the special forces and Serb paramilitary groups. Among the specific allegations made in the indictment was the 1995 Srebrenica massacre of up to 8,000 Muslim men and boys.

This indictment charged Milosevic with two counts of genocide and complicity in genocide (genocide being the most serious possible charge before the ICTY); ten counts of crimes against humanity (persecution, extermination, murder, imprisonment, torture, deportation and inhumane acts (forcible transfers)); eight counts of grave breaches of the Geneva Conventions of 1949 (wilful killing, unlawful confinement, torture, wilfully causing great suffering, unlawful deportation or transfer, and extensive destruction and appropriation of property); and nine counts of violations of the laws or customs of war involving, *inter alia*, attacks on civilians, unlawful destruction, plunder of property, and cruel treatment.

When asked how he pleaded to the Croatia indictment, Milosevic sought to make a speech rather than respond. Judge May cut him off from the microphone saying that, 'it was not the time for speeches'. As he had failed to plead, the Chamber entered pleas of not guilty on every count on his behalf. The same happened with the other two indictments.

IV The mechanics of evidence

There is extensive testamentary and documentary evidence on the events in Kosovo, Croatia, and Bosnia,[27] but evidence that is admissible in a criminal trial is much more limited. A court may restrict or exclude evidence on the grounds of reliability[28] or efficiency. One of the prosecution's first proposed witnesses was the ICTY's senior investigator for Kosovo. He had prepared a report based on 1,300 interviews by ICTY investigators, but the Chamber excluded his opinions and conclusions as hearsay.[29] The number of prosecution witnesses has also been considerably reduced from the total figure of 600 initially estimated by Del Ponte. In relation to the Kosovo indictment, the Chamber set the number of prosecution witnesses at ninety, with leave to apply for permission to present additional witnesses. The Chamber then indicated that further reductions would be necessary to meet the time limit of the end of June/beginning of July for the conclusion of the Kosovo case. Not all proposals to save time have been accepted, however. The Chamber denied the prosecutions motion to disclose witness statements to the accused solely in English. Article 21(4) of the ICTY statute requires that the accused be informed promptly and in detail in a language which he understands of the nature and cause of the charges against him, and the Chamber determined that the disclosure obligations in this particular case were 'so fundamental as to outweigh considerations of judicial economy'.[30]

In the early stages of the trial prosecution witnesses testified on a range of issues, including Milosevic's character, events that took place in the former Yugoslavia, and Milosevic's participation in those events. There has been expert evidence from police officials and military investigators, as well as from diplomats, historians, forensic pathologists, economists, constitutional lawyers, social scientists, journalists, and archaeologists. To establish his responsibility, the prosecution's witnesses will have to link the allegations in the indictments to Milosevic and his government's policies. Some of these witnesses will be former Serb government officials awaiting their trials in The Hague. One possible witness is the former Bosnian Serb president Biljana Plavsic.[31] She is the most senior Serb politician and the only woman brought before the ICTY. Protective measures have been granted for a number of witnesses,[32] but a prosecution motion to withhold witness identities until they testified was denied. The prosecution argued that non-disclosure would avoid any possibility of intimidation. The Chamber, however, considered that the proceedings must remain consistently transparent, and that withholding the names of witnesses would defeat that objective.

The first witnesses were Mahmut Bakalli, a former communist leader of Kosovo and now a member of the Kosovo Parliament, Peter Spargo, an Australian police officer who created maps for the ICTY showing the displacement routes from Kosovo, and a Mr Zeqiri, an Albanian farmer from Kosovo, who had allegedly lost twenty-six of the twenty-eight members of his family. All three witnesses were severely cross-examined by Milosevic both as to their evidence and their credibility. Milosevic has stated that he intends to call witnesses, including the former US President, Bill Clinton; the UK Prime Minister, Tony Blair; the former UK Foreign Secretary, Robin Cook; Madeleine Albright, the former US Secretary of State; and Kofi Annan, the UN Secretary-General. He would have to demonstrate to the Chamber that the evidence of such witnesses was relevant to the charges against him. In October 2002, Stjepan Mesic, the President of Croatia, became the first head of state to testify before an international criminal tribunal. One witness who refused to give evidence was held in contempt.

How quickly the trial progresses will partly depend on how much of the written evidence adduced by the prosecution is held admissible by the Chamber.[33] The potential documentary evidence is vast. In relation to the Kosovo indictment the prosecution initially intended to produce 500 documents, 167 extracts of video recordings, 775 photographs, 50 charts and sketches, 30 maps on paper media and an electronic map, 30 slides or other images, and hundreds of police forensic reports. Some of this material was either withdrawn by the prosecution or rejected or limited by the Chamber. For example, the Chamber agreed to view BBC news videos without the sound because the latter represented opinion or commentary.[34] In relation to the Croatia indictment, the documentary evidence represents 3,000 pages in English, along with videotapes, photographs, and forensic reports.

V Arguments of legality and legitimacy

In her opening address Del Ponte argued that the evidence would reveal co-ordination between the VJ, the MUP, and the other forces of the FRY and Serbia throughout the Kosovo campaign, and that the patterns of threats, abuse, property destruction, rape, and murder were relentlessly repeated by these forces.[35] Milosevic, however, vigorously denied the allegations of wrongdoing[36] and argued instead that responsibility lay chiefly with the Kosovo Liberation Army ('KLA') and NATO. The KLA constituted a terrorist threat to Serbia, against which Serbia lawfully defended itself. This defence did not include ethnic cleansing – on the contrary, the KLA ordered the Kosovo population to flee in order to attract NATO support, and NATO bombings caused further flight, destruction, and death.[37] NATO intervention was part of a larger strategy to secure global control. It stirred up conflicts between Slav and Muslim nations in the hope that they would destroy or at least weaken each other so much that control might be established over them. Serbia was the victim of these aggressive actions, whose real criminality lay in the killing of Yugoslavia.

Milosevic did not merely deny the accusations; he denied the legitimacy of the entire ICTY process. The ICTY was not appointed by the UN General Assembly, therefore it was illegal.[38] Its chief officers were also biased. The Kosovo indictment suggested that NATO did not commit aggression against Yugoslavia but rather that Yugoslavia committed aggression against itself. Discounting the devastating effects of seventy-eight days and nights of NATO bombing, during which 22,000 tonnes of bombs were dropped, itself showed partiality or bias on behalf of the prosecution.[39] If the Chamber refused to take these facts into account then it too was part of the machinery to commit a crime against his country and his people. Milosevic also particularly attacked the presence of a British judge as evidence of a biased tribunal.[40] Given the UK role in Kosovo, the Chamber could not be impartial.

The biased, false, 'absurd' indictments, including the attempt to blame Serbia 'for the armed secession of Croatia which provoked a civil war, conflicts and suffering of the civilian population'[41] revealed the real aim of the trial, which was to produce a false justification for the war crimes of NATO at the expense of the Serbian nation. He noted that the Kosovo indictment had been issued on the sixtieth day of NATO aggression against Yugoslavia, and that two and a half years after obtaining the Croatia and Bosnia indictments the prosecution was not ready to proceed with them.[42] Not only was Serbia on trial for defending itself, the trial was inciting further Albanian terrorism in southern Serbia. That terror, conducted under the auspices of the United Nations, had resulted in 33,000 people being chased out of Kosovo and Metohija. Furthermore, there was a parallel trial through the media. This was part of a 'media war designed to Satanise the Serbian people, the Serbian leadership, Milosevic and his family'.[43]

Milosevic also argued that his own treatment by the ICTY undermined its legitimacy. He considered that his imprisonment was the product of an illegal arrest. He also complained of his isolation from his family, that he was discriminated against in relation to family visits,[44] and that his visits and family conversations were monitored. He wanted the cameras removed from his cell and to meet his family in the absence of prison staff. He also wanted to communicate with the press as he claimed that lies were being printed about him. The response of the Chamber to the latter point was that the Rules of the Detention Unit forbade such communication. It is difficult to justify that blanket restriction.

Milosevic stated this litany of complaints orally before the Chamber. In addition, he presented two formal motions challenging the legality of the ICTY by reason of its unconstitutionality, its lack of an independent prosecutor or objective judges, its violations of his right to privacy and freedom of expression, its discriminatory territorial jurisdiction, its lack of competence by reason of his status as former president, and his unlawful surrender. The *amici* presented some similar arguments. They argued that the Chamber should address the jurisdictional issue by seeking an opinion from the highest judicial body of the UN, the International Court of Justice, which is also located in The Hague. They also put the arguments of bias and partiality, submitting that from Milosevic's perspective the ICTY was incapable of giving him a fair trial and faced unacceptable levels of pressure from external sources. An example of partiality was the court's order forbidding him from giving media interviews, while the prosecution faced no such restriction.[45] The *amici* also argued that trying Milosevic for actions as a head of state violated the principle of state sovereignty. Finally, questions were raised about the legality of Milosevic's extradition from Yugoslavia to The Hague.

The Chamber dismissed all of the arguments in a reasoned opinion[46] but Milosevic has challenged the legality of his detention and trial in other fora. He sought an order for his immediate release from the Regional Court in The Hague. The court refused, stating that it considered the ICTY to be independent and impartial. In December 2001, Milosevic also submitted an application against the Netherlands before the European Court of Human Rights in Strasburg.[47] This claimed that the ICTY was illegal and that his arrest and detention violated the following Articles of the European Convention on Human Rights: Article 5 (right to liberty and security), Article 6 (right to a fair trial), Article 10 (freedom of expression), Article 13 (right to an effective remedy), and Article 14 (prohibition of discrimination). In March 2002 the application was declared inadmissible for failure fully to exhaust domestic remedies.

VI Aims and objectives of this trial?

The final determination of Milosevic's guilt or innocence lies some time in the future. While this is the trial's fundamental purpose, it will not be its only consequence. Law reduces often highly complex stories through legal concepts of relevance and admissibility, and through the legal process important, and arguably new, stories may emerge. The narrative struggle in this trial will determine how much some of the bigger political legitimacy questions will be addressed in this forum. In her opening address, Del Ponte set out her aims and objectives in no uncertain terms.

> Today, as never before, we see international justice in action. . . . This Tribunal, and this trial in particular, give the most powerful demonstration that no one is above the law or beyond the reach of international justice. As Prosecutor, I bring the accused Milosevic before you to face the charges against him. I do so on behalf of the international community and in the name of all the member states of the United Nations, including the states of the former Yugoslavia. The accused in this case, as in all cases before the Tribunal, is charged as an individual. He is prosecuted on the basis of his individual criminal responsibility. No state or organisation is on trial here today. The indictments do not accuse an entire people of being collectively guilty of the crimes, even the crime of genocide. It may be tempting to generalise when dealing with the conduct of leaders at the highest level, but that is an error that must be avoided. Collective guilt forms no part of the Prosecution case. It is not the law of this Tribunal, and I make it clear that I reject the very notion. . . . [W]hile I bring the indictment as Prosecutor in the international public interest, I do not mean to ignore the victims of the crimes committed during the conflicts . . . [A]s Prosecutor, I do not directly represent any individual victim. I do, however, consider it to be part of my function in presenting the case to allow the voice of the victims to be heard. . . . With the trial of this particular accused, we reach a turning point of this institution. The proceeding upon which the Chamber embarks today is clearly the most important trial to be conducted in the Tribunal to date. Indeed, it may prove to be the most significant trial that this institution will ever undertake.[48]

Yet how comforting are these words? The trial raises difficult questions with respect to at least four identifiable groups: Serbia and the Serbian people; Bosnian, Croatian, and Serbian victims; other nations and organisations caught up in the conflict; and the ICTY itself. Del Ponte's confidence notwithstanding, the trial may complicate these questions more than it answers them.

To what extent is Serbia actually on trial in this case? Despite Del Ponte's express denial, Milosevic has repeatedly described the proceedings as a crime against his country and an accusation against the Serbian people. If, to some extent, Serbia is being placed under the microscope of international review, will the experience be similar to that of Germany following the Second World War? The Nuremberg trial contributed to Germany's re-acceptance into the community of civilised states, but did not lift from the German people the burden of collective guilt.[49] Conversely, the trial may contribute to feelings of denial and isolation. It has been widely reported that many Serbs find the actions taken against them incomprehensible given the role of Serbia in the Second World War, its ethnic kinship with Russia, and friendship with Italy and France.[50] A response to this feeling of betrayal by the outside world may be denial and historical reconstruction. There have already been reports of Milosevic being written out of Serbian history.[51]

Del Ponte has stated that she wishes the voices of the victims to be heard, but how can this be achieved? What role will the trial play in establishing the 'truth' of what happened, particularly as witnesses give oral evidence and the evidence of mass graves is presented?[52] To what extent can a criminal trial of this kind serve to provide a cathartic experience for victims, and ought this to be one of its aims? If so, how can the proceedings be structured to allow for Serbian, as well as non-Serbian, victims to tell their stories?

In the early stages of the trial Milosevic has drawn attention to the role of the KLA and NATO. Why have there been no indictments for alleged war crimes committed by members of the KLA? Del Ponte has been reported as saying that she would like to issue indictments but that there are problems in obtaining evidence.[53] Milosevic has claimed that Osama Bin Laden, allegedly responsible for the attacks on the United States in September 2001, was in Kosovo with the KLA.[54] Might such information redirect American attention to the Balkans as part of its 'war on terrorism'? Does NATO have immunity for the heavy toll of civilian casualties that resulted from its bombing campaign? If it does not, how are NATO, member states, and individuals to be held responsible for the alleged violations of international law committed against Serbia in respect of Kosovo?[55] Moreover, what of the other members of the international community, both those which supported and sustained the former Yugoslavia, Serbia, and Milosevic,[56] and those which failed to intervene to stop the ethnic cleansing and other atrocities?[57]

And, finally, can the independence and impartiality of the ICTY be credibly maintained? Both Milosevic and the *amici* have challenged the legitimacy of the process on the grounds of bias. Can it withstand the critiques of those who consider that the trial is merely another example of 'Victor's Justice' – 'a demonstration of power more than of justice?'[58] An 'International Committee to Defend Slobodan Milosevic' has been formed and attracted over 1,200 supporters, including the distinguished playwright Harold Pinter.[59] Perhaps the new permanent International Criminal Court, which is expected to begin work in 2003, will signal the end of all such *ad hoc* tribunals,[60] but will that tribunal end the debate over the validity of 'international justice' in the context of war crimes?

This volume has considered some of the most significant war crimes trials of the twentieth century. That century began with a failure for such trials when the Netherlands government refused to hand over the ex-Emperor of Germany to an international tribunal. In the *Milosevic* trial, the twenty-first century may begin with a success, or with failure of a different kind. Whatever its outcome, this trial may have deep and lasting significance for international law and international institutions. War crime trials have been defended as the means by which the most important international norms are finally, fairly, and peacefully enforced. If an individual trial fails to achieve these aims, it can undermine the validity of the trial process generally in this context. Del Ponte has also spoken of the trial's place in the history of conflict in the Balkans:

> I recognise that this trial will make history, and we would do well to approach our task in the light of history. The history of the disintegration of the former Yugoslavia and the fratricidal conflicts of another age which brought it about is a complex process which must be written by many people. This Tribunal will write only one chapter, the most bloody one, the most heartbreaking one as well; the chapter of individual responsibility of the perpetrators of serious violations of international humanitarian law. It is up to other courts to make the moral, historical, or even psychological diagnosis of the accused and to analyse the social, economic, and political dynamic which constituted the basic fabric of the crimes that we are going to consider.[61]

Even accepting her caveat, it is a heavy burden to bear.

Notes

I am grateful to Steve Wheatley, Steve Cooper, and Catherine Le Magueresse for their comments on drafts of this essay.

1 *Prosecutor* v. *Slobodan Milosevic*, Case No. IT-02-54. All of the case documentation and transcripts are available at the ICTY's website, www.un.org/icty.
2 Paul Akayesu was tried and convicted before the ICTR in 1998, confirmed on appeal in 2001, but he was a head of government, not a head of the state.
3 In Belgrade in November 2001, 'smiley glamour postcards' of suspected war criminals were on sale, E. Mahoney, radio review of 'Crossing continents – the new Serbia' (BBC, Radio 4), *Guardian* (16 November 2001).
4 See L. Sell, *Slobodan Milosevic and the Destruction of Yugoslavia* (Chapel Hill, N.C.: Duke University Press, 2002).
5 See D. Leurdijk and D. Zandee, *Kosovo – from Crisis to Crisis* (Aldershot: Ashgate, 2001).
6 See D. Doder and L. Branson, *Milosevic – Portrait of a Tyrant* (London: Simon & Schuster (Free Press), 2000); L. J. Cohen, *Serpent in the Bosom: the Rise and Fall of Slobodan Milosevic* (Boulder, Colo.: Westview Press, 2000).
7 A video of this speech was shown on the first day of the trial.

8 The others were Milan Milutinovic (as President of Servia, member of the Supreme Defence Council, and pursuant to his *de facto* authority); Nicola Sainovic (as Deputy Prime Minister of the FRY); Dragoljub Ojdanovic (as Chief of General Staff of the Yugoslav Army (the VJ); and Vlajko Stojiljkovic (as Minister of Internal Affairs of Serbia).

9 The UK website of the *Guardian* newspaper carried twenty-six pictures of arrest. It had an interactive website guide entitled 'Slobodan Milosevic on trial'.

10 May was also the pre-trial judge.

11 For the British *amicus* this included his wig.

12 On the lawyers generally, see B. Malkin, 'Killing time', *Lawyer*, 15: 3 (2001), 21–5.

13 See E. Vulliamy, 'Avenging angel', *Observer* (4 March 2001). (The article also considers the 'feminisation of The Hague Tribunal'.)

14 He was provided with relevant materials but refused to read them.

15 Order Inviting Designation of *Amicus Curiae*.

16 See note 55 below.

17 See 'Regulations to Govern the Supervision of Visits to and Communications with Detainees', ICTY Doc. IT/98/Rev.3.

18 A former US attorney-general.

19 Another legal adviser was a Mr Ognjanovic.

20 See the transcript of 11 December 2001 for the joinder application, which the *amici* supported. See Decision on Prosecution's Motion for Joinder, 13 December 2001.

21 Decision of 1 February 2002. See the transcript of 30 January 2002.

22 The original three case numbers were No. IT-01-50 (Croatia), IT-01-51 (Bosnia), and IT-99-37 (Kosovo).

23 See the transcripts of 12 and 13 February 2002. The chamber made it clear that it was willing to hear only very limited historical evidence.

24 Transcript of 13 February 2002.

25 See A. D. Amato, 'A brief review of the indictment against Milosevic and others', *International Peacekeeping*, 5: 3 (1999), 91–3.

26 Among the connecting links listed by the prosecution were the supply of personnel, payment of officers' salaries, supply of twenty-three military equipment and munitions, provision of training, sharing of twenty-four communication systems, sharing of intelligence, linkage between twenty-five radio/technical reconnaissance systems. It also sought to rely on the ICTY's Appeal Chambers' holding in the *Tadic Case* that, 'The armed forces of the Republika Srpska were to be regarded as acting under the overall control and on behalf of the FRY.' 35 I.L.M. 35 (1996) para. 162.

27 See K. Booth (ed.), *The Kosovo Tragedy – the Human Rights Dimensions* (Southgate: Frank Cass Publishers, 2001); Human Rights Watch, *Under Orders: War Crimes in Kosovo* (New York: Human Rights Watch, 2001).

28 In October 2002 the Appeal Chamber of the ICTY overturned the convictions of three individuals in the *Kupreskic Case*, IT-95-16. It held that the charges were too vague and general, and were dependent on the testimony of unreliable witnesses.

29 The Chamber may, in its discretion, admit hearsay evidence, but it is of limited probative value.

30 Decision of 19 September 2001.

31 A. Osborn, 'Fellow Serb turns on Milosevic', *Guardian* (12 October 2001).

32 Among the possible measures are expunging names and identifying records from the public record, non-disclosure to the public of any records identifying the victim,

the giving of testimony through image- or voice-altering devices or closed circuit television, assignment of a pseudonym or closed sessions of the Chamber. Milosevic complained of unfairness in the use of protected witnesses against him.

33 See Rule 92*bis* of the ICTY's Rules of Procedure and Evidence.

34 The videos showed people crossing borders and in camps, and damage from NATO air strikes.

35 Transcript of 12 February 2002, pp. 2–9.

36 See transcripts of 13 February, pp. 215–20; and 14, 15, and 18 February 2002.

37 Milosevic relied on a number of videos and an extensive number of pictures, for example, of bodies carbonised by NATO bombing.

38 His argument is that the ICTY was not based on a treaty to which states could or could not consent.

39 Another concern from a human rights perspective would be that predictions by Del Ponte that Milosevic would be found guilty violated the presumption of innocence.

40 I. Black, 'Milosevic attacks Hague Tribunal for British bias', *Guardian* (10 January 2002); Transcript of 9 January 2002.

41 Transcript of 29 October 2001.

42 Tapuskovic, one of the *amici*, also complained about this delay on the basis that the proceedings were not expeditious and effective, and 'thereby also one can ask how fair they can be'.

43 Transcript of 11 December 2001.

44 He was visited by his wife, Misa, known in Belgrade as Lady Macbeth, and members of his family. He complained to the Chamber when his wife was not given a visa to visit him.

45 See 'Tribunal warns Milosevic over jail interview', *Guardian* (25 August 2001).

46 Decision on Preliminary Motions, 8 November 2001. The decision was not appealed.

47 See www.echr.coe.int (Application number 77631/01).

48 Transcript of 12 February 2002.

49 See I. Buruma, 'The Hague vs Belgrade', *Guardian* (19 February 2002). Serbia has been admitted to the UN and the OSCE. See A. Bloed, 'OSCE news: Yugoslavia returns to the OSCE', *Netherlands Quarterly of Human Rights*, 18: 4 (2000), 531–2.

50 See T. Weymouth and S. Henig (eds), *The Kosovo Crisis – the Last American War in Europe?* (Harlow: Reuters, 2001).

51 See R. Carroll, 'Milosevic disappears from history', *Observer* (12 September 2001).

52 'Depressingly, the programme revealed was that many [in Serbia] prefer to live an "affected indifference behind which lies a seething resentment" '. Mahoney, 'Crossing continents'.

53 See 'Carla Del Ponte', *Guardian* (31 December 2001).

54 Milosevic catalogued attacks against the Serbs before and after the NATO bombings (transcript of 15 February 2002).

55 In *Bankovic and Others* v. *Belgium and 16 other NATO States*, the grand chamber of the European Court of Human Rights considered an application by a number of alleged victims of bombings of Radio Televizije Srbije ('RTS') in Belgrade by NATO forces in 1999. It found the application inadmissible because the applicants did not come within the jurisdiction of the respondent states, Application no. 52207/99 (12 December 2001). The ICTY prosecutor considered the evidence on the bombing campaign but found no grounds to prosecute.

56 See I. Traynor, 'Trying the tyrant we helped to create', *Guardian* (16 January 2002).

57 See B. Simms, *Unfinest Hour – Britain and the Destruction of Bosnia* (London: Allen Lane, 2001); N. Cohen, 'Betrayal in the Balkans', *Observer* (4 November 2001).

58 See S. Milne, 'Hague is not the place to try Milosevic – the tribunal is effectively the legal arm of NATO in the Balkans', *Guardian* (2 August 2001); N. Thorpe, 'Hague indictments spark Croatian crisis', *Guardian* (9 July 2001); J. Laughland, 'This is not justice', *Guardian* (16 February 2002).

59 See F. Gibbons, 'Free Milosevic, says Pinter', *Guardian* (26 July 2001).

60 See M. Caplan, 'The right way to try Milosevic', *The Times* (19 February 2002).

61 Transcript of 12 February 2002.

Index

amicus curiae 180–2, 190
appeals 87, 123–5, 149–50
Attorney General *see* law officers

capital punishment *see* punishment
clemency petitions 3, 37, 40, 88
confirmation of sentences 82–3, 112, 149–50
courts
  competence 58, 61–2, 64, 68–70, 126
  jurisdiction 7, 59, 82, 108, 110–11, 113, 116–17, 123–5, 127, 141, 188
  legitimacy 110, 114, 122–3, 126–7, 187–8
  structure 81, 115, 124, 139, 141, 180

death penalty *see* punishment
defence counsel 6, 15–17, 31, 43, 46–7, 63, 65–8, 150, 168, 171, 181–2
duration of trials 14, 64, 113, 123, 141–3, 157, 182–3

executions *see* punishment
evidence 6, 79–80, 86, 119–21, 157, 185
  character 36–7, 40–9
  documentary 60–1, 111–12, 186
  expert 6, 9, 22–39 *passim*, 157, 163–4, 169–70, 186
  oral 12–18, 62–3
  see also witnesses

habeas corpus 82–3, 88–9

imprisonment *see* punishment

judges
  attitudes 24–5, 29–30, 32, 39, 42, 83, 87–9, 97, 99, 145–9
  competence 3, 140–1, 167
  conduct 46–7, 61–3, 82, 91–2, 95, 142–3, 185
  see also courts
juries 22, 30
jurisdiction *see* courts

law officers 39, 42–3, 55, 57, 59–60, 84, 87–9, 91–3, 97, 138–9, 142, 149, 152
lawyers *see* defence counsel; prosecutors
length of trials *see* duration of trials

objectives of litigation 109
  ethical 113, 115–16
  financial 42
  historical 9, 159–60, 191

political 42–3, 54–6, 69, 109–10, 138, 145, 158–9
psychological 118–21, 158, 189
whether achieved 9, 68–70, 112–14, 123–4, 126, 151–2, 167–70, 188–91

press coverage 4–5, 43, 60, 81, 84–7, 91, 96–7, 150–2, 157, 170–1, 181, 187
procedure 5–7, 57, 64–8, 77–8, 82–4, 110, 117–18, 121, 141
prosecutors 5, 41–6, 67, 121, 124, 138–9, 143–5, 150, 181, 189–90
public opinion 3, 4, 55–7, 68–9, 91, 93, 126, 139–40, 150–1, 168
punishment
capital 38, 77, 79–88 *passim*, 95, 112, 117, 125–6, 146–50
imprisonment 79, 84, 87, 95, 112, 117, 148–9, 167

reports 2–4, 12, 14, 25, 38–9

Solicitor General *see* law officers

tribunals *see* courts

witnesses 22–8, 30–3, 41–4, 58, 61–3, 65–7, 120–1, 125, 157, 165, 170, 185–6
see also evidence